Love and Fr

Diverse Sexualities, Genders, and Relationships

Series Editors

Richard Sprott, PhD, California State University, East Bay
Elizabeth Sheff, PhD, Sheff Consulting

The Diverse Sexualities, Genders and Relationships Series highlights evidence-based approaches to understanding and serving diverse individuals and families whose relational or sexual practices or identities have been marginalized and understudied; reports of emerging empirical research on these topics; and analyses of the latest trends in cultural and societal developments on the status and place of diverse sexualities, genders and relationships. Books in the series emphasize the intersections of race, culture, age, social class, (dis)ability, and other factors that shape the social locations of relational, sexual and gender minorities as they intersect with institutions in fields such as education, law, medicine, religion, and public policy.

The books in this series will serve as sound and critical resources for the training and continuing education of professionals directly serving diverse communities, professions such as counseling, marriage and family therapy, social work, healthcare, criminology, human service and education. They will also be useful for educators teaching undergraduate and graduate level university courses in anthropology, cultural studies, gerontology, psychology, sexuality studies, sociology, and women's and gender studies. Finally, these books will interest educated laypeople who wish to better understand diversity among relational, sexual and gender minorities.

Titles in Series:

Love and Freedom: Transcending Monogamy and Polyamory by Jorge N. Ferrer

BDSM in Therapy: What Psychotherapists Need to Know about Working with Kinky People and Communities by Richard Sprott and Ryan Witherspoon

Mental Health Practice with LGBTQ+ Children, Adolescents, and Emerging Adults in Multiple Systems of Care by Cristina L. Magalhães, Richard Sprott, and G. Nic Rider

The Handbook of Consensual Nonmonogamy: Affirming Mental Health Practice by Theodore Burnes and Michelle D. Vaughan

Love and Freedom

Transcending Monogamy and Polyamory

Jorge N. Ferrer

ROWMAN & LITTLEFIELD
Lanham • Boulder • New York • London

Published by Rowman & Littlefield
An imprint of The Rowman & Littlefield Publishing Group, Inc.
4501 Forbes Boulevard, Suite 200, Lanham, Maryland 20706
www.rowman.com

86-90 Paul Street, London EC2A 4NE

British Library Cataloguing in Publication Information Available

Library of Congress Cataloging-in-Publication Data

Names: Ferrer, Jorge N. (Jorge Noguera), 1968– author.
Title: Love and freedom : transcending monogamy and polyamory / Jorge N. Ferrer.
Description: Lanham : Rowman & Littlefield, [2022] | Series: Diverse sexualities, genders and relationships | Includes bibliographical references and index.
Identifiers: LCCN 2021009188 (print) | LCCN 2021009189 (ebook) | ISBN 9781538156568 (cloth) | ISBN 9781538156575 (paperback) | ISBN 9781538156582 (epub)
Subjects: LCSH: Love. | Monogamous relationships. | Non-monogamous relationships. | Sex. | Interpersonal relations.
Classification: LCC BF575.L8 F47 2022 (print) | LCC BF575.L8 (ebook) | DDC 152.4/1—dc23
LC record available at https://lccn.loc.gov/2021009188
LC ebook record available at https://lccn.loc.gov/2021009189

♾™ The paper used in this publication meets the minimum requirements of American National Standard for Information Sciences—Permanence of Paper for Printed Library Materials, ANSI/NISO Z39.48-1992.

To Jenny
(1970–2019),
the love of my life,
who lived in love
and died in freedom

Contents

Acknowledgments

The individuals who have influenced and enriched this book's perspectives on intimate relationships are too numerous to mention here. Nonetheless, I want to explicitly thank the following friends, scholars, and colleagues (in alphabetical order): Ramon V. Albareda, the late Deborah Anapol, Veronica Balseiro, David Barba, Meg-John Barker, Erika Bennet, Karina Bertolotto, Sandra Bravo, Adi Leigh Brown, Nuria Costa, Adriana de los Rios, Gabriel Fernandez, Ignacio Forcada, Marta Grau, Scott Hanon, Francesca Hector, Sean Kelly, Michael Lerner, Samuel Malkemus, Robert A. Masters, Wendy-O Matik, Veronica Balseiro, Maria Pallota-Chiarolli, Eliana Perinat, Nathan Rambukkana, Kenneth Ring, Marina T. Romero, the late Jen Rothman, Mimi Schippers, Elisabeth Sheff, Maria Sideri, Renée Soule, Richard Tarnas, Lucia Telechea, Marie Thouin, Jenny Wade, Angela Willey, and Skylar Wilson.

Many thanks as well go to Elisabeth Sheff for kindly encouraging me to submit this work to Rowman & Littlefield's *Diverse Genders, Sexualities and Relationships* Series; to Richard Sprott for urging me to discuss intersectional sources of social privilege and oppression in the search for relational freedom; to the thirteen anonymous reviewers selected by Rowman & Littlefield for their careful reading of the manuscript and constructive suggestions; and to Rowman & Littlefield's executive acquisitions editor Mark Kerr for his enthusiastic support of the project and assistant editor Courtney Packard for her diligent care and professionality.

I owe special gratitude to my longtime editor Anna F. Doherty, who not only helped to significantly improve the presentation of my ideas but also strengthened some of my arguments through a number of important additions and qualifications.

Lastly, special kudos go to the real teachers of this work: those who have loved me, granted me the pleasure and honor to love them, and patiently (or impatiently) had to deal with my personal shortcomings and many errors on the path toward relational freedom. I humbly dedicate this work to them as well.

* * *

Permission to use material from the following publications has been granted:

Chapter 2. Ferrer, J. N. (2018). Mononormativity, polypride, and the "mono–poly wars." *Sexuality & Culture*, 22(3), 817–836.

Chapter 3. Ferrer, J. N. (2006). What's the opposite of jealousy? Questioning the Buddhist allegiance to monogamy. *Tricycle: The Buddhist Review* (Summer), 83–85; and Ferrer, J. N. (2007). Monogamy, polyamory, and beyond. *Tikkun: Culture, Spirituality, Politics* (Jan/Feb), 37–43, 60–62.

Chapter 4. Ferrer, J. N. (2018). Beyond the non/monogamy system: Fluidity, hybridity, and transcendence in intimate relationships. *Psychology and Sexuality*, 9(1), 3–20.

The subtle realms of love and freedom have been explored across cultures, with countless individual voices expressing human experience and desire through poetry, art, philosophy, hard politics, and soft conversation. Further, romantic relationships and psychological health have been studied from many scientific and philosophical perspectives. Nonetheless, new and uncharted relational territory continues to arise in contemporary Western culture, from our relationship with rapidly advancing technology to the effects of shifts in the planetary ecosystem. Intimate relationships are no exception.

Although the hefty burden placed by modern Western individuals on romantic love for achieving happiness can be rightfully questioned (e.g., Ben-Ze'ev & Goussinsky, 2008; Brake, 2012; Kipnis, 2003), fulfilling intimate relationships are not only essential for a meaningful life, but also are a major source of personal happiness and even psychophysical health (e.g., Diener & Seligman, 2002; Roberson et al., 2018; Simon, 2002; Waite & Gallagher, 2000). As a society, however, we struggle with how to successfully achieve and maintain intimate relationships, that is, reciprocal loving bonds involving erotic attraction, physical closeness, and emotional affection usually developed over a certain time[1]:

> We . . . feel like failures when love dies. We believe it could be otherwise. Since the cultural expectation is that a state of coupled permanence is achievable, uncoupling is experienced as crisis and inadequacy—even though such failures are more the norm than the exception. (Kipnis, 2001, para 8)

Many people hope that more years of therapy, workshops, psychological work, or today's fashionable mindfulness practices (e.g., Davenport & Scott, 2018) will eventually heal their intimacy wounds or allow them to "crack" the relational "code." Even after decades of seemingly failed relationships, others believe that they simply have not found their "soul mate" or a more compatible partner.

Perhaps, as Rainer Marie Rilke (1934) famously intimated, we have not been asking the right questions to live by. Are all these relational trials and tribulations really emerging from character flaws or bad luck? Is all this personal suffering (and money spent mitigating it) truly necessary? Does the widespread monogamy crisis arise from attachment issues, the in-vogue scapegoat for relational challenges (e.g., A. Levine & Heller, 2010; Tatkin & Hendrix, 2011)? It should be obvious that any black-or-white response to the above questions would be misleading. Nobody's upbringing is perfect. No one had faultless primary caregivers. We all have some degree of relational, emotional, or sexual healing to do—or intimate skills to learn and sharpen. Both personal and structural factors are intermingled in most modern relational ordeals, and are worth investigating (e.g., S. A. Mitchell, 2002; Illouz, 2019). Nonetheless, I strongly suspect that for an increasing number of people, the solution cannot be found in more therapy or relational providence.

In this book, I argue that the question to live by today is this: What if, rather than trying to conform to outmoded or inadequate relational structures, people boldly cocreate intimate lives more attuned to their essential dispositions, changing needs, and deepest desires? What if we exorcise the monocentric spell and realize that "the problem" might not be, after all, a problem? What I am suggesting is that *behind the inability to exclusively commit to a single person for life or an indefinite period of time, there may be emerging wisdom at play.*[2] In other words, some of the fears, conflicts, and challenges modern individuals experience in monogamous pledges may arise from an often-unconscious discernment of that relational structure as no longer appropriate for their personal development or even for our culture's historical moment. Positively framed, those difficulties may indicate that many people are ready to break away from monocentrism, become more autonomous agents in their relational choices, and perhaps even commit to something larger than any one self or single person (e.g., life, love itself, human flourishing).[3]

At this point, a reasonable assumption might arise that I must proactively correct: this book does *not* present a full-on case for open marriage, open relationships, polyamory, or other forms of so-called responsible or consensual nonmonogamy (CNM)[4] (e.g., Barker & Langdridge, 2010a; Beggan, 2021; Sheff & Tenese, 2015). While there is a modern crisis of monogamy (see chapter 1) and the exploration of alternative relational paradigms is paramount, I believe that more freely chosen, mindful monogamy will be—and should be considered—a valid player in twenty-first century's intimacy world. If in this book I briefly discuss polyamory's psychospiritual potential (chapter 3), it is largely because monogamy was and still is socially and religiously imposed in the West, and thus more severely constrains our relational choices than polyamory (e.g., Bergstrand & Sinski, 2010; Emens, 2004; Kipnis, 2003; Rosa, 1994). However, both monogamy and polyamory are often animated by two equally ideological (i.e., not evidence-based) interlocked sets of psychosocial attitudes leading to the unfortunate predicament of mutual judgment among monogamists and polyamorists that, somewhat tongue in cheek, I call the "mono–poly[5] wars" (see chapter 2).

Instead of building a case for any particular relational style, in this book I argue that (a) people have diverse relational dispositions, (b) developmental and sociopolitical conditions can call individuals to engage in different relationship styles at various junctures of their lives, (c) there are more and less constructive or mature types of both monogamy and polyamory, (d) people can follow a specific relationship style for the "right" or "wrong" reasons, and (e) all relationship styles can become equally limiting ideologies. After discussing how monogamy and nonmonogamy ultimately reinforce each other, I deconstruct the dichotomy between these relational styles through the articulation of several relational pathways to living *in-between*, *through*, and *beyond* the mono/poly binary (chapter 4). In other words, in the same way that the transgender and gender diversity movements dismantle the gender binary, I propose a parallel step with the relational binary. To this end, I have coined the term *novogamy* to refer to a diverse array of relational options and identities beyond the mono/poly binary (while mindful that many may prefer another term or eschew any categorization altogether). In any event, as nonbinary or transbinary relational modes can include the temporary or indefinite choice of monogamy and/or nonmonogamy, I also argue that my proposal avoids the elevation of novogamy as a "superior" relational style (see chapter 5).

Thus, the project of this book stands in full alignment with the recently articulated "queer intimacy paradigm" (Hammack et al., 2019), the goal of which is "to better reflect the lived experience of intimate diversity in the 21st century" (p. 582). Describing their work as "anchored in axioms that highlight diversity and pluralism in human intimacy," the authors wrote, "A queer paradigm stands to anchor our understanding of relationships in principles that recognize and value social creativity and integrity in the expression of desire" (p. 582). Among other important features, this paradigm challenges both the normativity and exclusive validity of binary accounts of gender, sexual orientation and identity, and relationship styles.[6] One aspect of what I am seeking to accomplish here is nothing more—and nothing less—than a "queering" of relational styles, arguably in a more radical (or at least more systematic) manner than anything done previously to my knowledge.

Although scholarly in nature, this book is animated by a practical thrust. Too often I have witnessed bitterness, distress, depression, and even existential anguish in people who were thriving in their lives but whose intimate bonds were lacking or disappointing. Conversely, I have consistently observed how many people with serious professional, economic, or personal challenges but fulfilling intimate lives both appear and report being fundamentally happy.

While this book can have a deep impact on readers' lives and includes practical suggestions to increase their relational freedom and assess relational success (chapter 5), this is not a "how-to" guide. The market is saturated with many fine books offering practical advice about how to navigate the stormy seas of contemporary relationships; for example, how to cultivate a mindful or mature monogamy (e.g., Brandon, 2010; Masters, 2007), constructively engage non-monogamous lifestyles (e.g., Taormino, 2008; Veaux & Rickert, 2014), or consciously design flexible relationships attuned to people's personal moments and dispositions (e.g., Barker, 2013; Gahran, 2017; Michaels & P. Johnson, 2015).

This book aims at radically opening the range of legitimate relational choices individuals and couples can make throughout their lives—beyond not only socially enforced monogamy but also the apparently compulsory choice between monogamy and polyamory or nonmonogamy. Understanding the emerging relational options of our times—as well as the forces conditioning them—can also counter the confusion and inadequacy many face today in the wake of repeated relationship "failures," clandestine affairs, or decreased sexual desire toward their partners. To this end, in this book I have developed a set of critical categories (see chapter 2) that can positively transform the way people live their intimate relationships and relate to others opting for different relational styles. My hope is that this work empowers people to live freer, more vital and creative, and ultimately more fulfilling relationships in which deeper and wider forms of love can flourish on Earth without unnecessary constraints.

Before beginning the discussion, it may be helpful to include a brief itinerary of the journey ahead.

Outline of the Chapters

Chapter 1, "Relational Freedom and the Crisis of Modern Relationships," sets the background for the rest of the book, starting with a discussion of the crisis of traditional lifelong monogamy and the problems of the currently prevalent serial monogamy paradigm. Building on the work of many scholars (e.g., Ashkam, 1984; Bauman, 2003; Cherlin, 2009), I suggest that the monocentric paradigm is foundationally afflicted by the tension between two essential human needs: the sexual need for diversity and novelty, and the emotional need for stability and constancy. After addressing the challenges of the deep structural change arguably necessary to relax this tension, I introduce the notion of *relational freedom*—the capability to freely choose one's relational style—in terms of relational integration, plasticity, autonomy, and transcendence. Six sources or levels of conditioning potentially constraining relational freedom are explored: evolutionary, biological, historical, cultural, social, and biographical. Finally, I suggest that to love as many people as one desires in constructive, nonharmful ways should be considered a human right as fundamental as the right to equality, free movement, or freedom of belief.

Chapter 2, "Mononormativity, Polypride, and the 'Mono–Poly Wars'," discusses how, both in everyday life and scholarly discourse, monogamists and polyamorists tend to unfavorably portray one another as somehow flawed, misguided, or, in a word, "inferior." To this end, I document and critically examine two pairs of interlocked psychosocial attitudes—monopride/polyphobia and polypride/monophobia—mediating this mutual competition and condescension in the context of Western mononormative culture. I then demonstrate the ideological nature of these "mono–poly wars" through a review of the available empirical literature on the psychological health and relationship quality of monogamous and polyamorous individuals and couples. The chapter concludes by outlining a critical pluralist approach that, eschewing universalizing hierarchies between monogamy and polyamory, suggests tools for not only making qualitative distinctions within and among relational styles but also enhancing the possibilities of relational freedom.

In chapter 3, "Sympathetic Joy: Beyond Jealousy, Toward Relational Freedom," I focus on the experience of jealousy as a major obstacle for relational freedom. To this end, I explore how the application of the Buddhist contemplative practice of sympathetic joy or *mudita* to intimate relationships can transform jealousy and expand relational choices. After reviewing relevant findings from the field of evolutionary psychology on the twin origins of jealousy and monogamy, I introduce the notion of *genetic selfishness* or the privileging of one's own offspring over anyone's else. Then, I argue for the possibility to transform jealousy into sympathetic joy (or *compersion*) and challenge the culturally prevalent belief that the only spiritually correct sexual options are either celibacy or (lifelong or serial) monogamy. To conclude, I suggest that the cultivation of sympathetic joy in intimate connections paves the way to overcome the "mono–poly wars" and empowers people to better exercise relational freedom.

Chapter 4, "The Dawn of Transbinary Relationships," presents a more sustained discussion of the conceptual and experiential territory beyond the non/monogamy system. To this end, I consider three plural relational modes—fluidity, hybridity, and transcendence—that not only disrupt and arguably outdo the non/monogamy system but also embody and develop the various competences of relational freedom. Moving beyond the mono/poly binary, I argue, opens up a fuzzy, liminal, and multivocal semantic–existential space this book terms *novogamy*. After describing several transbinary pathways (e.g., developmental, contextual, intrapersonal, transcategorical), I suggest that an increasing number of twenty-first-century individuals will very likely enact novogamous relational identities beyond the mono/poly binary. In closing, I address the concern that transbinary relationship modes may lead to a lack of coherent identity and consequent psychological fragmentation.

Chapter 5, "Relational Freedom and the Transformation of Intimate Relationships," expands on the critical pluralist approach animating the prior discussions of relational styles. This approach effectively avoids universal sequences or hierarchies among monogamy, nonmonogamy, and novogamy, while simultaneously providing tools for qualitative discernment both within and among relational styles. Building on this discussion, I address the thorny question of the possibility of relational freedom in the context of the typology of conditioning sources introduced in chapter 1. After discussing some avenues to enhance relational freedom in oneself and others—including working toward dismantling social privilege and oppression—I respond to the potential objection of privileging individual freedom over relational care and family values. Then, I critique the standard of longevity in the assessment of relational success and outline various alternative emancipatory, healing, and transformational criteria as more appropriate for any (sub-)culture that is free from monocentrism. Finally, I briefly consider the future of romantic love beyond monocentrism and its attendant myth of a single "soul mate" or "The One."

The book closes with a coda and two appendices. The coda, "After Covid-19," discusses the future of nonmonogamies in the wake of the Covid-19 pandemic. Appendix I, "Ten Theses on Relationship Styles," outlines the central arguments of the book. Appendix II, "The Alpha Male versus the Omega Man," suggests that the ongoing evolution of intimate relationships needs to be grounded on—and is gradually transforming—not only human sexuality but also sexual identity. Leaving the task of discussing such changes in the female gender for discerning women attuned to the spirit of the times (as well as for queer and transgender people in the case of nonbinary gender identities), here I focus on exploring one possible shift in male sexual identity: the movement from the traditional Alpha Male to what I name the *Omega Man*.

It is important to disclose that I write as a white, middle-class, cisgender, "queer" or mostly heterosexual male who has lived long periods of both monogamy and nonmonogamy (as well as periods of sexually active singlehood and three years of highly erotic asexual–aromantic celibacy), but who has not felt identified with—and has actually felt oppressed by—these categories for more than a decade. Thus, in addition to a caring commitment to nurture the diversity of life's nonharmful creative expressions, a personal sense of frustration animates this book's efforts to think beyond the binary and bring forth relational spaces wherein, to put it bluntly, I (and perhaps many others) can feel more *at home*.[7]

Finally, largely due to this personal location, this book focuses on—and limits its validity claims to—heterosexual relationships between cisgender men and women. Although ample references are made to research on lesbian, gay, bisexual, transgender, and queer (LGBTQ+) experience, only members of these populations (and more informed scholars) can establish the full relevance of this book's theses and proposals outside the cisgender paradigm. Likewise,

I do not discuss asexual and aromantic identities or orientations (see Bogaert, 2015; Chasin, 2019; Przybylo, 2019), although some asexual people's emphasis on plural affective bonds can be seen as a type of polyamory (Copulsky, 2016; Scherrer, 2010). Admitting that each particular case should be individually assessed for possible developmental or even psychiatric factors (see Brotto & Yule, 2016; S. B. Levine, 2017), my proposal of relational freedom certainly includes and legitimizes these existential options (cf. Schippers, 2020; Wilkinson, 2010). That said, my articulation of transbinary relational styles is partly inspired by the lived experience and testimony of the many courageous individuals who dared to challenge binary constructs in biological sex, gender identity, sexual orientation, and race (e.g., Brubaker, 2016; Firestein, 1996; Stryker, 2008). In my efforts to both describe and enact transbinary relationships, I humbly stand on the shoulders of all these often-unrecognized giants.

Notes

[1] While most intimate relationships are developed over time, some also include casual, occasional, or singular encounters (Bradbury & Karney, 2014; Giddens, 1992; W. B. Miller, 2018). It is also important to note that one can, of course, be intimate in a nonsexual way with friends, partners, and family members (Helm, 2010; Jamieson, 1998; Przybylo, 2019), as well as in erotic and/or emotional ways with things, places, nature, and the world itself (Anderlini-D'Onofrio & Hagamen, 2015; Barker & Iantaffi, 2019). Although there is no scholarly consensus on the definition of romantic intimacy, most researchers agree that some kind of merging of two (but arguably more) identities resulting in feelings of extraordinary closeness and belonging is involved (see Erber & Erber, 2017; H. Rubin & L. Campbell, 2012). Successful romantic relationships in the Unites States have been characterized by the following features: excitement about meeting the beloved, passionate intimate lovemaking, feeling comfortable and behaving in amicable ways with one's partner, listening to the other's concerns about her or his job, offering to help out in various ways, and perceived mutual altruism and passion (de Munck & Kronenfeld, 2016).

[2] While this positive reframing of the inability to commit (to a single person) might feel misguided or even uncompassionate, especially to those who have suffered deeply in the wake of clandestine affairs, I firmly believe that most honest individuals are struggling today with dyadic fidelity due to the factors discussed in this book. Of course, some people systematically cheat without scruples out of deficit, narcissism, psychopathy, or selfish reasons (e.g., Josephs, 2018; McNulty & Widman, 2014), but as monocentrism generates the very possibility of cheating (there is no adultery without monogamy), I still believe it valuable to inquire into the deepest motivations for their behavior.

[3] For a powerful essay arguing that a solution to both relational style hierarchies and the problems of emerging polynormativities (see chapter 2) is to love life itself, see Barker et al. (2013).

4 *Nonmonogamy* is a more encompassing term than *polyamory* and is used throughout this book. The standard objection against the term *consensual nonmonogamy* (CNM) is that it defines itself in relation to what is not (as in calling people of color "nonwhite"), thus strengthening the hegemony of its polar opposite and perpetuating what Willey (2006) called the "non/monogamy system." However, although other more positive terms have been proposed (e.g., *responsible multi-partnering*; see Deri, 2015), there appears to be no single term that can encompass every possible relationship except monogamy without somehow referring to the latter, leaving *nonmonogamy* and *CNM* as the best available options. The former includes any type of nonmonogamous relationship (including open marriage, swinging, and promiscuity), while the latter is normally used to refer to the consensual, long-term maintenance of more than one romantic, sexual, and/or emotional bond as in the case of most forms of polyamory and open relationships (see Barker & Langdridge, 2010a, 2010b; Haritaworn et al., 2006; Klesse, 2006; Sheff & Tenese, 2015). Swinging would be a consensual, short-term form of nonmonogamy (see Bergstrand & Sinski, 2010). The obvious prototype for *nonconsensual nonmonogamy* is clandestine adultery, cheating, or any other form of being sexually and/or romantically engaged without the knowledge and consent of one's partner(s). In the context of a couple or any other relational structure (i.e., triads, polyfamilies), both casual sex and promiscuity can be either consensual or nonconsensual.

5 Although this book mostly focuses on polyamory as the most popular version of nonmonogamy today (e.g., Andersen, 2012; Burleigh & Rubel, 2020; Haslam, 2005–2013; Hogenboom, 2016), much of what is discussed may well apply to other CNMs. In this spirit, I use the term *poly* (e.g., "mono/poly" wars, mono/poly binary, polyphobia) as a generic abbreviation for all types of CNM relations. As for the incidence of CNM in the United States, a recent survey showed that 4% of a representative sample is currently engaged in open/nonmonogamous relationships (E. C. Levine et al., 2018), and several studies indicated that one in five adults have engaged in a CNM relationship at least once in their lives both in Canada (Fairbrother et al., 2019) and the United States (Haupert et al., 2017). Further, an even more recent survey of a representative sample of 3,438 U.S. singles showed that one out of nine (10.7%) had already engaged in polyamory and one out of six (16.8%) desired to engage in polyamory (Moors et al., 2021). As for nonheterosexual populations, the only available U.S. nationally representative survey indicated that 32% of gay men, 5% of lesbians, and 22% of bisexually identified people reported being in CNM relationships (E. C. Levine et al., 2018). Unfortunately, no data are currently available for the occurrence of CNM in Europe, Australia, or other Western populations.

6 For earlier accounts of queer theory as instigating the collapse of all such oppressive binaries and the problematization, transgression, or transcendence of the boundaries between them, see Fuss (1991) and de Lauretis (1991).

7 See Barker and Iantaffi (2019) for a helpful discussion of the shared challenges of nonbinary identities, including "a sense of not completely fitting in either place" (p. 117), as well as "double discrimination from both sides of the binary . . . internalized shame . . . [and] trouble locating yourself in terms of privilege or oppression" (p. 118).

Chapter 1

Relational Freedom and the Crisis of Modern Relationships

Traditional monogamy is in a profound and apparently unsurmountable crisis. Despite having been the only legal form of marriage in the Western world for centuries, this long-standing relational model based on lifelong sexual exclusivity to one partner is afflicted by a legion of seemingly unresolvable problems.[1] Although many of the challenges faced by modern monogamous couples are not new (the history of monogamy is the history of adultery), they have reached unprecedented scope and magnitude.[2] The failure to sustain a long-term, emotionally and erotically fulfilling life in the context of sexually exclusive bonds frequently leads to a profound sense of disillusionment, confusion, frustration, and inadequacy. Those who do achieve an enduring partnership where emotional and even spiritual intimacy flourishes often do so by sacrificing the joy, vital regeneration, and transcendent powers of erotic passion (S. A. Mitchell, 2002; Perel, 2006). Sooner or later (and often sooner), active or passive aggression sneaks in through the back door of such stable, semi-happy relationships (Haag, 2011). One does not need to go to bed with Sigmund Freud to recognize the many polarizations, confrontational attitudes, and even violent behaviors that can emerge from the repression of sexual needs, desires, and potentials. This growing crisis contributed to a shift in the prevalent relational paradigm in the West from lifelong monogamy ("till death do us part") to *serial monogamy*: the practice of engaging in romantic or sexually exclusive relationships sequentially (e.g., Cherlin, 2009; J. D. Foster, 2016; Woodword Thomas, 2015).

In this chapter, I first outline the merits and problems of the serial monogamy paradigm, to establish that it does not provide a satisfactory solution to our modern relationships crisis. Then, after arguing that monogamy's central relational trials are based on the tension between two conflicting human needs (sexual diversity and emotional stability), I explore six sources of relational conditioning potentially shaping relational style choices: evolutionary, biological, historical, cultural, social, and biographical. Finally, I introduce the notion of *relational freedom* as a way to address the modern crisis of relationships, and conclude with a vindication of the fundamental human right to love (any number of people as one desires).

The Problems of Serial Monogamy

At first, serial monogamy offered several important advantages over traditional monogamy. Although views supporting serial monogamy began to appear in the eighteenth century (Dabhoiwala, 2012), this relational mode did not prevail in Western society until the late twentieth century with the introduction of divorce and the possibility of remarriage (de la Croix & Mariani, 2015; R. Phillips, 1988)—and, I would add, the invention of the birth control pill and the incorporation of women in the labor market, which made it far more possible for unhappily married women to find better companions (see Blow & Hartnett, 2005; K. P. Mark et al., 2011; Finkel et al., 2014).[3] In any event, serial monogamy has today become the normative project of romantic self-actualization in the Western world (Petrella, 2005). As Overall (1998) pointed out, "When simultaneous relationships are not recognized and validated . . . the only alternative to lifelong monogamy may appear to be serial monogamy" (p. 6). In this context, regardless of what may be professed at nuptial ceremonies, traditional marriage vows have given way to "more realistic" prenuptial agreements or relational pledges. In other words, an increasing number of couples understand not only that their love will change over time but also that their committed relationship might not last forever. In this way, serial monogamy avoids the self-defeating expectations of lifelong promises and their associated disillusionments.

Serial monogamy has two additional advantages over traditional monogamy. First, it allows individuals to mature through exposure to a greater diversity of sexual and emotional partners—and, at least in theory, without cheating. Second, serial monogamy gives people the chance to separate from bad matches, learn from mistakes, heal wounds through successive relations, and approach a new relationship with enhanced self-awareness and more seasoned intimate skills. Even if it is rarely consciously engaged in these ways, serial monogamy can thus potentially be a path of mindful sexual, emotional, and relational healing and growth.[4]

Despite these relative merits, there are at least five reasons serial monogamy is not the path to a better future for everyone's intimate relationships. First and foremost, the Romantic Love Myth ("find your soul mate and live happily ever after") holds an overpowering fascination for the Western psyche (see Ben-Ze'ev

& Goussinsky, 2008; Kern, 1992). Relentlessly reinforced by the movie and music industries, pop culture, social media, and Judeo–Christian religions, this myth leads numerous serial monogamists to eventually experience a sense of failure. Many today wonder, "What's wrong with me? Why can't I maintain a lasting relationship?" The Romantic Love Myth engrains an increasing sense of dissatisfaction in the serial monogamy paradigm.

Second, many people cherish the prospect of sharing a substantial part of their lives with the person they have deeply fallen in love with but are sabotaged by sexual habituation. Already identified in human beings by Kinsey et al. (1953), *sexual habituation* is a systematic decrease in sexual arousal after repeated exposure to the same stimuli or intimate partner (Dawson et al., 2013; W. H. James, 1981; Over & Koukonas, 1995). Even though serial monogamists have greater chances of sustaining sexual passion throughout life by finding a new partner each time insurmountable problems arise, serial monogamy simply avoids the problem of sexual dissatisfaction in long-term, exclusive relationships (Ryan & Jethá, 2010). Sexual habituation, usually kicking in after a few weeks or months of regular sexual intimacy, tends to become (at times unbearably) an unwelcome but permanent guest in the relationship after 2–3 years (E. Anderson, 2012; Donnelly & Burgess, 2008; M. Robinson, 2009). Decreases in the frequency and quality of erotic exchanges impact not only sexual satisfaction but also emotional closeness and relational well-being (E. Anderson, 2012; Tennov, 1979).[5] This downward spiral of sexual–emotional corrosion often results over time in passive aggression, interpersonal quarrels, frustration, clandestine affairs, and separation (Perel, 2017; M. Robinson, 2009).[6] Modern technology also intensifies and accelerates the pace of breakups and separations.[7] "Three out of five relationships were over in little more than a year" showed a 2009–2012 demographic survey of over 3,000 U.S. residents (see Regnerus, 2017, p. 157).[8] Changing partners every few months (or even years) does not usually forge the emotional and spiritual depth that many people long for when romantically bonding; serial monogamy cannot fulfill this dream.

In the early 1990s, feminist writer Sonia Johnson (1991) had already captured the hopelessness many experience after repeated attempts at monogamous relationships:

> Thousands of us are completely fed up with the self-betrayal of marriage of any sort, including the self-betrayal of "serial monogamy." (Perhaps "serial agony" is a more apt description.) The thought of going through even one more relationship cycle, to say nothing of one after another until we die—ecstasy, contentment, boredom, numbness, pain, misery, breakup, recuperation—makes us feel suicidal when it doesn't bore us senseless. (p. 118)

In short, serial monogamy does not offer the stability and security that draw people to monogamy in the first place. As Jackson and Scott (2004) observed,

"In a social climate where serial monogamy prevails, promising monogamy and assuming that the relationship will end if the promise is broken surely creates conditions for the ultimate insecurity" (p. 156). Bingo.

Third, serial monogamy may be playing an important role in the propagation of sexually transmitted infections (STIs). In comparison to people engaged in CNM, serial monogamists may not be as proactive about STI testing (after all, they are *monogamous*)—even when they tend to have unprotected sex soon after they begin a new exclusive relationship (Conley et al., 2015).[9] Considering both the transience of many serial monogamous relationships, and the periods of looser or even simultaneous sexual connections between those "steady" relationships, serial monogamists with undiagnosed infections from previous partners may inadvertently spread the transmission of STIs. Since about 30% of U.S. adults through age 60 "report having had overlapping sexual relationships at some point in their lives" (Litschi et al., 2014, p. 25), this issue should not be underestimated. In addition, the gap between serially monogamous partnerships is often shorter than the infection period of most STIs (which can last weeks or months), so "partnerships can be behaviorally serially monogamous but biologically concurrent" (Mercer et al., 2013, pp. 249–250). To make things worse, out of fear of rejection or social stigmatization, some serial monogamists may hide the fact that they have tested positive (e.g., for herpes) from a desirable future partner; in the modern world, having contracted an STI is often equivalent to becoming an untouchable (e.g., Blickford et al., 2007; Lee & Craft, 2010; Nack, 2000). Thus, contrary to popular belief, serial monogamy can be an acutely hazardous intimate relationship style.

Fourth, in some cases serial monogamy can have undesirable consequences for both children and adults. It has been linked not only to the "current epidemic of broken homes and single-parent families" (Ryan & Jethá, 2010, p. 300; cf. Cherlin, 2009) but also the production of legions of wounded ex-partners and the loss of friendships (see Squire, 2008). Illustrating both potential problems, a polyamorous mother poignantly wrote: "I'm not going to ditch one loved one just because I love someone else. That's . . . more like serial heartbreak! And what it does to the kids!" (Naomi, as cited in Pallotta-Chiarolli, 2010, p. 41). On the one hand, serial monogamy among people who procreate can have a negative impact on an increasing number of children. According to recent statistics, about 1.5 million U.S. children experience the divorce of their parents every year (Arkowitz & Lilienfeld, 2013); in addition, 26% of North American children are living with only one parent and 15% are living in households with step-parents (Pew Research Center, 2015). Even though in optimal conditions children appear to recover from the most harmful effects of divorce in 2–3 years (Arkowitz & Lilienfeld, 2013), research on children from stepfamilies shows important comparative dysfunctions, such as lower grades in school (Nusinovici et al., 2018), higher rates of depression (Strohschein, 2005) and drug use (Hemovich & Crano, 2009), greater antisocial and delinquent behavior (Fagan & Churchill, 2012), more psychophysiological health issues (Nunes-Costa et al., 2009), and more problematic intimate relationships as adults (Kelly & Emery, 2003; Wallerstein & J. M. Lewis, 2004), among others (for reviews, see Amato, 2001, 2010). It is important to note, however, that these findings do not necessarily prove that divorce or parental separation is the only or main cause of such detriments; for example, factors such as the level of conflict between parents—prior and during divorce (Kelly, 2000)—and type of child–parent relationship after divorce seem to be often decisive in this regard (e.g., Amato, 2014; Lansford, 2009). (One could also hypothesize that the shift from an emotionally, physically, or sexually abusive parent to a healthy step-parent could actually be beneficial for children.) Likewise, with the appropriate conditions (e.g., cooperative relationships between all parties), many children from divorced parents can receive the constructive support of two different families (see Cohen, 2018; Ebersohn & Bouwer, 2015). In any event, as discussed in chapter 5, alternative relational paradigms can arguably foster more optimal conditions for raising children by minimizing the impact of changes in their parents' intimate lives.

On the other hand, the rupture of partnerships intrinsic to the serial monogamy paradigm often leads to troublesome relations between people who once loved one another deeply. In serial monogamy, Overall (1998) wrote, "When a partner begins a new sexual relationship, it is likely the beginning of the end for the old" (p. 6). First, because most people today do not deal well with romantic endings, harmful feelings from breakups often emerge, hindering the transformation of romantic bonds into deep friendships with people they have loved—and often still love, even though in a different way (Conley & Moors, 2014; Fischer et al., 2005). Second, even when friendships with ex-partners are achieved, they often gradually dissipate or radically terminate once engagement in a new monogamous relationship begins (severing connections with ex-partners is a typical demand in a monocentric context; Foley & Fraser, 1998). What is more, especially during cohabitation or marriage, monogamous people tend to spend less solo time with their former friends (for heterosexual couples, especially those of the opposite sex) and to avoid interacting with new attractive friends in order to conform to their partner's preferences, minimize exposure to tempting alternatives, or due to the phenomenon known as "dyadic withdrawal" (M. P. Johnson & Leslie, 1982; Kalmijn, 2003; B. H. Lee & Sullivan, 2019). Actually, dyadic withdrawal is strongly advised by some relationships "experts": the first of Neuman's (2001) eleven secrets to a great heterosexual marriage is to "insulate and protect your marriage against emotional infidelity by avoiding friendships with members of the opposite sex" (p. 17). Thus, in the serial monogamy paradigm relationships with ex-partners are problematized by both the enhanced emotional pain after recurrent separations and the monocentric phenomenon of dyadic withdrawal.

These points should also be qualified. Emotionally integrated and stable people who have not experienced—or have significantly healed—sexual trauma or mental illness are increasingly able to both maintain wholesome friendships with ex-partners and support their new mate's connections with both ex-partners and friends (prior and new). Naturally, whenever the decision to end the relationship is not mutual (especially if triggered by a clandestine affair or falling in love with another person), a phase of distance can be necessary for the healing process that allows the new friendship to bloom. As Meg-John Barker (2013) wrote in one of the most sensate guides to contemporary intimate relationships, "As with needing time out from a conflict, we may need time out from the old dynamics of a relationship before new dynamics can emerge: time to grieve, to process what has happened, and to let the heat go" (p. 145). Thus, although many factors are at play in these dynamics and each case should be considered independently, serial monogamy can have a pernicious impact on both children and relationships with ex-partners.

Last, despite promising to expand the possibilities of finding love for everyone, serial monogamy is disadvantageous for women and may reinforce patriarchal supremacy. As Marlowe (2000) explained, serial monogamy allows men who have higher status or are more physically attractive to achieve polygyny in a supposedly monogamous society, as they can access younger females as they age.[10] Because most young men refuse to mate with older women, the unfortunate outcome is that an increasing number of mature women cannot find a partner, ending up lonely, frustrated, and understandably resentful toward men.[11] Although men can also experience difficulties finding partners as they age, the available empirical evidence supports the view that, through sequential re-partnering, serial monogamy enhances the reproductive success of U.S. men but not of women (see Jokela et al., 2010). In these ways, serial monogamy results in the perpetuation of a patriarchal society.[12]

In sum, despite its several virtues and advantages over traditional monogamy, serial monogamy often leads to a sense of personal failure and frustration after repeated efforts to sustain exclusive romantic bonds, is easily prey to sexual habituation, could be contributing to the spread of STIs, can have a negative impact on both children and relations with ex-partners, and may be inadvertently maintaining the Western patriarchal status quo. To fully comprehend why serial monogamy is not entirely working for many people, however, it is important to consider two conflicting human needs underlying relational choices and dynamics.

Two Conflicting Human Needs

One way to understand modern relational trials is to recognize two conflicting needs at the very core of most people raised in modern Western society: the sexual need for diversity, novelty, and erotic passion on the one hand, and the emotional need for stability, safety, and depth on the other. Researchers of marriage and intimate relationships have articulated this conflict in various ways. For example, Ashkam (1984) conceptualized this predicament in terms of tension between a simultaneous search for identity-development and stability in intimate relations. Likewise, the chief feature of Bauman's (2003) *liquid love* (his favored term for modern romantic bonds) is its contradictory longing for both individual freedom and relational security. Explaining the shift from lifelong to serial marriage in the United States over the last decades, Cherlin (2009) appealed to "the central place in American culture of both marriage [i.e., committed partnership and family life] and a kind of individualism that emphasizes self-expression and personal growth" (p. 8).[13] Most people in long-term monogamous relationships negotiate these fundamental needs by repressing or sublimating their sexual needs, or by finding minimally satisfying ways to meet those needs (Brandon, 2010; Haag, 2011; Perel, 2006).

The challenge is apparently insuperable because these two needs not only pull people in different directions but also seem to be utterly irreconcilable. Whereas secure attachment is based on stability and security, erotic passion usually requires novelty, adventure, and the unknown (Brandon, 2010). Thus, to become attached to a stable, reliable companion eventually leads to a decrease in sexual desire (Eagle, 2007). The renowned psychoanalyst Stephen A. Mitchell (2002) put it this way: "Love seeks control, stability, continuity, certainty. Desire seeks surrender, adventure, novelty, the unknown" (p. 91), so "our longing for safety and our thirst for passion pull us in opposite directions" (p. 113). These views are supported by research showing how *passionate love* (based on strong sexual desire) consistently turns into *companionate love* (based on caring friendship and intimacy) over time (Hatfield et al., 1984; Sprecher & Regan, 1998). Recently, Balzarini et al. (2019) associated passionate and companionate love with van Anders's (2015) two fundamental functions of intimate relationships: eroticism and nurturance. Both sexual eroticism and emotional nurturance are arguably animated by equally vital developmental pulls, and both serve fundamental roles in relationships. To privilege one over the other leads to individual or relational quandaries (and often both).

Historically, having affairs in the context of a long-term, committed relationship has been the most common—if suboptimal—"strategy" to address this tension (D. E. Schmitt, 2005a; Treas & Giesen, 2000). Developing this reasoning, Lawson (1988) argued that adultery often results from a tension between the Myth of Romantic Love—which frames marriage as a lifelong journey from the altar to death—and the Myth of Me—which privileges individual self-realization over relationships. This point is related to E. Anderson's (2012) argument that cheating is a rational response to the irrational predicament of mononormativity, which demands dyadic sexual exclusivity. In this context, E. Anderson pointed out that cheating not only rectifies the dissonance many people feel between their monogamous self-identity and their desire for sexual diversity but also allows them to access sexual variety while staying in a long-term relationship (cf. Mint, 2004). In other words, through adultery, an individual is able to experience emotional stability at home and sexual novelty and passion with temporary lovers.[14] In chapter 4, I discuss the arguably more constructive pathways that contemporary couples are creatively exploring to relax this essential tension and live more fulfilling sexual, emotional, and relational lives.

In light of these issues, practical guides on how to revamp monogamy written by couple counselors and relationship "experts" flood the market every year. The overriding aim of these guides is to offer advice about how to rekindle desire in sexually exclusive couples. Repeatedly, readers are reassured of the prospect of "reclaiming desire" (Goldstein & Brandon, 2004), "boost[ing] their marriage libido" (Robin, 2017), "resurrecting sex" (Schnarch, 2002), or having "ridiculously great sex" (Snyder, 2018) in the context of an upgraded "hot monogamy" (Love & J. Robinson, 2012), "red-hot monogamy" (Farrel & Farrel, 2006), "mature monogamy" (Masters, 2007), or "passionate marriage" (Schnarch, 2009). The fact that these books continue to appear and sell, however, attests to not only a seeming pandemic of impoverished sexual lives for long-term monogamous couples but also the books' ultimate failure in delivering the promised fruits.[15]

The Need for Deep Structural Change

Efforts to solve the problems of serial monogamy described above evoke the futile struggle of a homeowner stubbornly determined to restore a centuries-old house without changing its foundations or undertaking major renovations. It is vital to remember that the relational structure we have come to call "monogamy" probably emerged in the West about 8,000–10,000 years ago (Stearns, 2009). Some experts even place "arranged marriages" involving bride price or the like at 50,000 years ago (R. S. Walker et al., 2011, p. 2), and others suggest that *Homo erectus* (the direct ancestor of *Homo sapiens*) very likely pair-bonded monogamously 2 million years ago (Isler & van Schaik, 2012). Regardless, monogamy's origins entailed drastically different social, cultural, economic, and religious circumstances (for a review, see M. M. Dow & Eff, 2013). In particular, scholars have associated the origins of socially institutionalized monogamy with the birth of patriarchy, the advent of agriculture, the rise of private property, and the control of female sexuality to ensure paternity (e.g., Jackson & Scott, 2004; Ryan & Jethá, 2010; see also chapter 2, note 5). For many millennia and until the late eighteenth century, monogamous marriage was essentially a socially enforced financial and/or political transaction among patriarchal families—in which women had not much choice; neither the love–marriage linkage nor gender-neutral marriage laws became widespread until the late twentieth century (Betzig, 1992, 1995; Coontz, 2005; Yalom, 2001). In any event, as Dabhoiwala (2012) documented, most early civilizations—from Babylonian to Assyrian to Egyptian to Jewish to Greek and Roman—considered adultery a very serious offense and at times punishable by death: "The main concern of such laws was usually to uphold the honour and property rights of fathers, husbands, and higher-status groups" (p. 5). The most basic justification for sexual discipline and sexual policing of the female gender, he continued, "was the patriarchal principle that every woman was the property of her father or husband, so that it was a kind of theft for any stranger to have sex with her" (p. 27). Although mutual attraction (and even courtship) was not necessarily absent in arranged marriages, up to the mid-eighteenth century, marriages were essentially negotiated over marital property and inheritance laws (Dabhoiwala, 2012; Erickson, 2005).

Although modern Western couples are indeed more egalitarian, to claim that contemporary heterosexual monogamy is free from patriarchal tropes would certainly be preposterous. To be sure, with the emergence of romantic love over the last few centuries (along with, for example, the rise of individual rights and feminism; Coontz, 2005), marriage has moved toward a more gender-egalitarian relational mode based on free choice and increasing emotional and sexual democracy (see Giddens, 1992). As the new waves of feminism have proven, however, patriarchal sexism still breathes with ludicrous ease in Western culture (e.g., Bates, 2016), and the original patriarchal–capitalist ethos of control and possessiveness persists in the deep structure of contemporary monogamy (Barker & Ritchie, 2007; Jackson & Scott, 2004; V. Robinson, 1997). What is needed, thus, is not to Band-Aid, patch, or reinforce an outdated structure but to have the emotional, political, and spiritual courage to undertake major reforms and cocreate novel relational structures capable of meeting the challenges of our times.

Deep structural change is the mark of genuine growth and evolution. Despite how essential the uterus is for the growth of a new life, the fetus must eventually leave its protecting container in order to be born into a new—and far broader and richer—world. Despite how important it is for children to live in a safe home under parental care, they too eventually need to depart in order to get ahead with their own lives. A simple notebook may suffice for keeping track of information at the start of a new business venture; for success, one eventually needs a website and accounting software, or even a larger infrastructure with premises and colleagues to support the venture's growth and evolution. Likewise, individuals seeking to live more fulfilling relational styles may need to break free from the sociohistorical conditionings that have trapped their spirits in boxes far too narrow for the span of their wings.

The magnitude of these structural challenges should not be underestimated. Whether in culture, personal psychology, or intimate relationships, much unnecessary suffering stems from attachment to structures that once were necessary, optimal, or constructive but that no longer serve a positive function. In some cases, however, attachment to old structures emerges not simply from deeply engrained habits and the (normally unconscious) fears of the ego-death entailed by the birth of any new identity (e.g., Grof, 1985; Loy, 2000), but also from culturally transmitted relational conditioning. Kipnis's (2003) words get to the heart of the matter:

> It's clear that serial monogamy evolved as a pressure-release valve to protect the system from imploding. No, there is nothing wrong with the institution or its premises, no, you just happened to get the wrong person. But next time around you'd better make the best of it, because too many strikes and you're out— you're the problem. In serial monogamy, the players change, but the institution remains the same. (p. 176)

Generally speaking, researchers have discussed six levels of conditioning in the selection of relational styles: evolutionary, biological, historical, cultural, social, and biographical. Although all these levels interact in diverse and complex ways, for the sake of clarity I discuss them for the most part independently.

Levels of Relational Conditioning

Evidence for the *evolutionary* and *biological* shaping of human mating strategies and associated relational styles is controversial. Whereas some evolutionary psychologists have argued that relationships in archaic times were characterized by a mix of short-term (3–4 years long) serial monogamous relations (enough time to safely raise a single child through infancy) and clandestine adultery (as having other mates provided evolutionary advantages for both genders; Fisher, 1992, 2011), other scholars have argued for a radically promiscuous sexual prehistoric past that evolutionarily anchors and boosts modern nonmonogamous impulses (Melotti, 1981; Ryan & Jethá, 2010). Overall, the evidence suggests the existence of a diversity of evolutionarily shaped mating strategies—from lifelong monogamy to serial monogamy plus clandestine affairs to nonmonogamy (e.g., Buss, 2006; Buss & D. E. Schmitt, 1993; D. E. Schmitt, 2005b)—rendering the discernment of how these forces may affect individual relational choices rather speculative. On a biological level, several studies have suggested specific genetic and hormonal variables predisposing people to either monogamous or nonmonogamous lifestyles (e.g., van Anders et al., 2007; Walum et al., 2008; L. J. Young et al., 1999). As discussed in chapter 2, however, the available biological evidence is largely inconclusive, and, at least in some cases, ideologically suspect (see Brandon, 2010; Willey, 2016). In addition, I raise several interpretive questions and dilemmas in chapter 5 that problematize the value of that evidence in the assessment and pursuit of relational freedom. Thus, to appeal to either evolutionary or biogenetic forces to account for relational-style choices is fraught with substantial difficulties.

The particular impact of historical, cultural, social, and biographical factors—though far from being uncontentious—is more widely accepted by both scholars and researchers. For example, it is likely that *historical* factors have a significant weight in contemporary monogamous choices. Monogamy (both lifelong and serial) was gradually internalized worldwide over centuries of patriarchal social enforcement (Dabhoiwala, 2012; de la Croix & Mariani, 2015; M. M. Dow & Eff, 2013). Throughout the European Middle Ages, for example, Dabhoiwala wrote,

> Underpinning this unceasing watchfulness [of sexual behavior] was the continual indoctrination of the ideals of monogamy and chastity. That lust was a dangerous and shameful passion, that fornication was evil, and adultery criminal—these were doctrines drummed into every man, woman, and child, throughout their life, in speech and print, from every conceivable direction. *Most people internalized them profoundly* [emphasis added], even when they sometimes acted in contrary ways. (p. 24)

In other words, the historical imposition of monogamy may have resulted in a pandemic condition of *psychologically enforced monogamy*. This predicament explains why many self-identified feminist women,

> although they understand, in theory, the patriarchal origins of the practice of monogamy, they are nonetheless unable to free themselves of their socialization to the extent of being able to countenance nonmonogamous relationships for their lovers or even for themselves. (Overall, 1998, p. 2)

Modern research also supports the notion of psychologically enforced monogamy: Even coupled people with no explicit monogamy agreement employ "monogamy maintenance strategies" in response to extradyadic attraction (e.g., derogation, avoidance), which "suggests that individuals have internalized norms about maintaining exclusivity" (B. H. Lee & O'Sullivan, 2019, p. 1744). As with other interiorized values and ideologies (e.g., racism, patriarchy, heterosexism), psychologically enforced monogamy can—and does—therefore unconsciously affect seemingly conscious relational behaviors and choices, perhaps even effectively preventing people from considering the historically coerced nature of such choices.[16] Building on Hegel's and Nietzsche's reflections, critical theorists appealed to the notion of a "second nature" to refer to unconscious attitudes, habits, or behaviors so deeply engrained that they feel "natural" to their agents (see Archer et al., 2013a). In other words, some modern individuals may sincerely believe that they are preferring monogamy when in fact their choice has been historically shaped in such profound ways that the detection of its possibly unfree nature is exceptionally challenging.

Likewise, scholars have identified a legion of *cultural* forces contributing to the implementation of monogamous values—from legal mechanisms (L. S. Anderson, 2016; Emens, 2004) to psychotherapeutic narratives (Bergstrand & Sinski, 2010) to institutional regulations (Kipnis, 2003). As discussed in chapter 2, these forces empower culturally prevalent assumptions about the normalcy and naturalness of monogamy (Barker & Langdridge, 2010b; Pieper & Bauer, 2005), simultaneously marginalizing nonmonogamous alternatives (Conley, Moors et al., 2013). Even though mononormativity dominates the modern West, the 2000s and 2010s have witnessed many cultural counterforces shaping relational choices in alternative directions. I am not just referring to adolescents' and young adults' hook-up culture (Garcia et al., 2012; L. Wade, 2017) or the increasing social popularity of polyamory (e.g., Newitz, 2006; Pappas & LiveScience, 2013), but also to the larger-than-ever impact of online dating and free access to pornography in the West. As Regnerus (2017) argued, in addition to the introduction of effective contraception, online dating/meeting services and mass-produced, high-resolution pornography "have created a massive slow-down in the development of committed relationships, especially [monogamous] marriage" (p. 11). To be sure, some monogamous individuals and couples can use pornography to satisfy their need for sexual variety and enrich their intimate lives, and pornography's impact on relational satisfaction seems to largely depend on people's acceptance of pornography, possible use discrepancies between partners, and attachment style (e.g., Mass et al., 2018; Willoughby et al., 2016). However, regularly watching pornography—with its diverse erotic scenarios and virtually infinite objects of sexual desire—may also heighten people's fascination for a variety of sexual partners and decrease their attraction to the real (i.e., non-fantasy) partner(s) in their lives, thereby conditioning people's relational choices away from monogamy and contributing to marital separations (see Perry, 2018; Wright et al., 2017). For a balanced discussion of the perceived positive and negative effects of pornography use based on 430 qualitative interviews with men and women in heterosexual relationships, see Kohut et al. (2017). Online dating/meeting services such as OkCupid, Tinder, or Grindr are widely used for hooking up outside committed relationships and have wildly expanded the possibilities of finding sexual/romantic options beyond the traditional dyad (Regnerus, 2017; Slater, 2013). The infamous website Ashley Madison explicitly encourages infidelity through providing contacts for extramarital affairs to socially monogamous people (Brennan & Jaworski, 2015; Madison, 2017). Bottom line, whereas online dating clearly strengthens serial monogamy, it can also reinforce nonmonogamous feelings and behaviors.

The desire for monogamy has also been connected with the historically predominant nuclear family model of cohabitation in the modern West, which stereotypically consists of two children raised by their biological mother and father (Bengston, 2001). Building on attachment theory (Ainsworth et al., 1978; Bowlby, 1969), researchers have suggested that the infant's attachment to a primary caregiver serves as the foundation for exclusive attachment to a single person in romantic relationships (e.g., Fraley & Davis, 1997; Fraley et al., 2013; Hazan & Diamond, 2000)—which is not to say that all romantic bonds are attachment relationships (see chapter 4, note 4). In the nuclear family model, most children are tended by a single primary caregiver (usually the mother) during their early years of life, so an unconscious association between primordial love and monogamy might result (Benjamin, 1988; Chodorow, 1978). As Tsoulis (1987) pointed out, "By forcing women to be the main child-rearers, the consequence is that children begin their lives being totally dependent on one adult, which has important implications for the direction of their emotional development" (p. 25). Building on Tsoulis's reasoning, V. Robinson (1997) argued that people bring those feelings of exclusive dependency into adult sexual relationships, expecting one person to fulfill all their needs; when this does not happen, hurt feelings of rejection and loss ensue. Because not even the most devoted mothers can give constant unconditional love to their children, the argument proceeds, an unconscious search for such a loving referent is often launched in adulthood to complete what could not be realized in childhood (e.g., Chodorow, 1978). In the case of heterosexual females or homosexual males, the absence of a loving father could also have a similar impact. Bottom line, as Overall (1998) put it,

> if human socialization did not foster dependence upon one human being—in short, if the construction of gender were not the linchpin of patriarchy—the perhaps sexual exclusivity and inclusivity would not raise problem for women's (and men's) sexual relationships. (p. 15)

Even in those cases of a happy infancy where children receive generous amounts of unconditional love, those positive early imprints could lead to seeking the fulfillment of one's intimate needs in an idealized single person—and to disappointing frustration when this unrealizable project fails (see Charles, 2002). The neurochemical cascade catalyzed by the experience of falling in love can temporarily provide such a feeling of fulfillment, but the inexorable expiration date of this feeling can lead over time to further disappointment and even cynicism about love (e.g., Fisher, 2004; M. Robinson, 2009).[17]

Furthermore, particular *social* identities and locations—associated with various types and degrees of social privilege and oppression—can effectively condition people's relational choices. Consider the case of traditional heterosexual gender roles: due to patriarchal sexual double standards (Crawford & Popp, 2003; Valenti, 2008), women are usually judged more negatively than men as their number of sexual partners increases (Marks et al., 2017). Extrapolating from how differently men and women engaging in casual and promiscuous sex are seen in Western culture (e.g., Conley, Ziegler et al., 2013), I believe it safe to say that poly women tend to be pigeonholed as "sluts," "harlots," or even "sex-hungry nymphomaniacs" (e.g., Tanenbaum, 1999; A. M. Walker, 2017; Wolf, 1997), while men are more positively seen as "studs" or "playboys" especially by other men but also by mainstream culture in general (LeMoncheck, 1997; Moors et al., 2013). Indeed, Jenkins (2017) described this Western cultural predicament as the "slut-versus-stud phenomenon" (p. 139; see also Valenti, 2008). That said, men are not immune to anti-promiscuity attacks: some poly men (especially those who are socially successful) tend to be seen as narcissistic womanizers who objectify women either for their own sexual pleasure or to bolster their Alpha-male status, which may be the case in some cases but clearly not in others (see Appendix II; Sheff, 2006).

In addition, as intersectionality studies have shown, the forces regulating social oppression normally intersect—or, perhaps more accurately, are interlocked (see Razack, 2005)—in rather complex and multifarious ways.[18] With its origins in black feminist thought, the notion of *intersectionality* refers to the interdependent nature of the social systems of privilege and oppression shaping people's plural identities and subjectivities (Creenshaw, 1989; Carastathis, 2016); for example, a black woman of low socioeconomic status often experiences concurrent racial, class, and patriarchal coercion or domination. Although usually focused on the mutually reinforcing nature of gender, race, class, and sexuality, intersectionality studies can include the critical analysis of variables such as age, disability, education, occupation, perceived level of attractiveness, income, marital status, religion, and nationality, among others (Gopaldas, 2013). For example, a gay, white male surgeon with "effeminate" traits may be more stigmatized at his hospital workplace than a straight, blue-collar black man who works as an auto mechanic and stays in his racial "place" (R. S. Chang & McCristal Culp, 2002). Thus, all social locations can be examined for their potential advantages and disadvantages in different contexts.

Relational choices are not at all exempt from these intersectional influences. For example, the relational freedom of bisexual, dark-skinned, and/or "lower-class" women is severely constrained by cultural discourses depicting these populations' sexual agency as "immoral" or "perverted" (Bhattacharyya, 1998; Klesse, 2005, 2014). Commenting on her ethnographic findings, Sheff (2005) pointed out, "While all of the polyamorous women in my sample faced the social risks of stigma, the women of color felt at greater risk of stigma and consequences for engaging in polyamory than did the white women I interviewed" (p. 277; see also A. A. Alexander, 2019; Pain, 2019). As Clardy (2018) argued, African American poly men are also negatively stereotyped as hypersexualized womanizers or "players," with many enduring, detrimental consequences for their self-identity. Positively reclaiming the word "pervert," some African American poly people are even calling themselves "perverts of color" (see *Perverts of Color Zine: Celebrating the Diversity of Perversity*). From another perspective, one U.S. middle-aged black woman reported: "Being a Black polyamorous person is unique because we have the stigma of our own community's homophobia and inflexibility when it comes to different family dynamics" (cited in C. N. Smith, 2017, p. 125). As in the case of coming out as lesbian, gay, or bisexual (Moradi et al., 2010), it is likely that deviating from mononormativity can be more stigmatizing for people of color (especially those with a lower socioeconomic status) than for white folks, which could partly explain why the former might elect themselves out from polyamory research studies (see Sheff & Hammers, 2011). So, gender, sexual orientation, race, and class (among other social positionalities) are deeply interdependent structural factors conditioning—and often constraining—the possibilities of relational freedom.[19]

These historical, cultural, and social factors predictably intermingle with *biographical* conditions, yielding results that can contribute to both monogamous and nonmonogamous propensities. The presence of possible deficits in early relationships with primary caregivers (e.g., emotional neglect or attachment issues) would appear to powerfully reinforce the monogamous stranglehold on relational choices. For example, some people may feel strongly drawn to monogamy (and its promise of enduring love) in order to create safe or controlled conditions that minimize their being emotionally harmed or abandoned. Supporting this view, some studies showed that individuals with a high anxious attachment style are more prone to experience jealousy and hold more negative attitudes toward engaging in CNM (Moors et al., 2015; Moors, Selterman et al., 2017). On the other hand, suboptimal biographical experiences can also play a role in the choice of nonmonogamous lifestyles. For example, the presence of an invasive mother in childhood, repeated failed attempts to find motherly unconditional love in a romantic partner, or traumatic monogamous intimate experiences can lead some individuals to avoid romantic attachment to a single person and explore nonmonogamy. After being abandoned by two women in his youth, a poly man reported, "I find it so much more comfortable to have several relationships at once. You are never quite vulnerable in the same way if you have several relationships at once" (cited by Illouz, 2019, p. 173). The aforementioned studies also showed that people with high avoidant attachment style display more positive attitudes toward engaging in CNM (Moors et al., 2015; Moors, Selterman et al., 2017). One can also hypothesize that the overprotective attachment of a mother to her child, presented (excused?) as love can create a negative early association between love and lack of freedom. Father absence during early childhood has also been associated with sexual promiscuity and less predisposition to committed monogamy in both male and female college students and adults (Hehman & Salmon, 2019; Salmon et al., 2016)—even though these researchers' (arguably mononormative and nuclear-family centered) linking of father absence with "stressful childhood environment" can hide the possibility that, at least in some cases, the absence of an authoritarian or sexually repressive father figure actually allowed an increased sexual–relational freedom. In addition, early sexual abuse can lead to risky, impulsive, or submissive nonmonogamy, as it can render survivors less able to know, articulate, and enforce what they do and do not want in a sexual encounter or relationship (e.g., Harden et al., 2015; Senn et al., 2018).

In any event, as in the case of jealousy and other deep-seated emotions (e.g., Buss, 2000a), it can be theorized that the particular nature and seriousness of biographical issues modulates the influence of particular evolutionary, historical, and cultural forces on people's relational choices. This hypothesis is supported by transgenerational studies, which have provided ample evidence suggesting that personal trauma can make people more permeable to transgenerational traumatic influences, such as childhood abuse, patriarchal oppression, or slavery and torture (e.g., A. Harris et al., 2017). To complicate things further, clinical evidence suggests the possible impact of prenatal, perinatal, and transpersonal variables on individuals' psychological conditions and concerns (Allen et al., 1998; Essau et al., 2018; Grof, 1985). Although the precise ways these variables may impact relational dynamics and choices have not been studied, it would be a serious mistake to dismiss their possible formative role.

So, while historical and sociocultural factors affect each person's unique propensity for (or aversion to) monogamy or nonmonogamy, individual choices are often being made atop a biographical foundation that may be too flawed to be patched or papered over.[20] How to then constructively engage our modern crisis of relationships? I propose what I term *relational freedom*, outlined in the next section (and fully addressed in chapter 5).

Toward Relational Freedom

While monogamy in its various versions cannot provide a satisfactory solution to the current crisis of intimate relationships in the West, this book does not seek to enthrone one particular "antidote" to modern intimate maladies. My intention is not to "debunk" monogamy and pronounce either polyamory or novogamy (i.e., relationship styles beyond the mono/poly binary; see chapter 4) as the most suitable relational style for the twenty-first century. In contrast, one of this book's central arguments is that whereas types of monogamy, polyamory, and novogamy range from more fear-based to more life-enhancing, from more destructive to more constructive, and from more to less socially aware of social privilege, these relational styles cannot be placed in any universal developmental or evolutionary continuum. Put bluntly, one can choose any relational style for the "right" or "wrong" reasons. Two additional factors (discussed in chapters 2 and 4 in greater detail) further problematize the validity of proclaiming any relational style as paradigmatically superior. On the one hand, it is likely that human beings are endowed with diverse biological, psychological, emotional, and perhaps even spiritual dispositions that may predispose particular individuals to thrive in the context of different relationship styles. On the other hand, some people can be called to one or another relational style depending on different developmental junctures and sociopolitical situations. Thus, to arrange monogamy, polyamory, and novogamy in any universal or absolute sequential order is not only fallacious but also ideological and misleading (see chapter 5).

In any case, as the stress fractures on the foundations of mainstream monogamy reflect, it seems unquestionable that the modern West is undergoing the dawn of a new era, bringing unprecedented changes in the way sexuality and intimate bonds are both understood and lived (e.g., Bauman, 2003; Haag, 2011; Weeks, 2007; Witt, 2016). Such a shift can be understood—in an admittedly oversimplified manner—as an emerging arc of a larger historical process: from unconscious forms of monogamy and nonmonogamy (archaic era) to socially imposed polygyny and monogamy (agricultural, feudal, and modern eras), serial monogamy (modern/postmodern era), and now mindful monogamy, CNM, polyamory, and novogamy (metamodern or post-postmodern era).[21] This historical process can also be framed in terms of gender as a transition from pre/modern patriarchal[22] monogamy and polygyny to post/modern, more gender-egalitarian serial monogamy, and now to metamodern post-patriarchal monogamy, nonmonogamy/polyamory, and novogamy.

Several novel emancipatory possibilities in the relational realm have been emerging at least since the sexual revolution of the 1960s (Allyn, 2000; Hekma & Giami, 2014). Briefly, I propose that a significant percentage of the Western population is gradually achieving competence in the following four relational skills or capabilities:

1. *Relational integration*: The ability to mindfully integrate essential values of both monogamy and nonmonogamy in intimate relationships, such as stability and diversity, or commitment and freedom.
2. *Relational plasticity*: The capability to live monogamy and nonmonogamy sequentially or cyclically at different developmental junctures or situations without serious fears or conflicts.

3. *Relational autonomy*: The power to choose between monogamy and non-monogamy as one's temporary, indefinite, or permanent relational style increasingly free from biological, psychological, sociocultural, and religious pressures.
4. *Relational transcendence*: The capability to experience and live intimate relationships beyond the mono/poly binary and the non/monogamy system.

These competences both *shape* and *are* different expressions of what I call *relational freedom*[23]—a regulatory ideal or principle for critical deliberation (see chapter 5) characterized by mindful autonomy, the resolution of or significant progress on psychological fears (e.g., of intimacy, abandonment, engulfment), and increased emancipation from possible biological and sociocultural conditionings in the choice of relational style and the cocreation of intimate bonds. (Although not discussed in this book, it should be obvious that relational freedom is also facilitated by improved interpersonal communication and emotional intelligence skills.) While relational freedom may never be *fully* achievable, nonetheless some relational choices are freer than others.

Whereas in chapter 5 I describe some avenues to enhance relational freedom, here I want to underline that in order to freely choose a relational style—and, more troubling, to even know that the choice is free—one must overcome significant difficulties, particularly those presented by a mononormative context and yet more incisively in the case of marginal social groups. It might be argued that, as in the case of queer lifestyle choices in heteronormative cultures, nonmonogamous options are automatically marked with a stamp of greater freedom. After all, monogamy has been socially imposed in the West for centuries (e.g., de la Croix & Mariani, 2015; Herlihy, 1995; MacDonald, 1995) and continues to be enforced through a wide variety of cultural and institutional mechanisms (Bergstrand & Sinski, 2010; Emens, 2004; Kipnis, 2003; Rosa, 1994; Tweedy, 2011). Breaking away from monogamy, the argument goes, is far more likely to be a free choice than staying within the default monogamous mode. However, some people could also be driven or hastily turn to CNM or polyamory due to either repeated disappointments in monogamous relationships or certain psychosexual conditions. For example, some individuals may feel pulled to explore polyamory in the wake of frustrating monogamous experiences with jealous partners, traumatic abandonment, loss of autonomy, sexual habituation, or monotony and boredom. Others may experience serious conflicts in conventional monogamy due to biographically imprinted engulfment fears, commitment issues, or sexual addictions, among other possibilities.

In any event, given its many problems, *socially enforced* monogamy must be honestly scrutinized and, I argue, radically transformed.[24] Although the gray line between deficit-based motivations and *metaneeds* impelling individuals toward wholeness and self-actualization (Koltko-Rivera, 2006; Maslow, 1971) varies both historically and cross-culturally (Cianci & Gambrel, 2003; Tay & Diener, 2011) and should thus be individually discerned, to know with confidence that one's relational choices are free appears to be extremely challenging. An obvious first step (undertaken in chapter 2) is to critically examine mononormativity—and relational normativity generally—with the goal of supporting people to choose love more freely.

The Right to Love

To conclude, I propose that any relational normativity—whether mono or poly—infringes on a fundamental human right: the right to love any number of human beings in whatever mutually beneficial, personally growthful, and nonharmful manner one desires or feels called to do.[25] This account is aligned with Wendy-O Matik's understanding of radical love as "the freedom to love whom you want, how you want, and as many as you want, so long as personal integrity, respect, honesty, and consent are at the core of any and all relationships" (as cited in Labriola, 2013, p. 152). In this context, I submit that mononormativity violates the right to love more than one person in ways that can incorporate physical, sexual, emotional, and spiritual love. Likewise, emergent forms of polynormativity (see chapter 2) can be seen as infringing on the right to concentrate one's own sexual or emotional love on a single person temporarily or indefinitely. To love as many other human beings as one feels called to in consensually agreed ways, however, should be considered a human right as fundamental as the right to equality, free movement, or freedom of belief.

Furthermore, I propose that to give and receive embodied love is not only a human but also a spiritual right. In the wake of modernity's secularization process, it is worth noting here, important elements of the Judeo–Christian tradition were assimilated into Western cultural values (Areshidze, 2017; Habermas, 2002; Taylor, 2007), shaping most people's approach to love and relationships regardless of their secular or religious orientation (Kern, 1992; May, 2011; Willey, 2018).[26] In particular, mainstream Western culture inherited from puritanical forms of Christianity a rather dissociated vision of erotic love that, with a few historical exceptions (see Burrus, 2004; Williams, 1987), drastically divorced all things sexual from both spiritual pursuits and the divine (e.g., Boyarin, 1995; Irwin, 1991; J. B. Nelson, 1983). Whereas the Christian God was traditionally thought to love all beings nonerotically via *agape* (i.e., unconditional love that is absent of desire), the validity of sexual love was limited to monogamous, heterosexual relationships within divinely sanctioned marriages (Nygren, 1982).[27]

Although this book is not the place to develop this argument, I theorize that an increasing integration of sexuality and spirituality in people's lives is dramatically affecting essential aspects of the modern transformation of intimacy (e.g., R. Bell, 2007; Eliens, 2009; T. Moore, 1998). In the West's increasingly postsecular age (Habermas, 2008; King, 2009), for example, a growing number of individuals (in both Europe and the United States) consider themselves Spiritual But Not Religious (SBNR), freely adopting and adapting all sorts of spiritual orientations and practices into more "holistic" spiritual lives (Fuller, 2001; W. B. Parsons, 2018). Informed by a complex blend of Westernized forms of tantra (Urban, 2003), New Age spirituality (Hanegraaff, 1998), and modern sex-positive secular values (Kern, 1992), this "spiritual turn" (Houtman & Aupers, 2007) bridges sexuality and spirituality as well as reunites erotic, emotional, and spiritual love (e.g., J. Brown, 2019; Fuller, 2008; Ogden, 2006). Furthermore, as L. Phillips and Stewart (2008) argued, the connection between sexuality and spirituality affirmed by many non-Western religious traditions (e.g., African, Caribbean, Native American, Hindu) may be central to many queer and African American identities (e.g., Conner & Sparks, 2004; G. H. James & L. Moore, 2006).

Thus, whereas the right to love has historically been denied by mononormative structures with roots in the religious past of the West, secularization has led to a deconstruction of these values, the emergence of post-Christian and transreligious spiritualities, and the rise of more liberal monogamous and CNM relational styles.[28] Whatever one may think of these trends, I am convinced that they will not only substantially increase over the next decades but also gradually lead individuals to more clearly recognize—and perhaps eventually overcome—the obstacles imposed by cultural and relational norms onto the human right to love.

Notes

[1] For example, rising separation and divorce rates (e.g., Cohen, 2016; Wang & Schofer, 2018), a staggering number of clandestine affairs (e.g., K. Campbell & Wright, 2010; Treas & Giesen, 2000; Vangelisti & Gerstenberger, 2004), lack of libido and sexual dysfunctions (e.g., Charny & Asinelli-Tal, 2004; Frank et al., 1978), monotony and boredom (e.g., Haag, 2011; S. A. Mitchell, 2002; Perel, 2006), the repression of desire and sexless marriages (e.g., Fleisher & Foss-Morgan, 2016; Parker-Pope, 2009), Internet pornography addiction (e.g., Carnes et al., 2007; Todd et al., 2015; however, see Duffy et al., 2016; Levy et al., 2014), the normalization of casual sex (Illouz, 2019), accusations of emotional adultery (e.g., L. Collins, 1999; Potter-Efron & Potter-Efron, 2008), Internet romances and infidelities (Hertlein & Piercy, 2006; Vossler & Moller, 2020), Facebook infidelity (Abbasi & Alghamdi, 2017), cyber-affairs through avatars and virtual reality (e.g., C. Jones, 2010; Maheu & Subotnik, 2001), virtual brothels using teledildonics (wireless-synched sex toys; Wakeman, 2016), sexual–affectionate relationships with sexbots (e.g., Hawkes & Lacey, 2019; Levy, 2007), and domestic violence and abuse (e.g., Goetz et al., 2008; Wilson & M. Daly, 1996).

2 To be sure, some of these problems are both novel and controversial (e.g., emotional, Internet, and virtual infidelities), but consider the scale of contemporary sexual affairs. While reliable estimates are complicated by factors such as sample variability (e.g., married or nonmarried couples; see K. P. Mark et al., 2011) or what counts as infidelity for different people (see chapter 4), the ratios of clandestine affairs in the Unites States moved from 20 to 25% in men and 10 to 15% in women in the 1990s (Wiederman, 1997) to approximately 60% in men and 50% in women only a decade later (Tafoya & Spitzberg, 2007; Vangelisti & Gerstenberger, 2004). A more recent statistical report revealed that not only 57% of men and 54% of women admitted to have committed infidelity at some point in their (socially monogamous) relational trajectories, but also that 74% of men and 68% of women said they would have an affair if they knew they would never get caught (Statistic Brain Research Institute, 2016). Further, U.S. couples currently dating showed a 70% infidelity rate (Allen & Baucom, 2006). Infidelity was also identified as the most common "hard problem" in marriage and long-term relationships that both men and women reported to their confidants (e.g., close friends, siblings) in a national sample of 1,000 U.S. adults aged 25–70 (Seal et al., 2015). Poignantly, these numbers should be regarded as conservative because most of the studies "use only currently married couples in their samples, leaving out currently divorced persons whose marital breakup could very well have involved infidelity" (Bergstrand & Sinski, 2010, p. 146). Moreover, according to Brizendine (2006), human genetic studies show that "up to 10 percent of the supposed fathers researchers have tested are not genetically related to the children these men feel certain they fathered" (p. 88; cf. Baker & Bellis, 1995; but see K. G. Anderson, 2006). Thus, although most people in modern Western culture consider themselves—and are believed to be—monogamous, both anonymous surveys and genetic studies reveal that many are so socially but not biologically (see also Barash & Lipton, 2001; K. Campbell & Wright, 2010; D. E. Schmitt, 2005a). Infidelity is a major cause of marital separation both in the United States (Amato & Previti, 2003; Scott et al., 2013) and cross-culturally (Betzig, 1989), and clandestine affairs (or, in many cases, the jealous suspicion of them) are behind not only domestic violence but also many female murders in the United States (Ben-Ze'ev & Goussinsky, 2008) and across the world (Goetz et al., 2008; Wilson & M. Daly, 1996).

3 As de la Croix and Mariani (2015) observed, "Europe is nowadays almost completely serial-monogamous" (p. 570). They argued that monogamy was a precondition of serial monogamy: first, the rise of rich males propitiated the shift from polygamy to traditional monogamy, and then the overall enrichment of society (across genders) led to the shift to serial monogamy. Such a shift was also propitiated by changes in both social norms and legal reforms: the development of serial monogamy followed three steps that I believe can be safely extrapolated from Andersson's (2015) context of twentieth-century Sweden to most modern Western societies: (a) renegotiations of marital morality (early twentieth century), (b) the introduction of more liberal divorce laws (1960s and 1970s), and (c) increased acceptance of unmarried cohabitation (1970s to early twenty-first century). Thus, in addition to longer life expectations, the triumph of serial monogamy has been

shaped by multiple economic, sociocultural, political, and legal factors intertwined with psychosocial changes in marital and sexual ethics.

4   Culturally, it is likely that serial monogamy (and the conditions propitiating it) helped to debilitate the patriarchal ethos of traditional monogamy. In her authoritative history of marriage in the Unites States, Cott (2002) captured the patriarchal nature of traditional monogamy:

> Political and legal authorities endorsed and aimed to perpetuate nationally a particular marriage model: lifelong, faithful monogamy, formed by the mutual consent of a man and a woman, bearing the impress of the Christian religion and the English common law in its expectations for the husband to be the family head and economic provider, his wife the dependent partner. (p. 3)

This patriarchal view was threatened by both the increased freedoms that societal wealth and birth control brought to women, and the growth potential that a series of relationships offered to all genders.

5   Conversely, frequency of both sex and desired sex (or at least having "enough sex") has been empirically linked to relationship satisfaction in both married and unmarried couples (see Byers, 2005; Christopher & Sprecher, 2004; Muise et al., 2019; Muise et al., 2016; Pascoal et al., 2014; A. Smith et al., 2011). The relationship between sexual passion and intimacy is most likely bi-directional, that is, not only does infrequent sex erode intimacy but also decreased intimacy (e.g., in self-disclosure) suffocates the flames of sexual passion (see Baumeister & Bratslavsky, 1999; H. Rubin & L. Campbell, 2012). To complicate these matters further, the attachment style of individuals and their partners appears to impact the relational and sexual satisfaction of married couples (see Butzer & L. Campbell, 2008), even if affectionate touch (central to most sexual encounters) has been associated with greater well-being in romantic relationships regardless of attachment style (Debrot et al., 2020).

6   The renowned former monk and psychotherapist Thomas Moore (2002) wrote:

> The most common story I heard from people in psychotherapy dealt with a happy marriage in which one or both partners felt compelled to engage in an extramarital affair. The parties involved couldn't understand the reason for the overwhelming allure of another carnal liaison. They assumed something must be wrong in their marriage or in their own past. They never considered that there might be some deep need for orgy, for sex without the weight of moralism, or for enough and varied sex to offset the bodiless, passionless life that modern work and family values insist upon. (para. 15)

In addition, surveys show that the number of married couples who successfully navigate the so-called four- and seven-year itches has been decreasing over the last decades (e.g., Barber, 2002; J. Lewis, 2001). According to the United Census Bureau, for example, 8.8 years was the average length of U.S. marriages in 2009 (Kreider & Ellis, 2011) and it is estimated that 50–60% of today's marriages will end in divorce (Cohen, 2016). In addition—and crucially—none of the available statistical data include the surely much larger number of separations in unmarried couples.

7   When experiencing frustration in their intimate lives, people often turn to technology for the connection they are missing at home. Many people increase their interaction with social media friends, consciously or unconsciously (often

somewhere in-between) looking for other suitable, hopefully more satisfying partners (e.g., Abbasi & Alghamdi, 2018). Others start looking at Internet dating or meeting-services websites, at times even at the very sites where they met their current partner. As Slater (2013) showed in his study on modern mating, online dating's virtually infinite number of potential partners decreases relational commitment, facilitates separations, and reduces the mourning period after break-ups. It is no surprise that the President of the American Academy of Matrimonial Lawyers identified cyber-affairs and online infidelity as growing trends in people's reasons for divorce and separation (see Atwood, 2005). In addition, the widespread use of pornography can negatively impact relational satisfaction with one's partner (Wright et al., 2017) and "prompt an end to an unknown number of relationships" (Regnerus, 2017, p. 131; see also Perry, 2018). Bottom line, modern technology makes it far easier than ever to not only access sex but also find new available sexual partners, both of which impact relationship break-ups. For discussions of the potentials of cyberspace for flirting, see Whitty and Carr (2003). See also Cooper and Sportolari (1997) and Döring (2002) for online- and cyber-romance, L. Collins (1999) and Maheu and Subotnik (2001) for cyber-affairs and Internet infidelity, and C. Jones (2010) for virtual dating/sex through avatars. For a critical review of the literature on Internet infidelity, see Hertlein and Piercy (2006).

[8] In contrast to these data, a 2014 survey of about 15,000 U.S. residents age 18–60 showed that "account[ing] for the effects of age, we actually see a positive correlation. As length of marriage increases, sexual inactivity decreases" (Litschi et al., 2014, p. 34). However, the authors added, "It's important to remember that sexually-inactive couples are certainly more likely than sexually-active couples to get divorced (and so be absent from these analyses), deflating the sexual inactivity rates for those who remain married" (p. 34). Whereas further research to clarify this question is necessary, the clinical and empirical evidence strongly indicates a general decline in sexual desire and activity in regular partners over time (see Brewis & Meyer, 2005; Diamond, 2013; Klusmann, 2002; McNulty et al., 2016). Dearth of libido is, after all, one of the most common issues leading couples to commit infidelity and/or seek counseling (e.g., Atkins et al., 2001, 2005; Blow & Hartnett, 2005; Liu, 2000; Whisman et al., 1997).

[9] For the incidence of unprotected sex in self-styled monogamists, see Conley, Moors et al. (2012), Swan and S. C. Thompson (2016), and Warren et al. (2012).

[10] In general, rich, socially powerful, and attractive men appear to benefit more from serial monogamy than their female counterparts around the world (for a review, see Gangestad & Simpson, 2000). The reproductive advantages of serial monogamy for males have been documented even in Indigenous populations such as the preindustrial (1700–1900) Sami of Northern Europe, where men had greater probabilities of remarriage than women of the same age (Käär et al., 1998). However, this predicament is not as ubiquitous as one may think. As Borgerhoff Mulder's (2009) study showed, for example, Tanzania Pimbwe females benefit more than men from marrying multiple husbands sequentially through both the maximization of resources

needed for reproduction and perhaps other indirect benefits (e.g., pairing with males with high genetic potential).

11   Needless to say, not all single, mature heterosexual women suffer from this predicament. Questioning the cultural (and arguably patriarchal) conditioning that women's happiness requires being in an intimate relationship with a man, many mature but also young women live fulfilling—and even healthier—lives in either solitude or connection with circles of women, male friends, family members, and animal companions (e.g., DePaulo, 2006; Kutob et al., 2017; Stewart, 2018; Wilkinson, 2014). For critical discussions of the overall social stigmatization of singlehood in the modern West, see Budgeon (2008) and Wilkinson (2012).

12   However, one can legitimately ask: Are relational styles intrinsically more or less patriarchal (or benefiting men)? Putting aside blatantly patriarchal types such as historical polygamy (i.e., harems and the like; Betzig, 1986) and traditional marriage (i.e., as financial transaction of women among men; Coontz, 2005), modern strict monogamy (e.g., Cott, 2002; Stelboum, 2010), serial monogamy (e.g., Marlowe, 2000), polyamory (e.g., Regnerus, 2017), and hierarchical polyamory (Bachmann, 2018; Overall, 1998) have been all accused of favoring men. I return to these considerations in the next chapter, but here I want to propose that insofar as a patriarchal ethos dominates a culture, it seems inevitable that most relationships in that culture are tainted with patriarchal prejudices. That said, as Sheff's (2005, 2006, 2014) ethnographic research showed, although some men and women in polyamorous relations reproduce patriarchal power dynamics (cf. Pain, 2019), many actively resist them, and some poly women feel more empowered than in their previous monogamous relations. Likewise, many contemporary men and women in monogamous relations are intentionally attempting to engage them in more egalitarian, post-patriarchal ways (Finlay & Clarke, 2003; Haag, 2011). For a general review of the several ways contemporary patriarchal monogamy may be harming women (e.g., sexual dysfunctions and hypoactive sexual desire, domestic violence and sexual assault), see Ziegler et al. (2014).

13   This shift toward serial monogamy should be understood as part of a larger arc in the evolution of marriage in the Unites States, from the *institutional era* (based on securing basic needs like food, shelter, and protection; 1776–1850) to the *companionate era* (focused on romantic love and sexual passion; 1850–1965) and to the *self-expressive era* (centered on self-discovery, personal growth, and self-actualization; 1965–present) (see Burgess & Locke, 1945; Cherlin, 2009; Coontz, 2005). For a helpful overview of these eras and analysis of the positive and negative aspects of contemporary marriage from the perspective of Maslow's (1970) hierarchy of needs, see Finkel et al. (2015). Accepting the validity of this overarching trajectory, my sense is that many contemporary couples are moving toward a new era that—through a deeper empathic connectivity—includes currently vital values such as sociopolitical awareness, ecological sustainability, global concerns, and communion with the human and nonhuman worlds (see chapter 5; Rifkin, 2009).

14   For a witty—and deliberately polemical—defense of adultery in the context of modern Western mononormative culture, see Kipnis (2003). Compare Ben-Ze'ev

and Goussinsky's (2008) related argument that adultery actually helps to maintain the social institution of monogamy. In this regard, V. Robinson (1997) pointed out, "the rationale for infidelity is that marriages would not survive without it. But this tolerance of affairs by individuals and society, ensures the continued acceptance of the monogamous ideal" (p. 151). Similarly, VanderVoort and Duck (2004) wrote, "The implication [of the adulterer's need for therapy] is that it is the transgressor, not the structure [monogamous marriage], that needs adjustment" (p. 8). In referring to these works I am by no means justifying adultery. However, the above arguments are worth pondering—and the point remains that adultery exists only in a monocentric context. As Mint (2004) put it, "monogamy and cheating . . . are conceptually interdependent. . . . They represent two sides of the same coin, one shiny and one tarnished" (p. 61). In addition, the fact that "cheating" is typically

> weighed down with mononormative assumptions . . . cannot capture the differences between someone choosing not to mention one lover to another, a person having unprotected sex outside of the agreed-upon fluid bonded group and someone texting their fling without their partner's consent or knowledge to enjoy—and defuse—the exhilaration of a one night stand. (Kean, 2017, p. 33)

For a revealing analysis of the motivations for—and empowering impact of—affairs on married women (often in sexless or "orgasmless" marriages) who for a variety of reasons did not want to leave their husbands or family life, see Walker (2017); and for a nuanced discussion of adultery's diverse motivations and growth opportunities for individuals and couples, see Perel (2017).

[15] Interestingly, some of the authors of these self-help guides may be struggling in their own marriages. I became aware of this possibility when a famous couple who had coauthored several influential books on monogamous relationships attended a workshop I cofacilitated at Esalen Institute in Big Sur, California. Although this anecdotal datum may be obviously unrepresentative, it made me wonder—especially given the evident conflict of interest these couples face in publicly disclosing their challenges. After all, who would buy a book or attend a workshop on monogamous intimacy from a couple whose sexual life is barren?

[16] A tragic symptom of psychologically enforced monogamy, often amplified by cultural and biographical factors, is *internalized polyphobia*. As discussed in chapter 2, polyphobia is the deeply seated conscious or unconscious fear, aversion, or disgust toward polyamory (or nonmonogamies in general; see Halpern, 1999). Like homophobia, polyphobia can manifest both outwardly (toward others) and inwardly (toward oneself).

[17] In addition, the romantic lives of couples in general—and cohabiting couples in particular—are often negatively impacted by the economic pressures dictated by specific sociocultural structures associated with the now-in-decline patriarchal, nuclear family model (e.g., Apostolou & Wang, 2020; Bengston, 2001; Cohen, 2018), such as private property, neoliberal capitalism, gender division of labor, and the family as unit of consumption (e.g., Brecher, 2012; Macfarlane, 1986). In some cases, for example, adultery can be partly driven by the social isolation and yearning for community—or a larger sense of communion—intrinsic to the Western economic organization of marriage and romantic relationships into stand-alone pairings (cf. Conley & Moors, 2014; M. P. Johnson & Leslie, 1982). While it may

have had certain historical advantages for child-rearing (B. Berger, 2017), the privatized nuclear family favors—and arguably was historically impulsed by—a capitalist market economy in which each household then needs a fridge, a washing machine, a car, and so on (this ecologically pernicious system also produces more plastic, garbage, and disposable goods). For an historical overview of the use of nuclear family imagery in *US Weekly* magazine's advertisements of food, alcohol, cars, and insurances, see Heinemann (2018); for a critical analysis of how the nuclear family model may be detrimental for wholesome relationships between ex-partners after any of them remarries, see Ebersohn and Bouwer (2015); and for a discussion of how Western institutions' preoccupation with preserving the nuclear family can foster domestic abuse and in particular jeopardize the safety of women and their children, see Shoener (2014). Lastly, for a thorough analysis of the weakening of the patriarchal nuclear family in not only the West but also less-developed countries, see Castells (2010).

[18] For helpful discussions and critical perspectives on intersectionality studies, see McCall (2005), Nash (2008), M. T. Berger and Guidroz (2009), P. H. Collins and Bilge (2016), Hancock (2016), and P. H. Collins (2019).

[19] For key accounts of the import of intersectionality for the theory and practice of polyamory and alternative relationships, see Haritaworn et al. (2006), Patterson (2018), and Pain (2019). See Noël (2006), Petrella (2007), and Klesse (2014b) for critical analyses of the interface between class and polyamory; Pitagora (2016) for a discussion of intersectional stigma in kink-poly-identified people; Gusmano (2018) and Braida (2021) for two considerations of the stigmatization of intersecting bisexuality and polyamory; and Willey (2006, 2016) for an exposé of the racist biases underlying naturalizing discourses of both monogamy and nonmonogamy. Also see Raab (2014) for some constructive suggestions about how polyamory can overcome the traditional gender-specific division of labor. For fuller treatments of gender, race, and class inequality in contemporary cultural discourses about monogamy, nonmonogamy, and polyamory, see Rambukkana (2015), Patterson (2018), and Schippers (2016, 2020). Finally, in a section of this book's chapter 5, "Open Your Eyes to Social Privilege and Oppression—Your Own and Others," I discuss the value of the insights offered by intersectionality approaches in the search for relational freedom.

[20] It is important, however, not to read the previous account as suggesting that all relational choices necessarily have a deficit-based foundation. As discussed in chapter 2, individuals with a secure attachment style can also opt for both monogamy and CNM (e.g., Conley, Ziegler et al., 2012). For a discussion of how optimal early experiences and family dynamics may also shape adult relational dispositions, see chapter 5.

[21] Contrast this proposed arc with the traditional monocentric account of the evolution of marriage that was prevalent for centuries up to the 1960s and 1970s (and that still breathes with ease in many sections of contemporary Western culture; see chapter 2). As one early twentieth-century scholar described, "Marriage has evolved from the original permanent mating of the prehuman state to primal promiscuity,

consanguineous family, punaluan family, pairing family, patriarchal family, to strict female and loose male monogamy; and is gradually reaching . . . to strict male and female monogamy" (Talmey, 1938, p. 427). Besides the obvious monocentrism of the passage, contemporary evolutionary psychology has challenged the very idea of a single prehistoric mating strategy (e.g., Buss, 2006; D. E. Schmitt, 2005b).

[22] Whereas the question of patriarchal dominance in archaic times is controversial and ultimately speculative (as contingent on interpretations of pre-Axial archeological records; see Bamberger, 1974; Conkey & Tringham, 1998; Eller, 2000; Gimbutas, 1989; Long, 1997), it seems undeniable that a patriarchal ethos dominated most forms of polygynous and monogamous relationships and marriages cross-culturally over many centuries—or perhaps even millennia—up to the late twentieth century (e.g., Betzig, 1986; Coontz, 2005; de la Croix & Mariani, 2015; Summers, 2005; Yalom, 2001).

[23] This account of relational freedom in terms of relational integration, plasticity, autonomy, and transcendence has precedents in the literature. Relational integration is indebted to classical and modern articulations of open marriages (O'Neill & O'Neill, 1972), open relationships (Michaels & P. Johnson, 2015), "new monogamist" (T. Nelson, 2012, 2016) or "monogamish" relationships (Savage, 2012), and hierarchical polyamory (Veaux & Rickert, 2014). Relational plasticity is related to Bauman's (2003) liquid love (i.e., malleable romantic relationships), as well as to Giddens's (1992) plastic sexualities and Baumeister's (2000) theory of erotic plasticity, both of which are nonetheless focused on variability in sexual orientation (vs. relationship style; for an exceptional study exploring the interface between sexual fluidity and relational identity, see Manley et al., 2015). Relational autonomy is aligned to Giddens's (1992) confluent (i.e., contingent) love, and, perhaps more closely, to Eda's (2013) intimate agency, which "highlight[s] the capability of defining and redefining our own individual intimate relationships" (p. 13). Relational transcendence is connected to Pallotta-Chiarolli's (2010) multivocal border or *mestizaje* identity, as well as to certain forms of so-called relational anarchy (see Heckert & Cleminson, 2011). Although I believe this book presents the most thorough account on the transbinary (or novogamous) relationships shaped by these competences available so far, I list some precedents of these relational styles in chapter 4. Overall, relational freedom seems also central to modern "relationships by design" (Michaels & P. Johnson, 2015), nonbinary relational styles (Barker & Iantaffi, 2019), and other forms of fluid, plastic, or hybrid intimate relations discussed in chapter 4.

[24] I stress "socially enforced" to reiterate that I believe mindful, freely chosen monogamy is a legitimate player in the relational scene of the twenty-first century (see chapters 2 and 5). In this spirit, Orion (2018) called *consensual monogamy* the "love-based, egalitarian monogamy by *choice*, not by force or law" (p. 11) that many couples seek to cultivate today.

[25] This emphasis on personal growth does not seek to dismiss the value or validity of recreational sexuality (cf. Klesse, 2006). I believe that, unless practiced in a mechanical or dissociated way, sexual encounters can always have a regenerative,

transformational, and even self-transcendent impact (e.g., Kleinplatz et al., 2009; Malkemus & Romero, 2012; J. Wade, 2004). As S. A. Mitchell (2002) put it, for example, "The transcendent power of sexuality might be understood as emanating precisely from its potential to undermine everyday psychic structure, to destabilize the ordinary experience of self" (p. 86). Nonetheless, the choice of engaging sexuality for the sake of playful exploration or pleasure per se should be fully respected; for a pungent critique of the erasure of pleasure in contemporary sex research, see A. Jones (2019). Likewise, my emphasis on nonharmful sexuality does not exclude BDSM's consensual exchange of bondage, pain, or psychophysical restraint with the intention of eliciting pleasure or other desired sensations (e.g., Baumeister, 1988; Newmahr, 2010), altered states of consciousness (e.g., E. M. Lee et al., 2016; Zussman & Pierce, 1998), or spiritual experiences and transformation (e.g., Fennell, 2018; Harrington, 2016). For explorations of the overlap between BDSM and polyamory (e.g., emphasis on consent, openness to sexual diversity), see Sheff and Hammers (2011) and Pitagora (2016). Many of the above references on BDSM are drawn from Greenberg's (2019) article, "Divine Kink: A Consideration of the Evidence of BDSM as Spiritual Ritual."

[26] Although the United States is anomalous in the sense that modernity's "secularization" has not substantially decreased Christian fidelity or affiliation (e.g., Eisbruger, 2006), May (2011) convincingly argued that romantic love has gradually replaced Christianity as "the West's undeclared religion—and perhaps its only generally accepted religion" (p. 1). For a remarkable thesis developing this argumentative line, see Balstrup (2012); for an essay arguing that compulsory romantic love has replaced compulsory heterosexuality (and even compulsory monogamy) in the United Kingdom and other Western countries, see Wilkinson (2012).

[27] For a brief discussion of the possible connection between monotheism and mononormativity, see chapter 2, note 14.

[28] These trends have begun to impact conservative Christian individuals, communities, and even professional clergy. As Cox's (2009) ethnographic study documented, for example, some former and present evangelical Christians living in the southwestern United States challenge the heterosexual monogamy doctrinally imposed by their Church through a "desire to integrate sexuality and sexual service with spirituality and worship" (p. 63) and to enact a sacred sexuality.

Chapter 2

Mononormativity, Polypride, and the "Mono–Poly Wars"

onogamy and *polyamory* are loaded terms for almost everyone in
Western culture, tending to awaken visceral reactions ranging from
the radically positive to the extremely negative. On the positive side,
monogamy—generally referring to sexually exclusive, pair-bonding romantic
relationships—evokes a sense of stability and security, emotional depth and
fulfillment of romantic fantasies, enduring or everlasting love, shared labor and
resources, cohabitation and family, and moral and religious rectitude. On the
negative side, it conjures a loss of freedom and entrapment, routine and boredom, mate-guarding behavior and jealousy, adultery and affairs, patriarchal
domination and domestic abuse, and even passionate homicide. The same goes
for polyamory—a relational paradigm based on consensual, multiple affective
and sexual relationships.[1] Positively, the term is connected with sexual and
emotional freedom, personal empowerment, liberation from patriarchal oppression, ethical interpersonal behavior, honesty and communication, nonpossessive love and overcoming of jealousy, and psychospiritual growth. Negatively,
polyamory is linked with shallowness and irresponsibility, psychological imma-
turity and character flaws, attachment issues and inability to commit, promiscuity and philandering, hedonistic narcissism, lust and sexual greed, one partner
bullying the other into nonmonogamy, moral and spiritual failure, and religious
sacrilege or sinfulness.

Nothing indicates better that a phenomenon merits careful scrutiny than
its power to catalyze such drastically polar—and emotionally charged—reactions. Three factors seem to play a role in these conflicting responses. First,
these relational choices arguably appeal to the two equally legitimate but often
conflicting human needs introduced in chapter 1: the need for emotional (and
sexual, at times) stability and security, on the monogamy side; and the need

for sexual (and emotional, at times) diversity and novelty, on the polyamory side (e.g., E. Anderson, 2012; Ashkam, 1984; Brandon, 2010). Second, as with most existential options, monogamy and polyamory can cast both "light" and "shadow"—that is, both relational styles can be engaged with mindfulness, integrity, and respect, but also unconsciously, deceitfully, or out of insecurities, conditionings, and internalized ideologies (e.g., Anapol, 2010; Masters, 2007). Third, diverging reactions to monogamy or polyamory may be also rooted in genetic and biological variables (Z. Johnson & L. J. Young, 2015; van Anders et al., 2007; Walum et al., 2012); individual developmental junctures (Conley, Ziegler et al., 2012); sociopolitical situations (M. Robinson, 2013); cultural, political, and religious dispositions (Ho, 2006; S. M. Johnson et al., 2015; Kolesar & Pardo, 2019); and a variety of demographic variables such as political affiliation, educational level, income, and marital status (Balzarini, Dharma, Kohut, L. Campbell, Holmes et al., 2019). Taken together, these and other possible factors (e.g., gender variances and identity, sexual orientation) weave a very complex relational tapestry suggesting the need to dissect the roots of prevailing Western attitudes toward these relational identities, orientations, or choices (e.g., Barker, 2005; Klesse, 2014a; M. Robinson, 2013).[2]

My aim in this chapter is to examine some of the central dynamics mediating dominant social and scholarly views of monogamy and polyamory, as a groundwork for destabilizing the mono/poly binary and paving the way to enhanced possibilities of relational freedom (see chapters 4 and 5). To this end, I first introduce what I call the "mono–poly wars," that is, the predicament of mutual competition and condescension among monogamists and polyamorists,[3] and describe and document two pairs of interlocked psychosocial attitudes—monopride/polyphobia and polypride/monophobia—which, in the context of Western mononormative culture, shape and energize those wars. I then show the ideological nature of many of the assumptions behind these attitudes through a review of available empirical literature on the psychological health and relationship quality of monogamous and polyamorous individuals and couples. In conclusion, I argue for the value of holding a critically pluralist stance when contrasting monogamy and polyamory—one that underscores the benefits of having a greater diversity of relational choices (thus supporting relational freedom) while maintaining the grounds for critical discernment within and among relational styles.

The "Mono–Poly Wars"

Mononormativity and its discontents shape the predicament of mutual competition and condescension among monogamists and polyamorists that I call the "mono–poly wars." Although the origins of human monogamy are highly controversial and probably multifarious (e.g., Carter & Perkeybile, 2018; de la Croix & Mariani, 2015; M. M. Dow & Eff, 2013; Fisher, 1992; Lukas & Clutton-Brock, 2013), the ideal of a sexually exclusive couple as the optimal model for healthy relating has prevailed in the West for many centuries (Herlihy, 1995; MacDonald, 1990, 1995).[4] It is also well established that this ideal became normative and even today is socially enforced through a variety of cultural, institutional, and legal mechanisms (see Bergstrand & Sinski, 2010; Emens, 2004; Kipnis, 2003; Rosa, 1994; Tweedy, 2011).[5] Only to mention an example, although they were rarely enforced, at least up to 2015 the laws of twenty-two states in the United States included adultery prohibitions and related criminal convictions (including penitentiary time); as L. S. Anderson (2016) indicated, "The effect of these restrictions is to force everyone to create dyadic pairings as intimate associations, and to expect sexual exclusivity once the dyad is created" (p. 6). In this regard, Pieper and Bauer (2005) coined the term *mononormativity* "to refer to dominant assumptions of the normalcy and naturalness of monogamy, analogous to such assumptions around heterosexuality inherent in the term *heteronormativity*" (as cited in Barker & Langdridge, 2010b, p. 750). Similarly, Bergstrand and Sinski (2010) called *monocentrism* "the unquestioned assumption that monogamy, or marriage to one person only, is morally superior to all other marital forms" (p. 99). Whether one calls it mononormativity (Pieper & Bauer, 2005), monocentrism (Bergstrand & Sinski, 2010), monogamism (E. Anderson, 2012; Blumer et al., 2014), compulsory monogamy (Emens, 2004; Schippers, 2016; Willey, 2015), socially imposed monogamy (MacDonald, 1995), heteronormative monogamy (Noël, 2006), or "amatonormativity" (Brake, 2012; Jenkins, 2017), this belief system not only establishes the monogamous (and heterosexual) couple as natural, optimal, and morally loftier but also stigmatizes nonmonogamous alternatives as unnatural, dysfunctional, or even perverse (see Conley, Moors et al., 2013; Grunt-Mejer & L. Campbell, 2016; Hutzler et al., 2016; Mogilski et al., 2020; Sheff & Hammers, 2011).[6]

Probably in part as a defensive strategy against standard criticism, most poly authors sharply distinguish polyamory not only from monogamy and polygamy but also from promiscuity, casual sex, and swinging (e.g., Ritchie, 2010).[7] This move is understandable since nonmonogamous relationships strictly focused on sexual exchange are more likely to be socially stigmatized in Western culture (Matsick et al., 2014). As Klesse (2006) pointed out, "The presentation of polyamory as 'responsible non-monogamy' is based on the attempt to challenge the negative assumptions of non-monogamous people as promiscuous, over-sexed, self-obsessed, irrational and pathological" (p. 577). In addition, the emphasis on love (vs. sex) permits poly activists to present monogamous people as the ones who are sex-obsessed in their elevation of sexual fidelity to sacrosanct status (e.g., Rowan, 1995). Discourse in advocacy of both nonmonogamy and polyamory has consistently included both a vigorous critique of monogamy as patriarchal, capitalist, racist, hypocritical, or sexually and emotionally pernicious (e.g., E. Anderson, 2012; Barker & Ritchie, 2007; Jackson & Scott, 2004; V. Robinson, 1997; Rosa, 1994; Schippers, 2016; Stelboum, 2010; Willey, 2006); and the elevation of polyamory as biologically, psychologically, socially, morally, or spiritually natural or advantageous (see Petrella, 2007; Wilkinson, 2010; Willey, 2016).[8]

In addition to the scholarly arguments reviewed here, I have consistently observed, at the ground level of everyday conversation, that monogamists and polyamorists tend to look down on each other.[9] Monogamists generously but condescendingly assume that polyamorous people have not yet found "true love" or their "soul mate"—many confidently believe the polyamorous will then surely "convert" to monogamy. Likewise, candidly but patronizingly, many polyamorists believe that monogamous people have not yet accessed the nonpossessive essence of human love that would allow them to open up their "limiting" exclusive relationships. Vastly different interpretations of the historical and evolutionary evidence lead members of both camps to claim that monogamy or polyamory is the "natural" relational or sexual way of intimate bonding for humans (for a cogent critique of these "naturalizing" discourses, see Willey, 2016). What is more, in the eyes of their respective antagonists, both factions are seen as unmistakably patriarchal. Whereas polyamorists appeal to feminist accounts of the historical and structural links between monogamy and male's ownership of women for reproductive control (e.g., Barker & Ritchie, 2007; Jackson & Scott, 2004; Rosa, 1994), monogamists point to how closely polyamory resembles the male polygamous dream of having many female consorts, as evidenced in the historical reality of harems (see Betzig, 1986; Summers, 2005). These charges are often backed up with evolutionary arguments about males' pressure to secure paternity (e.g., Ryan & Jethá, 2010) and interest in increasing procreative power through spreading their genetic code (e.g., Buss, 1994), respectively.

In what follows, I argue that these "mono–poly wars" are rooted in—or mediated by—two pairs of interlocked psychosocial attitudes: monopride/polyphobia and polypride/monophobia. Before discussing the ideological nature of many of the claims used to back up these attitudes, I offer some examples from the literature.

On Monopride/Polyphobia

The monopride/polyphobia system is firmly rooted in mononormativity, which, as described above, "present[s] monogamous coupledom as the only natural and/or morally correct form of human relating" (Barker & Langdridge, 2010b, p. 750). Briefly, I use *monopride* to refer to the psychosocial consideration of monogamy as variously natural, optimal, or superior. While normally exalting the virtues of monogamy, monopride can also manifest in more concealed ways, such as in the denial or downplaying of the prevalence of affairs in the modern West despite overwhelming clinical and statistical evidence (see E. Anderson, 2012; Buss, 2000b; D. E. Schmitt, 2005a; Treas & Giesen, 2000; Whisman et al., 1997). Or it can take the form of perpetuating what Vaughan (2003) called the monogamy myth—that is, the belief that people are essentially monogamous and that affairs happen only to "bad" or "weak" people.

Monopride usually comes together with *polyphobia*, which has been defined as (conscious or unconscious) fear of or disgust toward nonmonogamy (Halpern, 1999), but which can take many forms. Butler (2004), for example, articulated it this way: "Those who . . . maintain modes of social organization for sexuality that are neither monogamous nor quasi-marital are more and more considered unreal, and their loves and losses less than 'true' loves and 'true' losses" (pp. 26–27). I became personally and painfully aware of polyphobia many years ago when a student of a graduate university where I was teaching in San Francisco, California, confessed to me during her exit interview that she never attended my classes because she had heard about my then-nonmonogamous lifestyle. As she was an international student from South Asia, I sympathetically situated her decision in a cultural context and did not confront her—but imagine someone telling you that they did not enroll in your classes because you were gay, female, transgender, or from Bangladesh. On another occasion, I learned that a university colleague did not invite me to his home gatherings because, having heard about my nonmonogamy, he was afraid that I would hit on his wife—as if being nonmonogamous entailed being a player and disrespecting other people's monogamous commitments! In any event, as illustrated here, polyphobia is rationalized through discourses that condemn nonmonogamy as psychologically immature, morally pernicious, and even religiously sinful (Christianity, the prevalent religion in the modern West, typically considers it a sin to have more than one sexual partner or espouse; see Fuchs, 1983; Witte, 2015).

Like homophobia, polyphobia can manifest both outwardly (toward others) and inwardly (toward oneself). When externalized, it usually leads to expressions of revulsion, social rejection, pathologizing, moral judgment, outrage, religious condemnation, or spiritual condescension toward polyamorous people.[10] When internalized, polyphobia can lead to feelings of inadequacy and self-loathing, or the painful sense that there must be something wrong with oneself if one desires to romantically or sexually love more than one person or is incapable of sustaining long-term monogamous bonds (see Introduction;

Halpern, 1999). The fact that many poly individuals rate monogamous people more positively than CNM folks in domains as diverse as trustworthiness, paying taxes on time, or even teeth flossing evinces the internalization of polyphobia in the poly population (Conley, Moors et al., 2013); however, when poly people are given the chance to assess their own specific relational style (i.e., open relationship, polyamory, swinging) instead of CNM in general (Balzarini et al., 2018), these ratings do not differ from their ratings for monogamous individuals. In any event, although the following claim needs to be empirically examined, I hypothesize that long-term internalized polyphobia can result in isolation, cynicism, self-destructive behaviors, drug abuse, depression, existential angst, and even suicide-related behavior (SRB), among other undesirable consequences (cf. Cramer et al., 2020; Hutzler et al., 2016; Séguin, 2019).

Examples of monopride and polyphobia abound in the literature. Jenkins (2015) referred to the belief that "the only metaphysically possible romantic love relationships are monogamous ones" (p. 175), and documented how most Western philosophers of love—such as Solomon (2006) and Soble (1987)—associate romantic love with sexual exclusivity (cf. McKeever, 2017). Likewise, Strassberg (2003) claimed that polyamorous people cannot experience the transcendent dimension of romantic love because they "are unwilling to fully surrender their individuality to their partner" (p. 561). She added, "The infinitude of polyamorous desire is incompatible with the full surrender of individuality that produces transcendental unity" (p. 562). Summing up the findings of the Hite's (1991) report on attitudes toward love and sexuality in England in the 1970s, V. Robinson (1997) pointed out, "Non-monogamy is associated with promiscuity and shallowness of emotions, whilst monogamy is seen as emotionally and spiritually superior to it" (p. 151). Couples counselor Kane (2010) exemplifies this mindset: "Monogamy is a vehicle for creating deep spiritual connection, and it supports sacredness and depth in ways that open relationships do not" (p. 8). He continued, "The spiritual value of monogamy can also be articulated by viewing how non-monogamous relationships are often felt to be superficial or lacking in intimacy" (p. 9). Charny (1992), another couples therapist, stated that sexual activity beyond the monogamous dyad is an unequivocal sign of relationship problems. Furthermore, women who have affairs are often associated with diagnostic categories such as "histrionic personality" (Apt & Hurlbert, 1994) and narcissism (see Buss & Shackelford, 1997). Although admitting no demonstrable causality, Regnerus (2017) pointed out that findings from the broad survey for his *Relationships in America* project suggest an association between greater number of sexual partners and history of sexual abuse. As these examples illustrate, both scholars and professional health providers tend to pathologize nonmonogamous relationships and individuals (for discussions, see Kisler & Lock,

2019; Schechinger et al., 2018; Weitzman, 2006; Zimmerman, 2012). Some psychotherapists have even been shown to perform microaggressions against their nonmonogamous clients (see L. S. Jordan et al., 2017; Kolmes & Witherspoon, 2012).

Some authors accept the "natural" presence of nonmonogamous feelings and desires, but recommend their transformation to achieve "superior" emotional and relational maturity. For example, Masters (2007) claimed that the achievement of "mature monogamy"—which he characterized as "liberating bondage" (p. 18)—entails the utter eradication of nonmonogamous behaviors, feelings, and desires. After stating that polyamory avoids romantic attachment, uses other connections as distractions or consolations, and confuses love with sexuality, Masters situated polyamory and mature monogamy in a developmental continuum: "multiple-partnership is an avoidance of mature monogamy . . . immature monogamy and multiple-partnership are two aspects of a stage of relatedness that must be outgrown" (p. 18). Thus, Masters's apparent polyphobia did not allow him to consider mature forms of polyamory.

Other scholars seek to ground their monopride (and explicit or implicit polyphobia) in biological or evolutionary arguments. Including polyamory as a viable alternative for some couples, Brandon (2010) wrote that although people should not be ashamed of their natural nonmonogamous instincts, they "can rise above [their] more animalistic drives" (p. xiv). Similarly, accepting that monogamy is not natural, Barash and Lipton (2009) wrote: "what truly distinguishes human beings from other animals" is precisely their capability to "counter some of their biologically given inclinations" (p. 56).[11] In addition to identifying the evolutionary "pay-offs" of monogamy, such as the value of cooperation for parenting, survival, and accumulation of resources (cf. Chapais, 2010; Opie, 2013; Tucker, 2014), Barash and Lipton claimed to identify a "pro-monogamy hardware" or "neural and hormonal infrastructure to support monogamy" (p. 128) consisting of what they called the Four Horsemen of the Monogamist: attachment theory, mirror neurons, neuroplasticity, and endogenous "love" hormones such as oxytocin and vasopressin. In a similar vein, anthropologist Chapais (2013) argued that the emergence of monogamous bonds granted hominids a crucial evolutionary advantage over other related and extinguished species. The account of monogamy as the distinguishing feature separating humans from animals, as well as the foundation of human civilization, was also vigorously defended by Tucker (2014).[12]

Monopride/polyphobia also draws on polyamory's perceived social perniciousness. The French conservative intellectual Faye (2014) wrote, "The transparent polyamory model . . . can only result in a multitude of micro-tragedies and, finally, in the solitude and isolation of everyone, culminating in social despair" (p. 42). From a legal standpoint, Strassberg (2003) wrote that poly-amory may threaten "fundamental aspects of the modern liberal state" (p. 563), such as "individual autonomy, the maintenance of distinctive public and private spheres, and individual reconciliation with social life and identi-fication with the state" (p. 562). Similarly, Raley (2018) defended the legal imposition of monogamy in terms of its promoting equality, companionate unions, social stability, and ordered liberty; and Kurtz (2006) argued that the U.S. government's support of polyamory would lead to an infidelity "pandemic" resulting in the end of monogamous marriage. What is more, A. Young (2004) wrote, "polyamorous relationships replicate the disposable throwaway values of our capitalist society, treating other people as objects to satisfy our cravings, interchangeably as we please, useful to us only as long as they work for our own purposes" (p. 39). In a similar vein, Regnerus (2017) argued that nonmonogamy is undemocratic, misogynist, and patriarchal because "monogamy means greater equality—more men and women have the opportunity to meet, marry, save, and invest for the long-term, instead of competing . . . for others' available attention" (p. 182). He also stated that "sexual objectification—the treatment of persons as objects—is unavoidable in a non-monogamous system" (p. 183). Further, Regnerus proposed that nonmonogamy moves people away from (Christian) religion and fosters the secularization of society (both framed as a negative). These statements should not be surprising, as Regnerus introduced his work as an attempt to help people achieving "things like commitment, stability, monogamy, tranquil-ity, and [traditional] family" (p. 20).[13] (For a discussion of the related claim that polyamory is pernicious for children, see chapter 5.) These illustrations of polyphobia can help to understand polyamorous people's experiences of fear, mistrust, and projections of hypersexualizing by monogamists (see Sheff, 2014).

As these examples show, monopride and polyphobia are two sides of the same worn and rusty coin, manifestations of a single psychosocial ethos seek-ing to perpetuate monocentrism in the modern West. Having illustrated the nature of monopride/polyphobia, I now turn to its converse system: polypride/monophobia.

On Polypride/Monophobia

Diametrically opposed to monopride, *polypride* stands for the consideration of polyamory as variously natural, advantageous, or superior. To my knowledge, Halpern (1999) provided the earliest exposé of this attitude: "one can begin to see oneself as more highly evolved and special for wanting and being able to do this really wonderful thing—loving more than one" (p. 159). Polypride is usually attended by *monophobia*—that is, a critical characterization of monogamy as unnatural, hypocritical, or morally and spiritually bankrupt. As Taormino (2008) put it:

> A disturbing trend among some nonmonogamous people is to turn their noses up at those who chose monogamy, casting them as naïve, boring, brainwashed, unfulfilled, and unevolved—as if everyone in an open relationship is worldly, exciting, freethinking, fulfilled, and evolved simply by being nonmonogamous! (p. 29)

Similarly, Sheff (2014) identified a poly "stigma against monogamists" (p. 65), which leads many poly people to describe "monogamous people as small and grasping, too weak to face the self-awareness boot camp that poly family life can be" (p. 65), in contrast to "poly people [who] are more evolved, stronger, and self-realized that mere monogamists" (p. 65). Although less frequently than polyphobia, monophobia can also be internalized by people who have adopted poly values, for example, in the form of subtle to harsh self-criticism for not being able to romantically love more than one person, hold simultaneous sexual–affectionate relationships, or experience compersion instead of jealousy (see Barker et al., 2013). In this regard, Portwood-Stacer (2010) reported, "Individuals who attempted to practice polyamory were ashamed when they found themselves experiencing feelings of possessiveness or jealousy" (p. 489). The rest of this section offers a selection of examples of polypride and monophobia.

To begin with, some scholars have presented polyamory as historically primordial, evolutionarily more complex, and sexually optimal. For example, polyamory has been portrayed as the natural human sexuality or "original love" (Easton & Liszt, 1997, p. 135) before the advent of the patriarchal control of women (cf. Anderlini-D'Onofrio, 2004b; Ryan & Jethá, 2010).[14] In addition to presenting polyamory as the relational style of pre-civilized (and thus more natural) ancient cultures such as precolonial Hawaii (Anapol, 2004; for critical discussion, see Willey, 2016), Anapol (2010) wrote that polyamory is "a more complex form of relationship for men and women who already master the basics of intimacy and are prepared to evolve into more complex social organisms" (p. 224). In the same vein, after equating individuals to atoms and couples and groups to molecules, P. J. Benson (2008) suggested the greater evolutionary complexity of polyamory: "Again with people as with atoms, more and more complex bondings are possible with larger and larger numbers, and along with the bondings come ever more complex and sophisticated interactions and capabilities" (p. xxi). Likewise, Kaldera (2005) reported that polyamory is at times considered to offer a "'grad school relationships' as opposed to [monogamy's] 'beginner relationships'" (p. xiii). In addition, polyamory is featured as more sexually emancipated or progressive than monogamy. For example, Easton and Liszt (1997) portrayed polyamory as "advanced sexuality" (p. 244), and Anapol (1997) coined the term *sexualoving* to describe the integration of sex and love in multiple intimate relationships—a skill that, by implicit exclusion, monogamous couples do not develop. Another advantage of polyamory is the avoidance of sexual dissatisfaction, infidelity, traumatic separations, and even violence—all of which are attributed to monogamy's allegedly intrinsic repression of natural sexual desires and proscription of sexual variety (e.g., E. Anderson, 2012; Bergstrand & Sinski, 2010). Polyamory's emphasis on transparent communication and boundary negotiations has been also related, with some empirical support but conflicting evidence (e.g., Copen et al., 2019; Lehmiller, 2015), to a safer sexuality (i.e., less risk of contracting STIs) than the widespread monogamous clandestine affairs (e.g., Conley et al., 2015; Conley, Moors et al., 2012).

Psychologically, in most poly guides, polyamory is portrayed as "a superior way of relating in that it enables and requires more personal autonomy, self-awareness and responsibility, and more mutuality, equality and negotiation within relationships" (Barker & Langdridge, 2010b, p. 754). Similarly, Petrella (2007) critically indicated, "Another very important theme is the construction of the polyamorous subject as an autonomous creature, psychologically self-contained and emotionally independent from any other being" (p. 157). Other authors stressed the higher degree of self-reflexivity, trust, and dialogical openness required in polyamorous relationships (e.g., Heaphy et al., 2004). These features, it has been argued, bring polyamory closer than monogamy to Giddens's (1992) "pure relationship," that is, a relationship based on choice, trust, and equality, as well as on emotional and sexual democracy (for critical discussions, see Jamieson, 1998; Stacey, 2011). In addition, polyamory's commitment to face, work with, and transform jealousy is praised over the typical monogamous treatment of jealousy as an inevitable negative emotion or even a sign of love (e.g., see chapter 3; Deri, 2015; Mint, 2010). One of the most vigorous and theoretically sophisticated accounts of polyamory's psychologically superior status is due to Bergstrand and Sinski (2010). Building on Peabody's (1982) work, these authors use Loevinger's (1976) model to situate monogamy, swinging, and polyamory in single developmental continuum. Whereas traditional monogamy adheres to Loevinger's conformity stage (where individuals observe socially sanctioned values such as the repression of nonmonogamous feelings or the normalization of jealousy), swinging represents the conscientious stage (where people transcend societal values and create their own standards, leading to the greater autonomy and interpersonal communication necessary to practice sexual nonmonogamy). In this context, polyamory embodies the more advanced autonomous stage, where persons celebrate individual differences and greater autonomy, leading to not only sexual but also emotional nonmonogamy.

Ethically speaking, polyamory is presented as more honest, responsible, and less hypocritical than monogamy and its adulterous affairs (Sheff, 2014). As Barker (2005) reported, some poly people believe that monogamous individuals are threatened by polyamory because it represents "an honest way of having more than one lover, something many monogamous people might do, or consider doing, but might not be open about due to the dominant culture rules around infidelity" (p. 81). Serial monogamy punctuated with clandestine adultery, some polyamorists argued, is in many respects not too different from polyamory, except that the latter is more honest, ethical, and less harmful (e.g., Munson & Stelboum, 1999). Similarly, after denouncing monogamy's violations and double standards, Heinlin and Heinlin (2004) asked: "Why are people so hypocritical?" (p. 103), approvingly citing the view that

> monogamy is for the young and idealistic. But for those who have tried monogamy and seen its flaws first hand [sic], non-monogamy is the logical next step. Our society would be much healthier if we were more honest to each other, better informed, and planned better to accept our non-monogamy and revel in our ability to love multiple partners simultaneously. (p. 103)

Double-guessing in a psychoanalytical fashion, Heinlin and Heinlin added, "Some of the most unlikely activists against non-monogamy are those who are fighting their own deep inner urges to be non-monogamous" (p. 188). Lastly, Chalmers (2019) philosophically argued that since sexual and romantic relationships add intrinsic value to people's lives (e.g., sexual pleasure, emotional support, self-knowledge), the monogamous restriction to a single partnership should be considered morally condemnable (cf. Cruz, 2016). These arguments suggest that polyamory is at times regarded as ethically superior to monogamy, which is then demoted as a coercive or hypocritical practice to be developmentally overcome as people achieve greater sexual and emotional maturity.

Finally, other scholars have perhaps exalted the sociopolitical and spiritual virtues of polyamory. On a political canvas, polyamory is often presented as a socially emancipatory relational style through which women (and men) can overcome patriarchal, racist, classist, and capitalist oppression (e.g., Easton & Liszt, 1997; Jackson & Scott, 2004; Pieper & Bauer, 2005; Rosa, 1994; Sheff, 2005, 2006). For example, Wolkomir (2019) presented polyamorous love as shaping relational configurations that can "erode masculine dominance and gender hierarchy" (p. 81). Although challenging heteronormative monogamy, Noël (2006) contended that "the majority of these [poly] writers limit polyamory's revolutionary potential by primarily addressing the concerns of white, middle-class, college-educated individuals" (p. 615). Likewise, Schippers (2020) wrote:

> Depictions of polyamorists as white, middle-class, conventionally attractive, young, and heterosexual and representations of polyamory as more enlightened

or fulfilling than monogamy, situate "acceptable polyamory" as the path to happiness and a good life. This simply replaces "good" monogamy with "good polyamory." (p. 132)

To counteract these ideological trends, Schippers (2016, 2020) persuasively argued for the emancipatory power of integrating polyamory with other progressive movements—such as feminist, queer, and critical race theory—to critique social, gender, and racial inequalities. In a similar vein, Shannon and Willis (2010) proposed that polyamory can reinforce the "queering" of political anarchism (i.e., via the inclusion of nonnormative sexual practices) and strategically support the struggle against institutional forms of domination. From a spiritual standpoint, Anapol (2010) framed polyamory as a growth accelerator and training ground to cultivate unconditional love. Since polyamory is often taken to be more attuned to the all-inclusive, nonpossessive essence of love, "polyamorists are portrayed as some wondrous beings who have an amazing capacity to have many lovers" (Wilkinson, 2010, p. 242)—or who are capable of "loving more" (Anderlini-D'Onofrio, 2010) or "without limits" (Anapol, 1997). In addition, Heinlin and Heinlin (2004) saw in polyamorous sexuality a gnostic path to the divine (cf. Easton & Liszt, 1997).

As suggested above, it is likely that the polypride/monophobia system largely emerged as a reaction to mononormativity, gradually giving shape to an emerging polynormativity. Although the term *polynormativity* normally refers to standards about the "right" way to be poly (e.g., couple-centered, love-based, or rule-regimented) in contrast to other forms of nonmonogamy (Barker et al., 2013; Schippers, 2016, 2020; Zanin, 2013; see also Haritaworn et al., 2006), I suggest that polynormativity can be extended to any discourse defending polyamory as the right, best, or superior way of intimate relating. This expanded use would also include Wilkinson's (2010) *polyromanticism*, which presents polyamory as an ethically superior nonmonogamy that only people with an extraordinary capability to love can live.

Monopride, Polypride, and Relational Narcissism

In sum, monopride/polyphobia and polypride/monophobia are the prevalent lenses through which both monogamists and polyamorists look (down) at each other; naturally, both camps denounce the open or hidden arrogance they perceive in each other. These patronizing attitudes not only result in unnecessary polarizations between people who have different dispositions or are at distinct developmental crossroads but also arguably impoverish human relationships. Due to the mononormative ethos of Western culture, it should be clear that monopride/polyphobia is by far more pervasive, and that polypride/monophobia can be understood (at least partially) as a reaction to the former.

As in the case of religious choices, however, human beings display a remarkable tendency to deem as universally superior their preferred relational style over others (for discussions of spiritual narcissism, see Ferrer, 2002, 2017).[15] Although cultural rankings regarding sexual orientation and gender identity have diminished over the last decades, relational hierarchies—whether understood in terms of identity or orientation (see Klesse, 2014a; M. Robinson, 2013)—thrive in both scholarly and popular discussions. These considerations lead me to suggest that *relational narcissism*, or the belief in the universal superiority of one's relational choice, might underlie both monopride/polyphobia and polypride/monophobia.[16] If so, private relational narcissism—intermingled with social, cultural, racial, and religious biases—may often lurk behind public and even putatively "scientific" stances on these relationship styles. The ideological nature of these belief systems, argued in the next section, is consistent with this contention.

The Ideological Nature of the "Mono–Poly Wars"

According to critical theory, a belief is *ideological* when it is not supported by empirical evidence (i.e., does not correspond to the facts) and was adopted in a situation of ignorance, coercion, or bondage (e.g., Geuss, 1981; M. J. Thompson, 2017). Ideological critique seeks to raise consciousness about the pseudo-objectivity of ideological beliefs and their tainted origin, and is thus foundational for feminist theory, queer and cultural studies, and multicultural approaches (Agger, 2013; Fay, 1987). In the context of the present discussion, beliefs about the preeminence of monogamy have very likely been acquired over centuries of mononormative indoctrination and coercion (E. Anderson, 2012; Bergstrand & Sinski, 2010), while beliefs about the superiority of polyamory arguably emerged as ideological reactions to mononormativity.

Despite the variety of arguments reviewed above for the advantageousness of monogamy or polyamory, the empirical evidence (including data regarding other types of CNM) reveals a more egalitarian and pluralistic scenario. To begin with, there are no statistical differences between people in monogamous and CNM relations regarding psychological well-being and pathology, including measures for self-esteem, neuroticism, mood stability, anxiety, or depression, among other markers (see Rubel & Bogaert, 2015). For example, both independent studies and reviews of the literature found no differences in the psychological health and relationship quality of nonmonogamous and monogamous gay men (e.g., Bonello, 2009; Bricker & Horne, 2007; J. T. Parsons et al., 2013), as well as of gay male and lesbian couples (Kurdek, 1988). In addition, against the widespread association of both long-term monogamy with healthy attachment style and nonmonogamy with attachment issues (e.g., Birnbaum et al., 2006; Brandon, 2010; L. C. Miller & Fishkin, 1997), research shows that a secure attachment style predominates in both monogamous and poly-amorous couples (see Conley, Ziegler et al., 2012), as well as in polyamorous people with their concurrent romantic partners (Moors et al., 2019). A recent study of 1,308 individuals (73% female) engaged in monogamous (85%) and CNM (15%) relations corroborated this outcome (Moors et al., 2015). This study also found a larger number of individuals with low avoidance style in CNM relationships than in monogamous ones—even if those with high avoid-ance were attitudinally more disposed to engage in nonmonogamy. A related study with gay, lesbian, and bisexual individuals demonstrated that although an avoidance style was positively correlated with willingness to engage in CNM, standardized personality factors such as high openness to new experiences and low conscientiousness better explained the disposition (Moors, Selterman et al., 2017). The link between secure attachment and nonmonogamy receives further support from research studies showing not only that polyamorous women were often exposed to strong mother figures during childhood (Franceschi, 2006) but also that no differences are discernable in relationship commitment between monogamous and polyamorous lesbian and bisexual women (Tibbets, 2001). These and other findings support Fern's (2020) important notion of *polysecurity*, that is, the capability of "being both securely attached to multiple romantic partners and having enough internal security to be able to navigate the structural relationship insecurity inherent to nonmonogamy" (p. 128). Healthy attachment, that is, may depend much more on one's inner psychological secu-rity (which normally translates into interpersonal security) than the relational style one prefers, selects, or somehow happens to be living.

As for relationship quality, when comparing sexually exclusive and sexu-ally open couples, no significant differences were found in marital adjustment and happiness (A. M. Rubin, 1982), sexual satisfaction (J. T. Parsons et al., 2012), relationship longevity and reasons for breakup (A. M. Rubin & Adams, 1986), or overall well-being and health (Fleckenstein & Cox II, 2015). A study of monogamous and nonmonogamous gay male couples concluded that despite the lack of social support both populations report receiving in the gay male community, both types of couples can enjoy lasting, happy relationships and satisfying sex lives within their primary relationship (Spears & Lowen, 2016). Another study found similar levels of relational satisfaction among monoga-mous and different types of CNM individuals (i.e., engaged in open relation-ships, polyamory, and swinging), even if those engaged in CNM reported slightly higher levels of sexual satisfaction (Conley et al., 2017). High levels of relationships quality were also discovered in a Canadian sample of 3,463 monogamous and nonmonogamous individuals (polyamorous and in open rela-tionships) individuals in a study controlling for sexual orientation, sex, age, and relationship duration (Séguin et al., 2017). Furthermore, a comparative study of 284 monogamous and polyamorous men and women found no significant group differences in scores indicative of relational quality (i.e., passion, trust, and attachment)—although poly men and women showed greater levels of intimacy as measured by the Intimacy Attitude Scale-Revised (IAS-R; Amidon et al., 1983; Morrison et al., 2013). Similarly, no differences were found in the relational satisfaction of monogamous and CNM couples (Mogilski et al., 2017)—a finding corroborated by another study comparing 206 monogamous couples and 142 CNM couples showing no significant differences in sexual motivations, sexual satisfaction, and overall relational fulfillment (Wood et al., 2018). Finally, a recent study found no differences in relational satisfaction between self-identified monogamous and CNM individuals as measured by the Relationship Assessment Scale (RAS) and the Relational Assessment Question-naire (RAQ; Garner et al., 2019).[17]

More broadly, two independent reviews of the literature (Conley, Ziegler et al., 2012; Rubel & Bogaert, 2015) show no evidence for monogamy as advantageous over polyamory on improved sexuality and relationship quality (cf. Kurdek & J. P. Schmitt, 1986), healthy or secure attachment style (cf. Moors, Matsick et al., 2017; Moors et al., 2019; Morrison et al., 2013), and benefits for family life and child rearing (cf. Pallotta-Chiarolli, 2010; Sheff, 2014). More theoretically but attuned to empirical studies, Brunning (2016) considered and rebutted four common monogamist arguments that polyamory entails commodification of relationships, avoidance of secure attachment, lack of sufficient practical and emotional resources to nurture relationships, and greater presence of jealousy. Summing up the empirical evidence, Rubel and Bogaert (2015) concluded, "Taken together, studies on marital satisfaction and happiness suggest that the quality of consensually nonmonogamous relationships is neither better nor worse than that of monogamous ones" (p. 977). As these studies and reviews establish, the common popular arguments for the advantageousness of either monogamy or nonmonogamy are not grounded in empirical evidence and thus qualify as ideological.

A major practical argument against polyamory (and nonmonogamy, in general) is that a greater number of sexual partners increase the risk of contracting HIV or other dangerous STIs (e.g., Aral & Leichliter, 2010). However, as the aforementioned literature reviews show, sexual safety is not necessarily contingent on being monogamous or being polyamorous (Conley, Ziegler et al., 2012; Rubel & Bogaert, 2015; see also Loue, 2006). One major factor at play is the staggering number of affairs (i.e., sexual relationships conducted without knowledge or consent of the intimate partner) in self-styled monogamous couples (see chapter 1, note 2). Summing up the available evidence, Buss (2000a) estimated that "approximately 20 to 40 percent of American women and 30 to 50 percent of American men have at least one affair over the course of the marriage" (p. 133), and pointed out that surveys suggest the chance of *either* member of a modern couple committing infidelity at some point in their marriage may be as high as 76%—with these figures increasing every year and with women's affairs equaling in number those of men (see Adamopoulou, 2013; Fincham & May, 2017; Vangelisti & Gerstenberger, 2004). Crucially, as Conley, Ziegler et al. (2012) discovered, individuals having clandestine affairs are less likely to practice safe sex—both in extradyadic encounters and with their partners—than those engaged in consensually nonmonogamous relationships (cf. Swan & S. C. Thompson, 2016; see chapter 1). In addition to corroborating these findings, Lehmiller (2015) reported that, among 556 surveyed participants, there was no difference in the percentage of STI diagnoses between monogamous and consensually nonmonogamous individuals. Interestingly, however, research also showed that most women who acquire HIV are infected by their primary partners after having had clandestine, unprotected sex with others (O'Leary, 2000). Indeed, in many of the world's areas such as rural Mexico, Nigeria, or Papua New Guinea, public health professionals have recognized that, due to the widespread unsafe extramarital sexual behavior of men, getting or being married increases or is even the greatest risk of HIV contagion for women (e.g., Hirsch et al., 2007; Newmann et al., 2000; D. J. Smith, 2007). Thus, although there is no question that sexual exclusivity would decrease the spread of STIs, the real issue appears to be not necessarily the number of partners (i.e., being monogamous or polyamorous) but the practice of safe sexuality and honest communication among intimate partners (no matter their number).

If neither very different relationship style has an innate advantage in terms of relationship health and outcome, then what else could drive relationship choice? In contrast to both mono- and polynormative claims, available empirical literature suggests that human beings are endowed with diverse personal orientations that may predispose them toward different relationship styles. Indeed, as mentioned above, research suggests that personality factors such as conscientiousness and openness to new experiences respectively predict monogamous or nonmonogamous dispositions better than attachment style (e.g., Moors, Selterman et al., 2017). In addition, many equally valid developmental trajectories may call individuals to engage in one or another relationship style either permanently or temporarily (Conley, Ziegler et al., 2012).

Whereas the psychological foundation for this diversity of mating responses requires further clarification, recent discoveries in neuroscience suggest the possibility of a biogenetic base for both monogamous and nonmonogamous tendencies. When scientists inserted a piece of DNA (a repeated polymorphism in the vasopressin receptor AVPRIA) from a monogamous species of mice (prairie voles) into males from a different—and highly promiscuous—mice species (montane voles), the latter turned fervently monogamous (K. A. Young et al., 2011; L. J. Young et al., 1999). Strikingly, some human males tending to pair-bonding behavior (e.g., marriage, cohabitation) carry an extra bit of DNA in a gene responsible for the distribution of vasopressin receptors in the brain (a hormone associated with attachment bonds), and that piece of DNA is very similar to the one found in the monogamous prairie voles (Walum et al., 2008; for a similar finding regarding an oxytocin receptor, see Walum et al., 2012). Although the implications of these findings for the understanding of human mating await further clarification (for discussion, see Numan, 2015), they suggest that a diversity of relationship styles—both monogamous and nonmonogamous—might be genetically imprinted in some humans.

However, several important questions arise regarding L. J. Young et al.'s (1999) seemingly impartial study. As Willey (2016) argued, it is important to be mindful of possible ideological biases in the attempts to "biologize" or "naturalize" either monogamy or polyamory.[18] In addition to serious methodological flaws in L. J. Young et al.'s research designs (crucially, in the test to measure the voles' alleged monogamy), Willey's ethnographic research in L. J. Young's laboratory found that monogamy was ideologically associated with optimal human development: "In this model, monogamy in voles is compared to social health, and promiscuity in voles to autism in humans" (p. 57); for an elaboration of this questionable comparison, see Lim et al. (2005) and McGraw and L. J. Young (2010). Another biological mark found in nonmonogamous men and women is higher levels of testosterone, a hormone commonly associated with male sexual drive (van Anders et al., 2007); however, it remains undetermined whether such higher levels (in relation to monogamous people, that is) are a cause or an outcome of this relational style (cf. Brandon, 2010). In any case, Willey's work is invaluable in revealing the ideological character of "naturalizing" discourses about not only monogamy but also polyamory; for a critical assessment of biogenetic evidence as the ground for relational style choices, see chapter 5.

In this regard, M. Robinson (2013) also critiqued the very idea of polyamory and monogamy as "natural" or fixed sexual orientations (like heterosexuality or homosexuality), and proposed instead to regard them as strategic identities that people (bisexual women, in her study) can freely select in different sociopolitical situations. In a similar vein, Klesse (2014a, 2016) discussed several potentially pernicious sociopolitical implications of regarding polyamory as a biologically engrained sexual orientation, such as the essentializing of polyamory and consequent loss of alliance with other nonmonogamous identities. These arguments may need to be balanced by a consideration of the many legal and antidiscriminatory benefits of regarding polyamory a sexual orientation (see Tweedy, 2011). In any event, this discussion is related to Barker's (2005) finding that whereas some people think of their polyamory as how they naturally are, others describe it as something they choose to do.[19]

What to make of all these rather disparate views? While further research is necessary to shed light on these questions, both my own research and personal experience suggest that people can be situated on a continuum from "very monogamous" to "very polyamorous" (cf. Barker, 2013), with many falling somewhere in between depending on diverse personal, social, cultural, and religious/spiritual variables. If this is the case, it is likely that those at both ends of the continuum may think of their relationship style as innate, and those falling somewhere in between may tend to describe it as a personal choice. These variables, and the fact that one's position on the continuum can change over time (i.e., relational plasticity), are important considerations in the exploration of relational freedom (see chapter 5). In any event, as extensive cross-cultural data convey, it seems unquestionable that "humans are designed and adapted for more than one mating strategy" (D. E. Schmitt, 2005b, p. 268). As stressed in the concluding section, however, this plurality of human mating choices should not circumvent qualitative distinctions within and among relational styles or orientations.

Beyond Hierarchy and Relativism

In this chapter, I have shown how monogamists and polyamorists disapprovingly—and often condescendingly—look down at one another as somehow flawed, misguided, or, in a word, "inferior." In addition, both camps claim the psychological, moral, or spiritual higher ground, pigeonholing their perceived opponents as suffering from attachment deficits, interiorized patriarchy, or spiritual short-sightedness. As discussed in chapter 5, questions can be raised about the overall tendency in the West to hierarchically frame binary distinctions and posit one pole as superior to the other (e.g., man/woman, straight/queer, monogamy/polyamory). This hierarchical ethos substantially prunes and inhibits the development of relational freedom, in the sense that individuals (consciously or unconsciously) upholding the absolute superiority or rightness of any particular relational style will be less inclined to consider other relational options, even those potentially more attuned to their personal dispositions or current developmental pulls.

In keeping with a critical pluralist approach to intimate relationships and relationship styles, one of my aims in this chapter has been to expose the ideological underpinnings of enthroning any particular relationship style—whether monogamy or polyamory—as somehow "superior" or the most appropriate relational style for the twenty-first century. As Willey (2016) wrote, "The privileging of any single model of intimacy . . . automatically boxes all other models and their 'adherents' as problematic" (p. 145). Likewise, Barker (2013; Barker & Iantaffi, 2019) argued against the positioning of either monogamy or polyamory (or any other kind of romantic or sexual love) as intrinsically superior to the other, situating these relationship styles in a fuzzy continuum of mono-to-poly degrees versus a binary choice (see also chapter 4). One of the most effective approaches I am familiar with for dismantling the "mono–poly wars" is Barker et al.'s (2013) proposal for a revolutionary love ethics that shifts polyamory's "meaning away from having 'multiple lovers' to 'multiple loves'" (p. 198). This revolutionary love ethics, they wrote,

> might queer polyamory by inviting us to love our bodies just as they are [as well as] to nurture our capacity to love other bodies, not just those that we find easy to desire sexually, but to express a loving-kindness toward all the bodies on Earth with whom our lives are entwined. (p. 200)

In other words, by emphasizing the love of life itself beyond sexual romance, such an ethics not only blurs the borders between monogamy and polyamory (and nonmonogamy in general) but may also reveal previously unnoticed or marginalized spiritual resources, thus inviting a broadly embodied approach to loving oneself, others, and the world (cf. Wilkinson, 2010). Schippers's (2020) "poly gaze" also undermines the "mono–poly wars" by inviting a way to critically read culture and live in the world beyond both mononormativity and (sexually and romantically centered) polynormativity, opening the ground for a wider understanding of love leading to a deeper commitment to each other and the planet.

More pluralistic accounts of relationship styles, however, should not necessarily lead to a trivializing relativism that is incapable of critical discernment. On the one hand, even if monogamy and polyamory (or nonmonogamy in general) cannot be hierarchically situated as wholes in regard to each other, particular qualitative distinctions can be made between them both in general and contextually. In other words, these relational styles can be "better" or more appropriate in different ways and situations or for different people in distinct moments of their personal trajectories; for example, whereas it is likely that monogamy offers the best relational container for the healing of many sexual-emotional traumas, polyamory may be a powerfully emancipatory relational choice for women who spent years controlled by patriarchal or jealous husbands. On the other hand, a variety of qualitative, emancipatory, and transformational criteria can—and, I will argue, should—be applied when assessing the relative merits and shortcomings of specific intimate relationships (see chapter 5). Thus, adopting a critical pluralist approach not only allows for greater perspicacity in assessing the situated value of any relational choice but can also expand people's unfettered consideration of a wider number of relational options.

Notes

[1] The term *polyamory* is a hybrid word etymologically meaning "many loves." Also known as responsible nonmonogamy (e.g., Anapol, 1997; Klesse, 2006), polyamory is both a philosophy of love and "a relationship orientation that assumes that it is possible to love many people and to maintain multiple intimate and sexual relationships" (Barker, 2005, p. 75; cf. Sheff, 2006). Polyamory has also been described as a form of nonmonogamy grounded in the belief in "people's capacity to share and multiply their love in honest and consensual ways" (Anderlini-D'Onofrio, 2004a, p. 165). As discussed next, polyamory is usually contrasted to not only monogamy and polygamy but also swinging, casual sex, and promiscuity. Understandably, scholars have critiqued the poly account of multiple long-term loving bonds being "responsible" nonmonogamy, as it implicitly demotes other nonmonogamous practices as less responsible or irresponsible, thereby marginalizing various class, racial, and queer populations (see Barker et al., 2013; Klesse, 2006; Noël, 2006; Petrella, 2007; Wilkinson, 2010). As Klesse (2006) pointed out, for example, the polyamorist privileging of love over sex "can be presented as being superior to other forms of non-monogamy that emphasize more strongly the pursuit of sexual pleasure" (p. 578). For some constructive suggestions about how polyamory can achieve greater socially emancipatory force, see Barker et al. (2013), Raab (2014), and Schippers (2016).

[2] Although this chapter cannot address relational malleability and gender differences, research shows not only that males and females can undergo important changes in their sexual and relational orientations (see Conley, Ziegler et al., 2012) but also that individual women show greater sexual and erotic plasticity than men over time, arguably due to a variety of evolutionary and sociocultural forces (Baumeister, 2000; Chivers et al., 2004; Symons, 1979). Whether such a sexual–erotic plasticity somehow translates into relational style plasticity (I suspect it does) is an open question for future research; indeed, the only available research study on the interaction between sexual fluidity and relational identity over time suggests that this is the case (see Manley et al., 2015).

[3] In what follows, I differentiate between monogam*ists*/polyamor*ists* (who ideologically hold their preferred relational style as natural, superior, or advantageous) and monogam*ous*/polyamor*ous* people (who do not). For different discussions of *monogamism*, see E. Anderson (2012), Blumer et al. (2014), and L. S. Jordan et al. (2017).

[4] The origins of socially imposed monogamy in the Western world have been traced to ancient Greece and Rome (Betzig, 1992; Scheidel, 2009), the Middle Ages (Betzig, 1995; MacDonald, 1995), and the Industrial Revolution (Gould et al., 2008). As de la Croix and Mariani (2015) summarized, "it seems safe to affirm that European countries, which were undoubtedly inhabited by polygamous societies before the Greco-Roman age, had become strictly monogamous after the spread of Christianity" (p. 570; see also MacDonald, 1990). Greco-Roman monogamy effectively shaped the Christian position on monogamy, replacing the highly polygamous (i.e., polygynous) Jewish matrix that birthed early Christianity; as Saint

Augustine famously said in the early fifth century, monogamy was "a Roman custom" (Scheidel, 2009). For a discussion of the modern naturalization and secularization of Christian monogamous marriage as emerging from the interface of European colonialist imagination and early scientific sexological discourses, see Willey (2018).

5   The shift from widespread polygyny to socially imposed monogamy has been variously explained as appealing to (a) optimization of social cooperation by powerful men (Betzig, 1986) and the minimization of rebellion by lower-class males (Lagerlöf, 2010) or kin groups (R. D. Alexander, 1987); (b) reduction of intrasexual competition leading to crimes, rapes, and murders by low-status men (Henrich et al., 2012); (c) women's preference for monogamy after the spread of capital and resources among men (Citci, 2014; Kanazawa & Still, 1999); (d) growing appreciation for quality (vs. quantity) of children in the wake of increased cost of education after the Industrial Revolution (Gould et al., 2008); and (e) reduction of bacterial STIs in large groups and populations prior to the invention of antibiotics, latex condoms, and other protective measures (Bauch & McElreath, 2016), among other hypotheses (for a helpful review, see M. M. Dow & Eff, 2013).

Whereas it is likely that most of these theories provide a piece of the puzzle, it seems undeniable that both the rise of democratic forces—gradually allowing increased political activity for women and lower-status men—and the influence of the Church's enforcement of a strict sexual ethics were pivotal factors in the widespread social imposition of monogamy (Cott, 2002; MacDonald, 1995). As monogamy might also been a major factor in the very emergence of democratic ideals and gender equality (Henrich et al., 2012), both monogamy and democracy seem to have synergically impacted each other through a relationship loop of mutual causality.

6   Although in this book I use *mononormativity*, *monocentrism*, and *socially imposed monogamy* rather interchangeably, at times one or another term will serve better to give the appropriate nuance to a particular passage or argument. Importantly, Brake's *amatonormativity* also denounces the demotion of friendships and other caring relationships that is implied in the cultural privileging of exclusive romantic bonds. For a revealing list of 50 cultural rules and customs (from bigamy laws to couples-massage deals to the standard car design for two adults) showing how mononormativity works in practice, see Kean (2015). As discussed in chapter 5, Schippers (2020) has developed what she calls the "poly gaze" as a critical lens to detect mononormative biases and assumptions in cultural forms such as films, music, journalism, social media, and so forth.

7   As Rambukkana (2015) argued, the culturally prevalent, essentializing portrayal of polygamy as patriarchal polygyny perpetuates mononormative values. Interestingly, both monogamous and polyamorous individuals tend to position themselves as superior to polygamous people (e.g., Klesse, 2006; Ritchie, 2010).

8   Although virtually all poly activists and scholars critique compulsory monogamy, some neither reject monogamy per se nor hold polyamory as categorically superior (e.g., Anapol, 1997, 2010; Barker, 2013; Taormino, 2008; Veaux & Rickert, 2014).

9   The following account is informed by almost three decades of personal exchanges in Spain and the San Francisco Bay Area, as well as many European (e.g., England, Germany, Italy), Asian (e.g., Japan, India, Indonesia), and Central and South American

countries (e.g., Mexico, Peru, Argentina). Although aspects of the following discussion might apply to other cultures, I limit its validity claims to modern Western countries (e.g., European nations, Canada, and the United States) and perhaps other industrialized, urbanized, secular, and capitalist societies (see Hall, 1992).

[10] Applying life history theory (LHT; see Del Giudice et al., 2015), Mogilski et al. (2020) argued that the stigmatization of CNM is likely connected with cultural associations of sexual promiscuity with so-called "faster life history" traits developed in response to stressful childhood environments associated with lower socio-economic backgrounds (e.g., higher impulsivity, risk-taking, competitiveness); such traits, they argued, render CNM individuals untrustworthy, unstable, and socially uncooperative despite the lack of empirical evidence supporting such attributes in CNM people. In addition, as in the case of gay males and HIV, many CNM individuals appear to be socially excluded due to the widespread but empirically unfounded belief that CNM people are more likely to contract and spread STIs (Balzarini et al., 2018; Conley, Moors et al., 2013). Students and staff members who participated in a qualitative study of nonmonogamy on a New Zealand university campus reported that disclosing their being nonmonogamous was even more challenging than discussing alternative gender and sexual identities (Brown, 2020). As Rodrigues, Fasoli et al. (2017) showed, the perceived sexual permissiveness of CNM people can even lead to "dehumanizing" this population, with many adverse consequences; for example, victims of sexual assault viewed as sexually promiscuous tend to be blamed for the assault. Although studies exist on the social stigmatization of poly people in general (e.g., Conley, Moors et al., 2012; Hutzler et al., 2016; Séguin, 2019) and poly bisexual women in particular (Baumgartner, 2021; Klesse, 2005), I am not aware of any empirical study on polyphobia and gender. Given the frequency of CNM among transgender people (E. C. Levine et al., 2018; Rossman et al., 2019), as well as the interest in CNM among sexual minorities in general (Moors et al., 2014), research on the specific ways in which internalized polyphobia may manifest in these populations is also imperative (see Cramer et al., 2020). Fortunately, recent research indicates that younger generations of adults, even if they continue having more positive implicit associations with monogamy, are more neutral toward CNM (A. E. Thompson et al., 2020).

[11] Despite the polyphobic tenor of their discourse, Barash and Lipton (2009) made a valid point: the fact that monogamy may not be "natural" for either animals or human beings does not necessarily discredit it as a valuable achievement or potentially fulfilling relational choice. As they observed, "biology is not destiny" and the equation of "natural" with "good" is fallacious (p. 14). Many natural phenomena (e.g., tuberculosis or earthquakes) are not desirable, and many valuable attainments (e.g., musical symphonies or medical advancements) are not natural. In any case, the likely "unnaturalness" of monogamy should warn people about the many trials involved in its long-term maintenance, as well as help them to more compassionately understand its perceived "failures" (see Brandon, 2010).

[12] Even if some of these claims for the archaic evolutionary advantage of monogamy are plausible (e.g., the positive impact of pair-bonding on raising children, social

intelligence, and cooperative skills; see Fletcher et al., 2015), many adaptations that may have conferred evolutionary benefits for survival in humanity's past are clearly obsolete today (e.g., our taste for sweets and fats; even infanticide and rape, as some evolutionary psychologists controversially claimed; see Thornhill & Palmer, 2000). In any event, my intention here is not to take a stance on these thorny debates but to denounce the use of admittedly speculative evidence for an archaic human monogamous past to justify and perpetuate monocentrism in the present.

[13] In addition to this polyphobic prejudice, researchers detected serious methodological flaws in Regnerus's (2017) work suggesting serious homophobic biases, in particular regarding claims about the disadvantages of children of gay parents compared to those from opposite-sex parents (see Cheng & Powell, 2015; Cohen, 2012). Needless to say, my selective (and mostly critical) discussion of Regnerus's work in this book does not reflect any endorsement of his overall project in general or these problematic biases in particular.

[14] Contesting the standard evolutionary narrative of an ancestral pair-bonding culture and archaically seated sexual jealousy, Ryan and Jethá (2010) argued for a more sexually licentious human prehistoric past and a link between the origins of patriarchy and the emergence of agriculture about 10,000 years ago; for critiques of this proposal, see Ellsworth (2011) and Saxon (2011). Although the emergence of agriculture (and thus of human settlements and private property) very likely increased men's concern for paternity and thus sexual possessiveness (e.g., Stearns, 2009), the exact (pre-)historical origins of sexual jealousy are probably manifold and far from clear-cut; after all, many hunter-gatherer cultures practice marriage (R. S. Walker et al., 2011) and sexual jealousy exists even in cultures practicing shared paternity (Beckerman & Valentine, 2002). In this regard, Raley (2018) argued precisely for the opposite view: the accumulation of wealth and increased inequality of resources caused by the agricultural revolution shifted hunter-gatherers' monogamy into patriarchal polygyny.

[15] As a student of religion, I have always been fascinated by the parallels between the "mono–poly wars" and the many-centuries-long conflict between monotheism and polytheism (e.g., Kirsch, 2004; Paper, 2005), for example, regarding the superiority of the One over the Many, questions around the exclusivity of loving devotion, God's expressed jealousy toward other Gods, and so forth. Given both Christian monotheism and its perhaps associated prescription for lifelong monogamy, thus, it should not be surprising that polyamorous people prefer "other" religions and are less likely to be affiliated with Christianity than monogamous ones (Balzarini, Dharma, Kohut, L. Campbell, Holmes et al., 2019; Kolesar & Pardo, 2019). Indeed, the word *polyamory* was originally coined by the Neopagan leader Morning Glory Zell, and many poly women (and men) have embraced Paganism (Christianity's historical antithesis) as their favored religion (see Kaldera, 2005). Likewise, it is not surprising that U.S. religious practitioners of Christianity and other theistic traditions (with the seeming exception of certain sections within Judaism) disapprove of polyamory more than Buddhists and secular individuals (Litschi et al., 2014). The religious underpinnings of the "mono–poly wars" are complex and

surely deserve an extended discussion; for some directions, see Rycenga (1995), Anderlini-D'Onofrio (2004b), Goss (2004), Willey (2006, 2018), and Kolesar and Pardo (2019).

[16]   Although a narcissistic personality structure can naturally accentuate relational narcissism, I submit that the latter is not necessarily associated with the former. In other words, I hypothesize that individuals scoring low on the Narcissistic Personality Inventory (NPI; Raskin & Terry, 1988) can hold their relational choice as universally optimal or superior due to a variety of cultural and largely unexamined factors (such as monopride or polypride).

[17]   As Balzarini, Dharma, Kohut, Campbell, Lehmiller et al. (2019) pointed out, however, most of these comparative studies failed to differentiate between hierarchical (one primary partner) and nonhierarchical (coprimary or nonprimary partners) polyamorous structures. Building on their own research and other studies (e.g., Mogilski et al., 2017), Balzarini et al. indicated that individuals report higher satisfaction with monogamous and primary (including coprimary) partners than with secondary ones (cf. M. E. Mitchell et al., 2014). Diverging from these findings, E. C. Levine et al. (2018) found that individuals in open relationships reported lower relational happiness and sexual satisfactions than those in monogamous relationships. Although in contrast to prior studies, E. C. Levine et al.'s research was conducted on a representative probability sample of 2,270 U.S. adults drawn from the 2012 National Survey of Sexual Health and Behavior (REF), the authors conceded that "It is possible that relationship and sexual satisfaction function differently in open relationships and other forms of CNM . . . [so] a lower average might not necessarily indicate lower satisfaction, but rather different standards for measuring satisfaction" (p. 1459).

[18]   For discussions of classical and contemporary critiques of the invocation of "nature" as normative standard in public life, as well as of essentialist naturalizing discourses in general, see Archer et al. (2013b).

[19]   For a popular discussion of the innateness of nonmonogamy, see Carey (2013). The question of the biogenetically innate versus socially or individually shaped nature of polyamory should be seen in the wider context of the essentialist–constructivist debate in the human and social sciences. Generally speaking, whereas essentialism posits universal, invariable, or biologically engrained features in human nature, social constructivism rejects any givens in the human condition, holding instead that such features are both variable and changing, as they are always already constructed by the various cultures, societies, and languages (e.g., Fay, 1996). For a lucid review of this debate in the study of human sexuality (that nonetheless ignores relational style choices), see DeLamater and Hyde (1998). Whereas the modern discipline of epigenetics (e.g., D. S. Moore, 2015) may eventually relax the tension between essentialism and social constructivism, epigenetic studies on human sexuality tend to privilege biological influences (see Balter, 2015).

Chapter 3

Sympathetic Joy

Beyond Jealousy, Toward Relational Freedom

A major roadblock to relational freedom is arguably the experience of jealousy, which has evolutionary, sociocultural, and biographical roots (Buss, 2000a; Pines, 1998; Zandbergen & S. G. Brown, 2015). In particular, jealousy may prevent many individuals predisposed to nonmonogamous relationships from living a CNM or polyamorous lifestyle, as the thought of their longtime dyadic partner loving or being sexual with anyone else can be emotionally unbearable. As Tsoulis (1987) pointed out, "Jealousy ensures the supremacy of monogamy and monogamous love [serving] a property-owning patriarchal culture as well" (p. 25). Over many decades, countless men and women engaged in long-term monogamous arrangements have sincerely told me that they would actually love to have other sexual partners or romantic connections, but they refrained from seeking them—because their current partner would then want to do the same, and they feared or could not accept that outcome. However, jealousy can affect nonmonogamous relationships as well: at least some polyamorous people may (consciously or unconsciously) select their lifestyle in order to minimize the stronger jealous feelings that a monogamous commitment to a single partner might elicit in them, or to avoid partners with high levels of jealousy. Thus, decreasing or overcoming jealousy can expand relational freedom independently of relational style, optimizing the free choice of intimacy modes attuned to changeable circumstances and developmental junctures.

Since Christianity's views of sex, sin, and marriage have such a deep effect on Westerners' relationship choices and assumptions (see Dabhoiwala, 2012; Fuchs, 1983; Weiser-Hanks, 2000), the pursuit of relational freedom requires a new approach to jealousy: Buddhism in particular offers a spiritual perspective and practice for moving beyond jealousy. This chapter explores how the extension of the Buddhist contemplative quality of sympathetic joy or *mudita* from its original context to intimate relationships can transform jealousy and thus support greater relational freedom.[1] After reviewing contemporary findings from the field of evolutionary psychology on the twin origins of jealousy and monogamy, I introduce the notion of *genetic selfishness* or the privileging of one's own progeny over anyone else's. Then, I argue for the possibility to transform jealousy into sympathetic joy, and challenge the culturally prevalent belief that the only spiritually correct sexual options are either celibacy or (lifelong or serial) monogamy. To conclude, I suggest that the cultivation of sympathetic joy in intimate bonds paves the way to overcome the "mono–poly wars" and empowers people in the exercising of relational freedom.

Sympathetic Joy and Jealousy in Relationships

In Buddhism, sympathetic joy (*mudita*) is regarded as one of the "four immeasurable states" (*brahmaviharas*) or qualities of an enlightened person, and it refers to the human capability to participate in the joy of others—to feel happy when others feel happy (the other three are loving-kindness or *metta*, compassion or *karuna*, and equanimity or *upeksha*; see Pandita, 2017; Tuffley, 2012). In its original cultural context, Buddhist practitioners first practiced sympathetic joy in relation to friends or loved ones, then directed it to people toward whom they felt neutral, and finally toward difficult or hostile people, until the practice would encompass all beings (e.g., Buddhaghosa, 1976). As with the other immeasurable states, the Buddha also advised people to send *mudita* in all directions, first North, then South, then East, and West (Tuffley, 2012). The practice of *mudita* entails the meditative repetition of phrases such as "I am happy that you are happy," "May your happiness and good fortune not leave you," or "May your happiness not diminish," pausing after each phrase to allow the words to reverberate in the heart (e.g., Salzberg, 1995). In some contemporary accounts, practitioners are recommended to begin the practice with themselves, with phrases such as "May I be happy" or "May my happiness continue" (e.g., Germino, 2019).

Although with different emphases, a similar understanding can be found in the contemplative teachings of other religious traditions where they talk about empathic or appreciative joy. For example, in Christianity, the practice of *agape* or selfless love includes desiring the well-being and happiness of all human beings (e.g., West, 2007). In Sufism, opening the "eye of the heart" is said to allow one to see the divine mystery everywhere and thus rejoice in the presence of anyone's happiness (e.g., Ozturk, 1988). According to these traditions, the cultivation of sympathetic joy can break through the allegedly false duality between self and others, being therefore a potent aid on the path toward overcoming self-centeredness and achieving liberation from egocentric concerns and associated perspectives.

Intimate relationships offer human beings—whether spiritual practitioners or not—a precious opportunity to taste the experiential flavor of sympathetic joy. Most psychologically balanced individuals naturally share to some degree in the happiness of their mates. Bliss and delight can effortlessly emerge within as one feels the joy of a partner's ecstatic dance, enjoyment of an art performance, relishing of a favorite dish, or serene contemplation of a splendid sunset. This innate capacity for sympathetic joy in intimate relationships often reaches its peak in deeply emotional shared experiences, sensual exchange, and lovemaking. When we are in love, the embodied joy of our beloved becomes extremely contagious.

For the vast majority of people, however, if my partner's sensual or sexual joy arises in relation to someone other than me, the immediate reaction would not be expansive openness and love, but rather contracting fear—in the context of romantic relationships, jealousy appears to function as a hindrance to sympathetic joy. The *APA Dictionary of Psychology* defined *jealousy* as "a negative emotion in which an individual resents a third party for appearing to take away (or likely to take away) the affections of a loved one" (VandenBos, 2007, p. 506).[2] Underscoring the mutually reinforcing nature of jealousy and monogamy, feminist scholars Jackson and Scott (2004) wrote:

> Meaningful relationships are perceived as threatening because they trigger the fear of losing one's own relationship, but the threat of being traded in for a new model is a product of the monogamous ideal where being involved in two meaningful relationships entails a forced choice between them. (p. 156)

In any event, the fear of being displaced by another person in a valued relationship seems central to all forms of jealousy, not only romantic ones. Indeed, that fear can quickly convert into anger, and at times (too often), even violent rage. The change of a single variable (i.e., another person instead of oneself) can rapidly turn the selfless contentment of sympathetic joy into the "green-eyed monster" of jealousy, as Shakespeare famously called this compulsive emotion (Buss, 2000a).

Perhaps due to its prevalence, jealousy is widely accepted as "normal," inevitable, and even a desirable virtue in most Western cultures and by numerous scholars (e.g., Kristjánsson, 2002; Neu, 2000; Pines, 1998; Salovey, 1991; Toohey, 2014). Extolling the virtuous nature of jealousy, for example, Kristjánsson (2002) wrote,

> Jealousy is a necessary condition of pridefulness, and hence . . . it both acts as an important guardian of self-respect and also contributes, at a deeper level, to the formation and maintenance of personhood. The emotion of jealousy in this sense is a value which should be fostered rather than discouraged in moral education. (p. 136)

Further, beginning with Freud (1955), who considered the absence of "normal" levels of jealousy pathological, some modern clinical psychologists and relationship counselors understand jealousy as a healthy sign of care (e.g., Stirling Hastings, 1996). Indeed, its violent consequences have often been regarded as understandable, morally justified, and even legally permissible (as late as the 1970s, Texas, Utah, and New Mexico law considered the homicide of one's adulterous partner "reasonable" if it happened in the moment the affair was discovered; Buss, 2000a). Even when jealousy was considered pathological, the U.S. legal system (at least up to the 1990s) tended to treat the (usually male) perpetuators of "crimes of passion" rather generously as "sick" individuals who could not control their violent impulses (Mullen, 1993). Not surprisingly, women have suffered the most numerous and severe consequences of sexual jealousy across cultures, suggesting a central role of patriarchy's control of female sexuality in male jealous violence (Goetz et al., 2008; Vandello & Cohen, 2003; Wilson & M. Daly, 1996). The overwhelming majority of cases of battery and spousal murders worldwide are caused by jealous violence (M. Daly et al., 1982; Hupka & Ryan, 1990; H. Johnson et al., 2008); tragically, about 30% of women murdered in the United States were the victims of former or present jealous husbands or boyfriends (Ben-Ze'ev & Goussinsky, 2008). Although there are circumstances in which the mindful expression of rightful anger (not violence) may be a temporary appropriate response (see Masters, 2006)—for example, in the case of cheating and the adulterous breaking of monogamous vows—jealousy frequently makes its appearance in interpersonal situations where no betrayal has taken place, or when one rationally knows that no real threat actually exists (e.g., watching a partner dance with an attractive friend at a party).

That said, jealousy should be neither glorified nor demonized. Even though this chapter advocates for its transformation, certain jealous reactions can indeed signal that a relationship may be somehow out of balance or that "something" needs to be addressed. It is perfectly understandable, for example, to feel annoyed or frustrated if your partner takes you dancing and leaves you sitting by yourself the entire night while passionately dancing with another person—or if your partner ignores you throughout a cocktail party while actively flirting with everybody else. In these and similar cases, the emergence of discomfort or jealous feelings may be simply saying that something is "off" with the situation.

This chapter focuses on the more common aspect of jealousy—which arises from a complex mix of evolutionary forces, sociocultural scripts, and biographical factors—standing as a significant barrier to relational freedom, and on sympathetic joy as a means of moving beyond jealousy. In general, the awakening of sympathetic joy in observing the happiness of one's mate in relationship with perceived "rivals" is an extremely rare pearl to find in Western societies. To begin exploring why jealousy is so ubiquitous, I turn to the discoveries of modern evolutionary psychology.[3]

Genetic Selfishness: An Evolutionary Account of Jealousy and Monogamy

Whereas jealousy is not exclusive to monogamous bonds (Bergstrand & Sinski, 2010; Deri, 2015; Easton, 2010), the origins of jealousy and monogamy are intimately connected in the human primeval past. Jealousy very likely emerged around 3.5 million years ago in our hominid ancestors, as an adaptive response of vital evolutionary value for both biological sexes (Buss, 2000a). Whereas the reproductive payoff of jealousy for males was to secure certainty of paternity and to avoid spending resources in support of another male's genetic offspring, for females it may have evolved as a mechanism for guaranteeing protection and resources for biological children by having a steady partner.[4] In short, jealousy very likely emerged in humanity's ancestral past to reserve males' effort for their biological children and to ensure male providers for females' children. Even if children were eventually raised cooperatively and women with children felt less need to be "protected" and "provided" by men (see Hrdy, 1999, 2009), this does not alter the fact that ancestral women almost certainly experienced disadvantages if their mates left them to support other women and children. For this reason, evolutionary psychologists argued, even today men tend to experience more intense feelings of jealousy than women do when they suspect sexual infidelity (vs. emotional infidelity), while women are more likely than men to feel threatened when their mates become emotionally attached to and supportive of another woman (Buss, 2000a; Buunk & Dijkstra, 2004; Sesardic, 2002).[5] Although evidence exists for the cross-cultural presence of this gender-specific evolutionary logic in relation to jealousy (Buss, 1994, 2000a, 2006; Buunk et al., 2007), evolutionary feminists and other researchers have challenged such biologizing and stereotyping of sex differences, not only identifying serious methodological flaws in the relevant studies but also providing disconfirming evidence (see DeSteno et al., 2002; Eagly & Wood, 2013; C. R. Harris, 2003; Hrdy, 1997). Fortunately, the tension between evolutionary psychologists—who underscore nature and biological determinism—and feminist evolutionists—who stress nurture and sociocultural construction (Liesen, 2007)—has been relaxed by the emergence of more holistic biosocial approaches. With differences emphases, these approaches take into account the combined forces of culture and biology while rejecting both biological determinism and extreme forms of social constructionism (e.g., A. Campbell, 2012; Eagly & Wood, 2013; H. Johnson, 2012; Nicolas & Welling, 2015). Thus, it is likely that a complex intertwining of both biogenetic and sociocultural forces shape a diversity of gender-specific jealousy patters across cultures.

In any event, from a strictly evolutionary standpoint the main purpose of both monogamy and jealousy appears to be to secure the dissemination of one's DNA; however, most instinctive reactions that may have had evolutionary significance in ancestral times do not make much sense in the modern world. As evolutionary psychologist David Buss (1994) put it, most human mating mechanisms and responses are actually "living fossils" (p. 222) largely shaped by the genetic pressures of human evolutionary history. For example, many single mothers today do not need or want financial (or even emotional) support from their children's fathers, yet still feel jealous when their ex-partner bonds to another woman. In addition, most contemporary individuals suffer from jealousy independent of whether they want children or plan to have them with their partners. This biological "hangover" is a significant impediment to relational freedom, as it often leads to the restriction of both one's partner's relational choices and, at times, even one's own.

Indeed, jealousy ultimately serves a biologically engrained form of egotism that might be called *genetic selfishness*: the privileging of one's own progeny over anyone else's.[6] As Hrdy (1999) showed, for example, many primate males invest much more heavily in offspring likely to be their own—a behavioral pattern clearly magnified in the human male. Genetic selfishness is so archaic, pandemic, and deeply seated in human nature that it goes largely unnoticed in contemporary culture and spiritual circles. As an example, in the movie *Cinderella Man* (Howard et al., 2005), an officer from the electric company is about to cut the power to the residence of a family with three children who will very likely die without heat—it is winter in New York at the time of the Great Depression. When the children's mother appeals to the officer's compassion, begging him not to turn off the power, he responds that his own children will suffer the same fate if he does not do his job (because he will be fired). As I looked around the theater, I noted a large number of people in the audience nodding their heads in poignant understanding. Instinctively, it can seem both humanely understandable and morally justifiable to favor the survival of one's own offspring over that of others, but the officer's decision raises vital questions. What if by saving my own child I am condemning to death three or four other children? What if I am condemning ten, one hundred, or one thousand? My aim in raising these questions is not to offer solutions, but merely to convey how tacitly genetic selfishness is embedded as "second nature" in the human condition.

After introducing this understandably controversial notion more than a decade ago (Ferrer, 2007), I was reassured by the fact that a mother of the moral and intellectual stature of Marcia Angell (2016) shared similar feelings. In her provocative essay, Angell denounced the potential selfishness entailed by parents' focus on their own progeny over anyone else's, as well as its pernicious social consequences such as lesser solidarity with the poor and unwillingness to pay higher taxes (and, I would add, hiding immense fortunes in undeclared offshore accounts). As Milanovic (2020) pointed out, a major motivation of the elites' investment in gaining political influence is to be able to determine "the rules of inheritance, so that financial capital is easily transformed to the next generation" (p. 14), which naturally leads to "the reproduction of the ruling class" (p. 14). Bottom line, genetic selfishness promotes plutocratic capitalism, weakens democracy, and perpetuates socioeconomic inequality.

This discussion of the deeply seated evolutionary origins of jealousy raises two further questions: Can jealousy be truly transformed? What emotional response can take the place of jealousy in human experience? Both Buddhism and contemporary research on polyamory offer some answers.

Sympathetic Joy and Compersion

At first sight, Buddhism seems to speak directly to the issue of jealousy. In Vajrayana Buddhism, jealousy is considered an imperfection (*klesha*) associated with attachment and self-centeredness that is transmuted into sympathetic joy, equanimity, and wisdom by the power of the Lord of Karma, Amoghasiddhi, one of the Five Dhyani Buddhas (Buddhas visualized in meditation; see Thrangu Rimponche, 2013). From the green body of Amoghasiddhi emanates his consort, the goddess Green Tara, who is said to also have the power of turning jealousy into the ability to dwell in the happiness of others. While it may look as if the green gods and goddesses of the Buddhist pantheon have defeated the green-eyed monster of jealousy, however, closer inspection indicates otherwise.

The problem is that the Buddhist terms translated as jealousy—such as *issa* (Pali), *phrag dog* (Tibetan), or *irshya* (Sanskrit)—are more accurately read as "envy." In the various Buddhist descriptions of "jealousy," one generally find illustrations of bitterness and resentment at the happiness, talents, or good fortune of others, but very rarely, if ever, contracting fear and anger in response to a mate's sexual or emotional connection to others. In the *Abhidhamma*, for example, jealousy (*issa*) is considered an immoral mental state characterized by feelings of ill will at the success and prosperity of others (Dessein & Teng, 2016). In this regard, Chögyam Trungpa (1991) wrote, "It is not exactly jealousy; we do not seem to have the proper term in the English language. It is a paranoid attitude of comparison rather than purely jealousy . . . a sense of competition" (p. 32). All these descriptions in fact refer to *envy*, which the *Oxford English Dictionary* defines as "feel[ing] displeasure and ill-will at the superiority of (another person) in happiness, success, reputation, or the possession of anything desirable" (1989, 5.316) and not to jealousy, which is a response to the real or imagined threat of losing one's partner or valued relationship to a third party (see Clanton, 2006). Since Buddhist teachings about jealousy were originally aimed at monks who were not supposed to develop emotional attachments (even those who engaged in tantric sexual acts; Faure, 1998; Harvey,

2000), the lack of systematic reflection in Buddhism upon romantic jealousy should not come as a surprise.

Nonetheless, the Buddhist concept and practice of *mudita* has much to offer in transforming jealousy to sympathetic joy. The relevance of sympathetic joy for intimate relationships becomes more visible when juxtaposed with contemporary research on the phenomenon of compersion in polyamorous people. Since jealousy has no antonym in the English language, the Kerista community (a polyamorous group located in San Francisco that was disbanded in the early 1990s) coined the term *compersion* to refer to the emotional response opposite to jealousy (Kerista Commune, 1984).[7] *Compersion* is usually defined as "the feeling of taking joy in the joy that others you love share among themselves" (Ritchie & Barker, 2006, p. 595). While the term emerged in the context of the practice of *polyfidelity* (faithfulness to many; see Kerista Commune, 1984), the feeling of compersion can also be extended to any situation in which one's mate feels emotional or sensuous joy with others in *wholesome and constructive ways* (e.g., de Sousa, 2017; Deri, 2015). In these situations, one can rejoice in one's partner's joy even without loving or knowing the third parties.[8]

It is perhaps easiest to explain this emphasis on "wholesome and constructive ways" through a personal vignette. In the context of an open relationship with a woman with whom I was deeply in love, I once experienced a wave of anger and overall emotional distress at the imagined thought of her being penetrated by another man. As I looked deeply into my emotions, a different version of that scenario eventually emerged, in which the man having sex with my partner was *loving her well*—with passion, yes, but also with care and respect, as well as honoring my connection with her. I then realized that my original anger emerged in relation to an imagined predator male who was sexually objectifying my partner in selfish, patriarchal, or misogynist ways. When the new image appeared, all emotional distress subsided, and warmth and love toward both my partner and the other man spontaneously arose in my heart. What is more, I experienced a sense of both gratitude and brotherhood toward that man who loved well my partner and whose presence in my life was giving me the opportunity to work on my potential negative reactions to something that was actually good and beautiful. On another occasion, my partner experienced my care toward a woman I was in relationship with as a portal to sympathetically love a woman she had not had the chance to meet. These experiences suggest that the traditional account of compersion as exclusively focused on one's partner is somewhat myopic; compersion can potentially be extended to all the people engaged in open relationships, even to third parties one has not met.

These and other experiential accounts of compersion (see Deri, 2015; Duma, 2009) problematize Mogilski et al.'s (2019) utilitarian hypothesis that, instead of being the emotional opposite to jealousy, compersion is actually the feeling of satisfaction based on the expectation of personal or relational benefits (e.g., increasing sexual or romantic opportunities for both partners). Although the perception of such benefits may foster or enhance the emergence of compersion, I believe it is fallacious to reduce the latter to the former. Whereas further research into compersion is necessary to elucidate its various components and facilitating conditions, compersion is reportedly felt as a tangible presence in the heart whose awakening may be accompanied by waves of warmth, pleasure, and appreciation at the idea of one's partner loving others and being loved by them in nonharmful and mutually beneficial ways (Anapol, 1998; Chambliss, 2017; de Sousa, 2017).

In this light, I suggest that the term *sympathetic joy* can encompass compersion as a novel extension of *mudita* to the realm of intimate relationships and, in particular, to interpersonal situations that conventionally evoke feelings of jealousy. Although learning about the possibility of experiencing compersion can help some people to more easily enact it (see Deri, 2015), it is one thing to intellectually grasp the notion and quite another to live it. Given the deeply rooted nature of jealousy discussed in this chapter, it is likely that the cultivation of sympathetic joy is for most individuals a gradual (and perhaps an always-in-progress) affair contingent on a variety of conditions, such as strength of one's primary relationship bond, attachment style, personal self-esteem, or the level of perceived threat in the opening of one's partner to other potential partners (e.g., DeSteno et al., 2006; Rodriguez et al., 2015). Illustrating the gradual progression in the process of freeing oneself from jealousy, some polyamorous people in Britain coined the term *wibble* to refer to the temporary feelings of insecurity or discomfort one can feel when seeing a partner being sensual or affectionate with another person (Easton, 2010; Posey & Fowler, 2016; Veaux & Rickert, 2014). Thus, jealousy and compersion should not be understood in a black-or-white canvas or as mutually exclusive, but rather as elements of a person's emotional spectrum that can perfectly coexist, yielding many gray possibilities in-between (see Balzarini et al., 2020).

In any event, the practice of sympathetic joy may be helpful on the practical level, as regardless of one's relational style (e.g., monogamous or nonmonogamous), anyone experiencing jealousy can intentionally cultivate their desire for not only the happiness of their loved partner but also the happiness of their (real or imagined) "rivals" or third parties.[9] In the context of open relationships or jealousy-triggering social situations in both poly and mono relationships, for example, one may begin the practice of sympathetic joy with oneself ("May I be joyful"), then proceed with one's partner ("May my partner experience joy with this person"), before extending the practice to the person interacting with one's partner ("May s/he experience happiness with my partner"), and ending with a more integrative statement such as, "May this relationship bring joy and growth to me, my partner, and this third person."[10] Needless to say, the practice does not need to be undertaken just individually; it can be practiced with one's partner(s), as well as in small groups of intimately related or unrelated people struggling with jealous feelings.[11] In all cases, the statements can be uttered either for oneself in silence or aloud, as well as by combining inner repetition with outer verbalization.

Despite how challenging or counterintuitive desiring joy for those third parties may seem, it is important to remember that this long-standing Buddhist practice was partly devised to transform a person's negative emotions toward people experienced as difficult or even hostile. Although empirical research is necessary to establish the effectivity of *mudita* practice in the context of romantic relationships, the potential value of the practice receives indirect support from the "threatened self" theory of jealousy, according to which jealous feelings endanger the integrity of the self-system (Baumeister et al., 1996; DeSteno et al., 2006; Harris & Darby, 2010). In this model, threatened self-esteem is considered the main mechanism of jealousy, which explains coercive (and even violent) efforts at protecting one's respectability in light of the perceived loss of social status stemming from the usurpation of one's romantic relationship (especially in patriarchal "cultures of honor" where losing a woman to another man leads to decreased reputability; see R. P. Brown et al., 2018; Vandello & Cohen, 2003). Interestingly, several psychologists have argued that one of the main psychological effects of most types of Buddhist meditation is to promote changes in the self-system (e.g., Engler, 2003; Epstein, 2007). In particular, Buddhist meditation appears to simultaneously strengthen the functional dimensions of the self-system (e.g., reality testing, integration of experience, mediation of conflicts) and relax its representational ones (i.e., the "I" experience, internalized representation of others; Epstein, 2007). If this is so, it is evident why *mudita* practice can be an effective antidote to jealousy: through the practice, one can learn to disidentify from narrow egoic self-representations (desiring happiness to others goes against the dualistic egoic tendency to split one's own well-being from others') while reinforcing one's capability to metabolize challenging experiences and resolve inner tensions in the context of an expanded sense of selfhood. It seems reasonable to think that such a combined effect would have an impact on people's self-esteem and associated reactions when facing jealousy-triggering situations. Thus, I suggest that both monogamous and nonmonogamous people struggling with jealousy may benefit from cultivating sympathetic joy toward partners, third parties, and perceived "rivals."

I believe the transformation of jealousy through the cultivation of sympathetic joy bolsters the awakening of the heart's most lofty potentials. Although to love without conditions is generally easier in the case of brotherly and spiritual love, I suggest that as human beings heal the historical split between spiritual love (*agape*) and sensuous love (*eros*; see chapter 1; Irwin, 1991; Nygren, 1982), the extension of sympathetic joy to more embodied forms of love (including sexual ones) can become a natural development. As jealousy dissolves, universal compassion and unconditional love become more easily available to the individual.

In addition, when embodied love is emancipated from possessiveness, a richer range of spiritually legitimate relationship options organically emerges. As people are freed from certain basic fears (e.g., of abandonment, of unworthiness, of engulfment), new possibilities for the expression of embodied love open up that may feel natural, safe, and wholesome rather than undesirable, threatening, or even morally questionable. In short, once jealousy loosens its grip on the contemporary self, love can attain a wider dimension of embodiment in human lives that may naturally lead to the mindful cultivation of more inclusive intimate connections.

As the practice of sympathetic joy fosters relational freedom, intimate inclusivity is facilitated that can manifest in many ways. A greater number of people may opt for CNM relational styles that would be unthinkable without a substantial transmutation of their previous jealous feelings. In both monogamous and nonmonogamous contexts, such greater inclusivity can also nurture larger circles of significant friends and emotional bonds for all genders. As Butler (2004) wrote regarding nonmonogamous relationships, "Sexuality outside the field of monogamy well may open us to a different sense of community, intensifying the question of where one finds enduring ties" (p. 26). Further, sympathetic joy can counter the monogamous phenomenon of "dyadic withdrawal" discussed in chapter 1, which is often fueled by people's uneasiness toward their partners' old or new friends, especially those of opposite gender in a heterosexual context. In addition, regardless of their relational style, sympathetic joy can drastically change competitive relationships among women and among men, and in particular help men to break emotional isolation and develop deeper connections with other men, against traditional gender programming in the United States and other Western countries (e.g., Baker, 2017).[12]

Before closing this section, an important caveat: as in the case of achieving relational freedom (see chapters 1 and 5), it should be obvious that the chances of successfully transforming jealousy through sympathetic joy are contingent on a plethora of sociocultural forces and locations. For example, in the aforementioned "cultures of honor" (Nisbett & Cohen, 1996), such as Mediterranean, Middle Eastern, Latin and South American, and southern United States, "a man who allows his partner to stray may be seen as less of a man," and thus not being worthy of respect (Vandello & Cohen, 2003, p. 998). In these contexts, jealousy is seen as an entirely legitimate emotional reaction that protects the reputability of men and their families. Further, it has been widely documented that this patriarchal value system (aptly called *machismo* in Spanish-speaking countries; Torres et al., 2002) culturally justifies jealous aggression and violence toward women as proper responses to "restore" men's honor (e.g., R. P. Brown et al., 2018; Dietrich & Schuett, 2013). Thus, it is reasonable to extrapolate that men from marginal ethnic groups (or subgroups upholding similar values as "cultures of honor") in the United States and other Western countries may experience greater challenges in transforming jealousy—or even considering that such an endeavor is a "good" thing. Although discussing other social factors goes beyond the scope of this chapter, it is very likely that many variables (e.g., class, age, perceived level of attractiveness, sexual orientation; see S. L. Hart & Legerstee, 2010; Sheets & Wolfe, 2001) powerfully intersect with gender and ethnicity, impacting the possibility—and even perceived desirability—of transforming jealousy.

In any event, the practical question remains: How then can one develop sympathetic joy in one's relationships and intimacy? Whereas polyamory authors have offered a variety of practical hints to foster compersion (e.g., Anapol, 1998; Chambliss, 2017; Hypatia from Space, 2018; Labriola, 2013), no systematic practice to effectively develop it has yet been established. Given Buddhism's time-honored pedigree, I suggest that modern people seeking to transform jealousy may want to explore sympathetic joy through the extension of the Buddhist practice of *mudita* to their intimate relationships. In so doing, it is important to recognize that, in addition to sociocultural and psychological narratives, religion is another force legitimizing sexual exclusivity—and thus jealousy—through its common condemnation of nonmonogamy.

Religious Decrees on Sexual Behavior: Justifying Jealousy

While sympathetic joy can be also cultivated in monogamous relationships, its extension to sensuality and sexuality has traditionally been proscribed by conventional monogamy's insistence on sexual exclusivity (Jenkins, 2015; McKeever, 2017)—an insistence not limited to Christianity. In addition to the traditional Christian prescription of lifelong monogamy and the fact that lifelong or serial monogamy are still widely considered the only or most "spiritually correct" relationship styles in the modern West (e.g., Masters, 2007; Strassberg, 2003), many influential contemporary Buddhist teachers in the West make similar recommendations.

Consider, for example, the popular Buddhist teacher Thich Nhat Hanh's (2007) reading of the Buddhist precept of "refraining from sexual misconduct." Originally, this precept meant for the monks to avoid engaging in any sexual act whatsoever, and for lay people to not engage in a list of "inappropriate" sexual behaviors having to do with specific body parts, times, and places (Faure, 1998). In *For a Future to Be Possible*, Thich Nhat Hanh explained that the monks of his order follow the traditional celibate vow in order to use sexual energy as a catalyst for spiritual breakthrough. For lay practitioners, however, he read the precept to mean avoiding all sexual contact unless it takes place in the context of a "long-term commitment between two people" (p. 29), because he perceived an incompatibility between love and casual sex (monogamous marriage is a common practice for lay people in his order). In this reading, Thich Nhat Hanh reinterpreted the Buddhist precept as a prescription for long-term monogamy, excluding the possibility of not only responsible CNM but also spiritually edifying, occasional sexual encounters (e.g., J. Wade, 2004). (It is important to note, however, that "long-term commitment" is not equivalent to "monogamy," since it is perfectly feasible to hold a long-term commitment with more than one intimate partner.)

In *The Art of Happiness*, the Dalai Lama (Tenzin Gyatso, 1998) also assumed a monogamous structure as the container for appropriate sex in intimate relationships. Since reproduction is the biological purpose of sexual relations, he pointed out, long-term commitment and sexual exclusivity are desirable for the wholesomeness of love relationships. Needless to say, the reduction of sexuality to reproduction blatantly overlooks its recreational, bonding, regenerative, healing, transformational, and spiritual functions, among others (e.g., Chopel, 1992; Eliens, 2009; M. Robinson, 2009).

Despite the great respect I feel for these and other spiritual teachers who speak in similar fashion (see Edelstein, 2011), I must confess my perplexity. These assessments of appropriate sexual expression—which have become influential guidelines for many contemporary spiritual seekers—are often offered by celibate individuals whose sexual experience is likely to be limited if not nonexistent. A major lesson from developmental psychology is that an individual needs to perform several developmental tasks to gain competence (and wisdom) in various domains: social, cognitive, emotional, romantic, and so forth (see Havighurst, 1972; Roisman et al., 2004; Seiffge-Krenke & Gelhaar, 2008; Uhlendorff, 2004). Even when offered with the best of intentions, advice about aspects of life in which one has not achieved developmental competence through direct experience may be both questionable and misleading. When this advice is given by figures culturally venerated as spiritual authorities, the situation becomes even more problematic. In the context of spiritual practice in particular, these assertions can arguably be seen as incongruent with the emphasis on the direct knowledge characteristic of Buddhism (e.g., Jayatilleke, 1980). As the Buddha himself famously said in the *Kalama Sutta*:

> Don't go by reports, by legends, by traditions, by scripture, by logical conjecture, by inference, by analogies, by agreement through pondering views,

by probability, or by the thought, "This contemplative is our teacher." When you know for yourselves that, "These qualities are skillful; these qualities are blameless; these qualities are praised by the wise; these qualities, when adopted and carried out, lead to welfare and to happiness"— then you should enter and remain in them. (As cited in Thanissaro Bhikkhu, 1994)

Although this passage should not be (narcissistically) understood as always following one's own sense of what is true, this text encourages practitioners to question adopted beliefs and test them against their direct experience.

In any case, the romantic sexual exclusivity promulgated by many influential spiritual teachers inadvertently fuels possessiveness and jealous tendencies (see McKeever, 2017), attitudes that are regarded as negative or defiled by those religious traditions. In the next section, I argue for a wider, more pragmatic understanding of spiritual wholesomeness in the context of intimate relationship styles, which resolves this contradiction.

Spirituality and Relationship Styles

From a psychospiritual standpoint, an intimate relationship can be viewed as a structure through which human beings can not only sexually and emotionally mature but also learn to express and receive love in many forms. As discussed in chapter 2, human beings are likely to be endowed with diverse dispositions that may predispose them toward different relationship styles—asexuality, singlehood, serial monogamy, open marriage, swinging, and polyamory, among other possibilities—either for life or at specific junctures in their paths (see chapter 4). Thus, the culturally prevalent belief that the only psychospiritually correct sexual options are either celibacy or monogamy is a myth that may be causing unnecessary suffering and that needs, therefore, to be laid to rest.

In fact, it can be perfectly plausible to simultaneously hold more than one loving or sexual bond in a context of mindfulness and spiritual aspiration. This exploration can create unique opportunities for the development of emotional maturity, the transmutation of jealousy into sympathetic joy, the emancipation of embodied love from possessiveness, and the integration of sensuous and spiritual love. In addition, engaging in CNM might *in some cases* be crucial both to overcome codependent tendencies and to foster the health, creative vitality, and perhaps even longevity[13] of today's often-suffocated (e.g., by work, finances, family demands) marriages and intimate relationships (see Conley & Moors, 2014; Finkel et al., 2014).

A popular objection to CNMs is that people already tried them in the 1960s and 1970s: they did not work out, they replicated patriarchal dynamics, and, ultimately, many people got hurt. Even if historical attempts at gender-egalitarian nonmonogamous relationships were indeed not too successful or sustainable (e.g., Allyn, 2000; Sweetman, 2019; Wayland-Smith, 2016), to disregard a potentially emancipatory cultural development because its early manifestations did not succeed may be unwise. Looking back at the history of emancipatory movements in the West—from feminism to the abolition of slavery to the gaining of civil rights by African Americans—one can see that the first waves of the Promethean impulse have frequently been burdened with problems and distortions that only much later could be recognized and resolved. This book is not the place to review this historical evidence but to dismiss CNM because of its previous failures may be equivalent to having written off feminism on the grounds that its first waves "masculinized" women (so they could succeed in a patriarchal world) and failed to reclaim genuine "feminine" values or truly free women from patriarchy.[14]

That said, the following qualification seems to be in order: although I firmly refuse to declare CNM or polyamory more spiritual or evolved than monogamy (see chapters 2 and 5), it is likely that, in many cases, people who have not mastered the lessons and challenges of the dyadic structure may not be ready to take on the challenges of arguably more complex (at least at the interpersonal and communicative levels) forms of relationships (for discussions of relational and emotional complexity in polyamory, see Beggan, 2021; Ben-Ze'ev & Brunning, 2018; Moors et al., 2019). Importantly, this consideration does not entail framing polyamory as an absolutely more complex relational structure than monogamy. On the one hand, it should be obvious that different relational styles have their own distinctive interpersonal, communicative, and emotional challenges. On the other hand, it is likely that the complexity of those challenges is strongly shaped by the degree of emotional intelligence, secure attachment, empathy, and communicative skills of the people involved in a relationship regardless their number. Nevertheless, it seems unquestionable that (minimally successful) polyamory requires high-level competence in simultaneously holding multiple emotional perspectives and realities, managing different attachment orientations, and negotiating conflicting needs and desires. Further, it is important to note that in the same way homosexual and bisexual people have the right to make mistakes in their socially disadvantaged and thus arguably "more complex" relationships, polyamorous people should be allowed to do so in theirs—including, if they are so inclined, learning how to do poly relationships without dyadic exprience. In addition, it may be also the case that some people cannot or do not want to engage in dyadic relationships due to their very strong poly dispositions and may thus not need any prior dyadic "practice."

Interestingly, the Buddha himself encouraged polyamory (polygyny, actually) over monogamy in certain situations. In the *Jataka 200* (the Jatakas are stories of the Buddha's former births), a Brahmin asks the Buddha for advice regarding four suitors who are courting his four daughters. The Brahmin says, "One was fine and handsome, one was old and well advanced in years, the third a man of family [noble birth], and the fourth was good" (Cowell, 1895, p. 96). The Buddha answers, "Even though there be beauty and the like qualities, a man is to be despised if he fails in virtue. Therefore the former is not the measure of a man; those that I like are the virtuous" (Cowell, p. 96). After hearing this, the Brahmin gives all his daughters to the virtuous suitor. Although the meaning of the story should be situated in a cultural context dominated by patriarchal polygyny, the fact remains: the Buddha favored a poly arrangement over several monogamous marriages.

As the Buddha's advice illustrated, several forms of relationship may be spiritually wholesome (in the Buddhist sense of leading to liberation) according to various human dispositions and contextual situations. Historically, Buddhism hardly ever considered one relational style intrinsically more wholesome than others for lay people, and tended to support different relational styles depending on cultural and karmic factors; for example, as Buddhism spread, teachers accepted the sexual norms of the cultures in which it expanded, rather than imposing the norms of the Indian culture in which Buddhism originated (see Harvey, 2000; Sangharakshita, 1999). From the Buddhist perspective of skillful means (*upaya*) and of the soteriological nature of Buddhist ethics, it also follows that the key factor in evaluating the appropriateness of any intimate connection may not be its form, but rather its power to eradicate the suffering of self and others. Although Buddhism denounces sexual craving (as well as any other craving) as not conducive to liberation and thus unwholesome, freedom from craving is not intrinsically linked to sexual exclusivity or any particular intimate relationship style (see O'Connell Walshe, 1975). There is much to learn today, I believe, from the nondogmatic and pragmatic approach of historical Buddhism to intimate relationships—an approach that was not attached to any specific relationship structure but was essentially guided by a radical emphasis on liberation from suffering and the awakening of the human heart.

Taking Steps beyond Monogamy and Polyamory

In this discussion, I am obviously cherry-picking and magnifying a historical tendency in the diffusion of Buddhism for my own purposes. Any minimal analysis of Buddhist approaches to sexual relationships will reveal all types of sexually repressive, relationally coercive, patriarchal, and misogynist tendencies that were at times both contradicted and contested from within the tradition (see Cabezón, 2017; Faure, 1998, 2003). It also goes without saying that Buddhism is not a monolithic entity, but a highly pluralist, multivocal tradition whose different schools may be at odds with one another on all matters sexual and intimate (Faure, 2009). Nonetheless, I believe there is value in drawing on the broader strokes of Buddhist tradition as we seek a foundation for relational freedom from religious mandates.

It is my hope that this chapter contributes to the extension of spiritual virtues like sympathetic joy to all areas of life—and in particular to those that due to historical, cultural, and evolutionary reasons have been traditionally excluded or overlooked, such as sexuality and romantic love. Perhaps the greatest expression of spiritual freedom in intimate relationships does not lie in strictly sticking to any particular relationship style—whether monogamous or polyamorous—but rather in a radical openness to the dynamic unfolding of life that eludes any fixed or predetermined structure of relationships (see chapter 5). Moving beyond jealousy to sympathetic joy is one key to overcoming the "mono–poly wars" (see chapter 2) and destabilizing the mono/poly binary (see chapter 4). In the open space catalyzed by this movement, an existential stance more conducive to increasing our capability to exercise relational freedom can begin to emerge.

I also hope that gaining awareness about the ancestral—and mostly obsolete—nature of the evolutionary impulses that direct many human sexual/emotional responses and relationship choices may empower individuals to consciously cocreate a future in which expanded forms of spiritual freedom may have a greater chance to bloom. Who knows, perhaps as spiritual practice is extended to intimate relationships, new petals of liberation will blossom that may emancipate not only minds, hearts, and consciousness but also bodies and sexualities. In this light, I can envision—and invite others to join in—an "integral *bodhisattva* vow" in which the conscious mind renounces its own full liberation until the body and the instinctive world can be free as well.[15]

Notes

[1] This essay was originally commissioned in 2006 by the editors of *Tricycle: The Buddhist Review*, who resolved to publish a shorter version with the title, "What's the Opposite of Jealousy? Questioning the Buddhist Allegiance to Monogamy" (Ferrer, 2006). The full version appeared in the politically progressive magazine *Tikkun* (Ferrer, 2007). Both the abbreviated and full versions were then reprinted in several Buddhist magazines—such as *Dharma Vision* and *Turning Wheel*—and the shorter version was selected for the e-book *Tricycle Teachings: Love and Relationships* (Tricycle, n.d.). This chapter is an updated version containing many new materials and references.

[2] Although usually framed as an emotion, jealousy is also understood as having cognitive, behavioral, and emotional components (Pfeiffer & Wong, 1989), to which I would add somatic and instinctual dimensions that are arguably conflated in the literature with the emotional; for example, Enciso Domínguez (2018) distinguished between the emotional (i.e., verbally articulable, socially constructed) and affective (i.e., physical feelings that are hardly articulable) aspects of the experience of jealousy. Even when exclusively conceptualized as an emotion, researchers disagree about whether jealousy should be understood as a specific emotion or a blend of other emotions such as anger, fear, and sadness (Harris & Darby, 2010).

3   My discussion of certain findings of evolutionary psychology does not mean that I endorse the discipline's universalist, reductionist, and deterministic genetic explanations of human social behavior, which tend to overlook the importance of individual, sociocultural, and political factors in human affairs. In addition, as discussed next, feminist scholars have identified patriarchal biases in this field, in particular its biological essentializing of sex differences and the suggestion that females' preferences for wealthy and powerful males contributed to the emergence and perpetuation of patriarchy (e.g., Hrdy, 1997; Liesen, 2007). For an anthology summing up these and other criticisms, see Rose and Rose (2000), and for responses from the evolutionary psychology camp, see Barkow (2006). Another systematic response to these criticisms that nonetheless offers a helpful summary of the controversies and limitations of the field can be found in Confer et al. (2010). For the debate between evolutionary psychology and feminism, see also Buss and Malamuth (1996), Vandermassen (2005), and, especially, C. A. Smith and Konik (2011).

4   As discussed in chapter 2 (note 12), this standard evolutionary narrative of an ancestral pair-bonding culture and archaically seated sexual jealousy was challenged by Ryan and Jethá (2010), who argued for a far more sexually promiscuous human prehistoric past. Despite its lay popularity, evolutionary psychologists have critiqued Ryan and Jethá's work due to important omissions, misinterpretations, and highly selective use of the presented evidence (e.g., Ellsworth, 2011; Saxon, 2011). However, feminist scholars have also charged the standard narrative with similar problems, such as methodological flaws, cherry-picking of evidence, and overlooking of female psychology and behavior (see Liesen, 2007; Nicolas & Welling, 2015). For a critical discussion of the adoption of Ryan and Jethá's proposal, as well as evolutionary discourses in general, in polyamory rhetoric and self-help books, see Lerum (forthcoming).

5   Although this gender difference in jealous responses has received empirical support, research also shows that whereas emotional jealousy is more contingent on gender than culture, sexual jealousy is more contingent on culture than gender (Zandbergen & S. G. Brown, 2015). In addition, many other variables—such as degree of self-esteem, attachment style, relationship status, and power within the relationship—significantly impact the nature of both men's and women's jealous responses (e.g., Berman & Frazier, 2005; Burchell & Ward, 2011; DiBello et al., 2015; Harris & Darby, 2010). Thus, although research has found evidence of jealousy even in children's first year of life (S. L. Hart, 2010), it is likely that evolutionary, socialization, and psychological forces intermingle in complex ways in the jealous responses of both all genders generally and those of particular individuals (for discussions of the evolutionary–socialization debate in the understanding of jealousy, see Fenigstein & Peltz, 2002; Michalski et al., 2007). Central to this book's focus, even though jealous responses were found to be weaker in CNM individuals than monogamous ones, the gender difference has been found to be operative in CNM relationships in relation to primary (vs. secondary) partners (Mogilski et al., 2019).

6   Genetic selfishness should not to be confused with Dawkins's (1978) infamous "selfish gene" theory, which reduces human beings to the status of survival machines at the service of gene replication. Whereas the qualifier *genetic* appears to limit the

validity of the term to heterosexual couples, many same-sex and queer relationships have biological children through artificial or in vitro insemination, sperm donation, or surrogacy, with one or more of the parents genetically linked to the child. In the case of adopted children, the term would obviously not work but, as adoptive parents tend to also favor the well-being and survival of their children, I argue that the principle is equally valid in these cases.

[7] Interestingly, there is no antonym for jealousy in any of the languages I am familiar with.

[8] Empirical research on compersion shows that its connection to relational satisfaction may depend on not only relational style and goals but also gender. Specifically, compersion is (naturally) more positively related to relational satisfaction in open or polyamorous relations than in monogamous ones, and to experience compersion had a significant impact on the relational satisfaction of women (especially those in open relationships), but not of men (Aumer et al., 2014).

[9] I am leaving aside here the adulterous breaking of monogamous vows—in these cases, the (at least temporarily) reasonable anger experienced may render the practice of sympathetic joy toward both one's partner and third parties both unrealistic and inappropriate.

[10] Whereas sympathetic joy can thus be cultivated in monogamous relationships in any jealousy-triggering situation, its extension to one's partner's sexual connections is prevented by conventional monogamy's emphasis on sexual exclusivity (Jenkins, 2015; McKeever, 2017). However, the sexual dimensions of the practice should be relevant to the increasing number of so-called "new monogamists" or "monogamish" couples (see chapter 4; Haag, 2011; Nelson, 2012; Savage, 2012).

[11] For a brief but important essay denouncing the way most self-help guides inadvertently foster neoliberalism in emphasizing the individual person's overcoming of jealousy, see Cardoso (2018), who also stressed the arguably more effective—and politically revolutionary—collaborative power of community work in such a transformation.

[12] Times are changing: for example, many undergraduate heterosexual men tend to value their so-called "bromantic" bonds (i.e., emotionally close relationships with men) more than their romantic bonds with women (S. Robinson et al., 2017); and men between 20 and 40 display a diverse array of connectedness patterns problematizing the traditional view of men as being less invested than women in cultivating emotional bonds (McKenzie et al., 2018).

[13] Although desirable and growth-promoting in many cases, I do not think of longevity as the paramount or even a central benchmark to assess the success of intimate relationships. Instead of this arguably monocentric standard (clearly a residue of the traditional vow of lifelong monogamy), I suggest that more appropriate criteria are the quality of relationship (cf. Deri, 2015; Rowan, 1995), as well as its healing, transformative, and emancipatory power (see Chapter 5).

[14] For a succinct account of the three waves of CNM in the United States (i.e., nineteenth-century transcendentalism, twentieth-century countercultures, and the current Internet-impacting era), see Sheff (n.d.).

[15] In Buddhism, the bodhisattva vow entails the renunciation of liberation—variously understood as achieving nirvana or realizing the emptiness (i.e., lack of intrinsic existence) of self and phenomena—until all sentient beings are freed as an act of compassion (Goodman, 2009; Leighton, 2012). Since the conscious mind is the seat of most individuals' sense of identity, however, an exclusive liberation of consciousness can be deceptive insofar as one can believe that one is fully free when, in fact, essential dimensions of the self are underdeveloped, alienated, or driven by egoic or selfish tendencies (as the numerous sexual abuses perpetuated by many recognized spiritual teachers attest; see Edelstein, 2011). Thus, my use of the term *bodhisattva* does not suggest a commitment to early Buddhist accounts of liberation as the extinction of bodily senses and desires and release from the cycle of transmigratory experience or *samsara* (S. Collins, 1998; Harvey, 1995). For an extended discussion, see Ferrer (2017).

Chapter 4

The Dawn of Transbinary Relationships

U sually regarded as antagonistic binary opposites (see chapter 2; Jenkins, 2015; McKeever, 2017), monogamy and nonmonogamy can be better understood as mutually constituting each other within the single discursive field and cultural system of *non/monogamy* (Willey, 2006). Indeed, monogamy and nonmonogamy should not be considered as disconnected polar realities, but instead as "aspects of a single system for relating sexually, romantically, socially, and culturally, with multiple parts and different articulations" (Rambukkana, 2015, p. 15). In the same way that monogamy creates adultery (Kipnis, 2003; Mint, 2004) and adultery helps in turn to maintain the social institution of monogamy (Ben-Ze'ev & Goussinsky, 2008), patriarchal polygamy perpetuates monogamous heteronormative attitudes and behaviors by enthroning a male figure who enjoys diverse female monogamous commitments (e.g., Jacobson & Burton, 2011)—usually with detrimental impact on women, especially on senior wives (e.g., Al-Krenawi & Kanat-Maymon, 2015). Other factors problematize the traditional polarization between monogamy and nonmonogamy. For example, *polyamory* means "many loves," yet leading poly author Anapol (2010) understood polyamory to include freely chosen (vs. compulsory) monogamy. In addition, research has shown that monogamous tropes are reproduced in many polyamorous relationships (Barker, 2005; Finn, 2010; Finn & Malson, 2008; Jamieson, 2004), even if practitioners from all genders actively resist such pressures (Rambukkana, 2015; Sheff, 2005, 2006). Polyamory's privileging of romantic love or emotional commitments over purely sexual encounters can also be seen as reinforcing the values of mainstream monogamy (Barker et al., 2013; Posey & Fowler, 2016). Finally, the academic emphasis in assessing the "personal and political significance of a relationship solely in relation to its non/monogamy risks encoding mononormative assumptions about what makes a relationship significant into the scholarship itself" (Kean, 2017, p. 20). Thus, to understand monogamy and polyamory as polar or opposite realities deceitfully hides their systemically reinforcing nature.

Since the 1990s, both authors and scholars have issued pleas to deconstruct or overcome the mono/poly binary.[1] In this regard, I locate here S. Johnson's (1991) and Overall's (1998) exposés of the monogamy/nonmonogamy dichotomy as contingent on patriarchy, Anapol's (1997, 2010) account of polyamory as following the free flow of love beyond any particular relational structure, Willey's (2006) and Rambukkana's (2015) aforesaid articulations of the non/monogamy system, my own reflections on the psychospiritual value of moving beyond monogamy and polyamory (Ferrer, 2007), Frank and DeLamater's (2010) discussion of fluid boundaries across different relational styles, Heckert's (2010) related account of intimate relationships in terms of *nomadic boundaries*, Pallotta-Chiarolli's (2010) notion of *mestizaje* as a fluid relational identity between being monogamous or being polyamorous, Barker's (2013; Barker & Iantaffi, 2019) and M. Robinson's (2013) accounts of monogamy and nonmonogamy as a continuum (vs. an either/or binary), Cantor's (2014) resistance to both monogamy and polyamory as equally restricting labels, Michaels and P. Johnson's (2015) proposal for designer relationships inclusive of all relational styles, and Green et al.'s (2016) finding that the actual practice of modern marital monogamy cannot be captured by the standard monogamy/ nonmonogamy opposition. Although these works have provided a helpful beginning for thinking beyond the binary, the conceptual and experiential territory outside the non/monogamy system has not been discussed in a thorough and systematic manner.

Building on these and other developments, this chapter offers an introductory overview of nonbinary or transbinary relational identities or orientations.[2] What relationship types may lie beyond the non/monogamy system, and how might such transbinary relationships embody or enhance relational freedom? Seeking to open new trails for thinking and living *in-between*, *through*, and *beyond* the mono/poly bipolarity, I discuss three plural relational modes—fluidity, hybridity, and transcendence—that disrupt and arguably overcome the non/monogamy system. In the same way that the transgender and gender diversity movements surmounted the gender binary (e.g., Brubaker, 2016; Butler, 2004; Stryker, 2008)—and bisexual, pansexual, and queer scholars and practitioners challenged the sexual orientation binary (e.g., Callis, 2014; Elizabeth, 2013; Firestein, 1996)—I propose that a parallel step can, and should, be taken with the relational style binary. Moving beyond the mono/poly binary, I argue, opens a fuzzy, liminal, and multivocal semantic–existential space that, for lack of a better term, I call *novogamy*. After exploring several transbinary pathways, I conclude by briefly considering future prospects for the growth of novogamous (or transbinary) relational styles in Western society, as well as addressing one common concern regarding fluidity, hybridity, or ambiguity with regard to self-identity and related psychological issues.

Beyond the Mono/Poly Binary: An Outline of Transbinary Relational Modes and Pathways

In this section, I outline three modes or strategies to move beyond the mono/poly binary framework—fluidity, hybridity, and transcendence—each of which can manifest through several pathways.[3] In terms of the relational freedom competences introduced in chapter 1, the fluidity mode corresponds to relational plasticity and autonomy, the hybridity mode to relational integration, and the transcendence mode to relational transcendence. Before proceeding, three caveats are necessary.

First and foremost, whereas some of these pathways may be considered more effective than others in overcoming the mono/poly binary, others may be understandably seen as privileging either monogamy or nonmonogamy. These appraisals are to some extent inevitable. In the white-or-black non/monogamy world prevalent in the modern West, the choice between these binary relational styles typically takes the form of a zero-sum game where one person's gain necessarily results in another's loss. In this context, there is no way out: one must be *either* monogamous *or* nonmonogamous, sexually exclusive with one partner or not, and so forth (see Barker & Iantaffi, 2019). After repeated expositions of my transbinary relational style over the years, for example, some close friends still see me and describe me as a polyamorous man. The message is clear: if you are not monogamous, you *must* be polyamorous. In this chapter, I reject this limiting either/or logic and invite readers to try both/and—or win/win—lenses when considering the ensuing discussion.

Second, given the vast diversity of human dispositions (e.g., biographical, sexual, cultural, religious), some readers may resonate more with one or another path; put negatively, some paths may generate incredulity, dismissal, or even aversion. Taken together, however, I firmly believe that the surveyed relational modes and pathways are effective in, if not entirely dismantling, at least seriously undermining the mono/poly binary. At any rate, I am convinced that this exploration opens avenues to think and live intimate relationships in more spacious ways than those allowed by the Procrustean non/monogamy system.

Finally, as chapter 5 establishes, no universal developmental sequence or hierarchical relationship is maintained among relational styles (monogamy, nonmonogamy, novogamy) or transbinary modes and pathways. Although some pathways are mutually exclusive and others can be lived concurrently, all of them should be regarded, in principle, as equally valid options when engaged with integrity, care, and awareness of social privilege and oppression. That said, the rest of this chapter discusses three transbinary (or novogamous) modes: fluidity, hybridity, and transcendence.

The Fluidity Mode

The fluidity mode matches well what Brubaker (2016) called the oscillating form of the *trans of between*, which entails a back-and-forth movement between two established categories (e.g., male and female in transgender identities). In the context of this chapter, the *fluidity mode* entails different types of shifts between monogamy and nonmonogamy. This mode was foreseen by Giddens's (1992) notion of *plastic sexualities*, which he described as late modernity's growing trend toward the continuing renegotiation and malleability of relational commitments based on people's changing needs and desires (cf. Eda's [2013] concept of *intimate agency*). It is also similar to Heckert's (2010) *nomadic boundaries*, where "participants in a relationship create space to discuss, define and refine boundaries, which are always open to change" (p. 261). In chapter 1, I wrote about the main features of the fluidity mode in terms of two competences of relational freedom: relational plasticity (i.e., the capability to live monogamy and nonmonogamy sequentially or cyclically) and relational autonomy (i.e., the capability to more freely choose between monogamy and nonmonogamy as one's relational style).

An increasing number of today's self-styled monogamous couples redefine their relationships in ways that can include temporary or contextual nonmonogamous arrangements (e.g., Haag, 2011; Perel, 2006)—as the sociological reality of so-called "new monogamist" and "monogamish" relationships attest (Morris, 2014; T. Nelson, 2012, 2016; Savage, 2012). Furthermore, some sort of fluidity is intrinsic to the prevalent paradigm of serial monogamy (many partners sequentially), which at times not only is punctuated with adultery but also can entail periods of concurrent dating of various potential partners between monogamous commitments (Kipnis, 2003; Mercer et al., 2013; Petrella, 2005). The rest of this section discusses four pathways fluid relationships can take: developmental, definitional, interpersonal, and contextual.

Developmental Path to Relational Fluidity

In this path, individuals or couples shift from mono to poly orientations or vice versa according to emerging developmental needs (e.g., sexual, emotional, relational, psychospiritual). Reflecting on this path, Sumerau and Nowakowski (2019) wrote, "We have shifted back and forth between monogamous at times and polyamorous at times based upon our individual and collective needs and desires" (p. 122). In other words, developmental factors can lead people to choose monogamy or nonmonogamy as their most suitable relational style at different life stages (see Conley, Ziegler et al., 2012; Michaels & P. Johnson, 2015). This trend is arguably connected to the "psychologization" of the modern West (Taylor, 1989) and the increasing consideration of intimate relationships as a (and for some, *the*) central arena for personal or psychospiritual growth (e.g., S. Levine & A. Levine, 1995; Masters, 2007; Welwood, 1996). Although the very idea of "relationship as work" has its pitfalls (Kipnis, 2003; Petrella, 2007), it seems largely uncontroversial that both individuals and relationships have evolving needs, and that intimate bonds may call for structural changes to remain growthful, fulfilling, and alive.

This developmental movement between monogamy and nonmonogamy (or vice versa) can take various trajectories. Due to sexual habituation, incompatible sexual needs or desires, or renegotiations after infidelity, for example, couples beginning in a strictly monogamous relationship might open it up to include sexual encounters with others in order to stay together while minimizing sexual frustration (e.g., E. Anderson, 2012; Haag, 2011; T. Nelson, 2012; Perel, 2006). Conversely, some people can first choose nonmonogamy but eventually decide to be sexually exclusive, either temporarily or permanently. After a long trajectory of relational self-exploration, polyamory researcher Sheff (2014) concluded, "I both believe and can practice polyamory, but I am not polyamorous by orientation. . . . Because I seem to prefer monogamy when I am emotionally invested, I do not identify as polyamorous" (p. 112). As Conley, Ziegler et al. (2012) pointed out, both sequences may be particularly significant at different phases of life: whereas nonmonogamy may allow young people to explore a diversity of partners before settling into a suitable monogamous pairing, with time such a relationship may become monotonous and, building on the trust forged by years of exclusive commitment, a couple may then explore open relationships or polyamory. In addition, variables such as gender, sexual identity, and relationship style can shape radically different sexual–relational trajectories (see Hammack et al., 2019; Manley et al., 2015).

These multiple sequential variations strongly suggest that there is no linear or paradigmatic developmental progression between monogamy and nonmonogamy (or vice versa). Complicating things further, individuals and couples may move through just one or many different mono-to-poly or poly-to-mono cycles in their lives (e.g., Sumerau & Nowakowski, 2019). Hence, the fluid movement between monogamy and nonmonogamy should be seen as plural, nonlinear, and potentially dialectical or spiral. In sum, the developmental path allows individuals and couples to freely adjust their relationships style to fit their unfolding needs for further growth.

Definitional Path to Relational Fluidity

The second path to deconstruct the mono/poly binary is based on the empirically established fact that what counts as monogamy and nonmonogamy varies from person to person (Frank & DeLamater, 2010; Wosick, 2012). Here *fluidity* refers not to mono/poly shifts in individuals or couples but to interpersonal differences in people's definitions of non/monogamy and in/fidelity. Despite the standard belief that monogamy equals sexual exclusivity, self-identified monogamous couples and individuals understand infidelity (and thus monogamy) in drastically different manners. For some married couples, out-of-town or conference sex does not count as cheating, but for others cybersex, pornography use, sexting, masturbation, fantasizing about a third party, close opposite-sex friendships, or even going to the cinema with someone of the opposite gender are considered transgressions of the monogamous vow (see Barker, 2013; Frank & DeLamater, 2010). Not surprisingly, individuals' different (and often tacit or unexamined) definitions of fidelity can lead to troublesome surprises, as members of any couple can inadvertently break their partner(s)' monogamous rule if what counts as infidelity for each of them has not been thoroughly discussed and agreed upon (e.g., Warren et al., 2011). More controversially, many married women who have affairs through the Ashley Madison website "redefined 'commitment' to mean a resolution to remain in the marriage" (Walker, 2017, p. xxxviii) even if they enjoyed sexual or emotional intimacy with other partners. The idea that engaging in extradyadic emotional relationships is not linked to lower commitment to a primary partner is controversial (e.g., Leeker & Carlozzi, 2014) but has received some empirical support (e.g., Lee & O'Sullivan, 2019).

This state of affairs has led researchers to understand fidelity as a fluid continuum ranging from sexual and emotional to sexual but not emotional and to neither sexual nor emotional exclusivity (e.g., Wosick, 2012). In this vein, E. Anderson (2012) described four types of monogamy: physical (sexual), desirous (reflecting desires and fantasies), social (how one is seen by society), and emotional (exclusive romantic attachment but sexual openness). The combination of emotional fidelity and sexual openness—aptly called *monogamy of the heart* by LaSala (2004)—has historically been a central feature of various alternative lifestyles such as open marriages (Mazur, 1973), hierarchical polyamory (i.e., involving primary/secondary partners; Veaux & Rickert, 2014), swinging (Bergstrand & Sinski, 2010), and many bisexual (K. Mark et al., 2014; Rust, 1996) and gay male relationships (E. Anderson, 2012; Spears & Lowen, 2016). Exemplifying this stance, a gay male respondent reported:

> Emotionally monogamous, absolutely. The fact that I have sex outside the relationship and he may or may not have sex outside the relationship, in absolutely no way takes away from the fact that we are completely and totally committed

to each other and totally in love and we will spend the rest of our lives together and we both know it. (As cited by Adam, 2010, p. 64)

Nowadays, the distinction between sexual and emotional monogamy is also becoming increasingly common in married heterosexual couples (Haag, 2011; Swan & S. C. Thompson, 2016). In her study of contemporary fidelity, Wosick (2012) observed that such a distinction "provides the opportunity to remain emotionally monogamous while engaging in extradyadic sexual behavior (or to remain sexually monogamous while emotionally engaging with other partners)" (p. 186). As for the latter possibility, Sheff (2014) coined the term *polyaffectivity* to describe deeply emotional bonds with no sexual exchange in polyamorous relationships, and Kingma (1998) wrote about *emotional spouses* or persons with whom one can have a deeply emotional bond with no sexual component. The popular notion of "work spouses" who enjoy a platonic intimacy at the workplace (which may also channel sexual attraction into productive collaboration) can also fit into this category (e.g., Eyler & Baridon, 1992).

To these forms of fidelity, one might add *spiritual fidelity*, in which two or more people share a deep sense of spiritual communion (or soul union) that allows for a variety of sexual and emotional bonds beyond the confines of their relationship. In addition, Wosick-Correa (2010) coined the term *agentic fidelity* to refer to the free commitment to established needs and boundaries characteristic of most polyamorous couples. In any event, what seems clear is that, as Wosick (2012) stressed,

> the conduit for commitment in today's relationships is not necessarily sexual or emotional exclusivity but rather kinds of fidelity that involves agency and continued emphasis on feeling special. . . . the new benchmark of intimacy [is] the opportunity to set one's own standards. (p. 39)

In sum, as fidelity itself is variously defined, the non/monogamy system has no foundation of shared understanding on which to rest. The definitional path establishes that monogamy and nonmonogamy are so variously demarcated (and thus lived) that any generic clear-cut distinction between these categories is implausible: individuals and couples are therefore free to negotiate and renegotiate their own definitions and meanings.

Interpersonal Path to Relational Fluidity

This path leading beyond the mono/poly binary emerges from the recognition that in a relational context, some individuals may stir (either provisionally or indefinitely) a desire for monogamy, while others may arouse nonmonogamous dispositions. The strength of sexual attraction and emotional intimacy, for example, may lead some people to engage in both monogamous and polyamorous relationships in ways that fall beyond their previous expectations or known dispositions. Substantiating this point, a longitudinal study exploring the interplay between relationship style and sexual identity in 61 monogamous and 55 polyamorous individuals revealed that "relational identity sometimes also shifts to coincide with romantic and sexual partner choices" (Manley et al., 2015, p. 177). Two other important variables shaping this path are gender and sexual orientation. Some bisexual or "curious" individuals may feel more monogamous toward people of their own gender and more poly toward people of different gender identities, or the other way around (e.g., S. J. Daly, 2021; Toft & Yip, 2018). Generally speaking, if people can be situated along a continuum from "very monogamous" to "very nonmonogamous" (see chapter 2), this interpersonal path may speak more—or be more available—to those falling somewhere in-between.

Engagement in this path may be contingent on not only personal factors (e.g., Barker, 2005) but also numerous cultural (e.g., Ho, 2006), sociopolitical (e.g., M. Robinson, 2013), and religious/spiritual variables (e.g., Kolesar & Pardo, 2019). For example, a cross-cultural analysis of contemporary forager cultures revealed that amount of males' food provisioning is a major factor in women's valuing of monogamy over polygyny or vice versa (Marlowe, 2003). In addition, diverse sociopolitical conditions can influence people's propensity to follow the monogamous or nonmonogamous feelings they might experience toward different people (see "Contextual Path to Relational Fluidity" section). Finally, adherence to particular religious traditions or spiritual beliefs could be a major factor in people's openness to monogamous and nonmonogamous feelings, desires, and behaviors in relation to potential partners (Balzarini, Dharma, Kohut, L. Campbell, Holmes et al., 2019; Litschi et al., 2014).

To be sure, the Western mononormative ethos enforces the belief that not desiring monogamy is an unequivocal sign of lack of care or of not having found true love (or one's soulmate, or "The One"; see chapters 2 and 5). Although desiring a closed container to explore and deepen intimacy with a person who awakens intense sexual–emotional feelings might be natural for many, especially at the onset of a relationship (e.g., E. Anderson, 2012), wanting monogamy or nonmonogamy does not need to inevitably correlate with more (or less) love or attraction. For some poly people, for example, maintaining a connection with their lovers may not interfere with but rather support their exploration of a potential primary relationship. Therefore, it is fallacious to regard the desire for a monogamous (or polyamorous) relationship as inevitably correlated with a greater or lesser degree of love or attraction. In my personal case, I was in an open relationship (from its very beginning to its end) with the person I have loved most deeply in my life; we chose this relationship mode due to contextual circumstances (we lived on different continents), developmental factors (my partner was leaving an asexual marriage and needed to explore her sexuality), capability for compersion (see chapter 3), and the relatively high relational freedom we both had somehow achieved in our lives.

Bottom line, the assumption that love—if deep and real—inevitably entails desiring and demanding sexual and/or emotional exclusivity is another mono-myth that must be laid to rest. The interpersonal path reflects the reality that different individuals can awaken different desires within, including diverse sexual and relational potentials, dispositions, or behaviors.

Contextual Path to Relational Fluidity

In a general sense, the contextual path acknowledges that people's relational desires and behaviors can change in different places, cultural environments, or sociopolitical circumstances. Almost anyone who has lived abroad or traveled extensively can probably attest that different geographical/cultural matrixes can activate distinct personal dispositions (e.g., Bushell & Sheldon, 2009; see also "Intrapersonal Path to Relational Hybridity" section). When traveling, the "movie" of one's life can dramatically change; one can not only feel but arguably *become* a different person. In addition, cultural environments such as particular clubs, gatherings, or events can also be situational factors affecting people's behaviors. As Taormino (2008) put it in reference to swinging and BDSM, "For some people exploring sex with others is specific to a place" (p. 133). Lastly, M. Robinson (2013) described how bisexual women can strategically flow from monogamy to polyamory when in different sociopolitical milieus:

> Periods of polyamorous identity may provide bisexual women with greater visibility, a sense of dominance and normative belonging in the bisexual com-munity. . . . At the same time, monogamy enables some women to . . . obtain a feeling of emotional security and social acceptance, while distancing them from the stigma of bisexual stereotypes. (p. 33)

Thus, geographical, cultural, political, and environmental factors can and do impact the range of people's sexual–relational tendencies, responses, and actions.

This path is connected to the so-called free passes some self-identified monogamous individuals give their partners when traveling, or when their partners' lovers live in a different city or country. In her study of modern hetero-sexual marriages, for example, Haag (2011) wrote about the "fifty-mile rule" (p. 224; see Brandt, 2002), according to which both men and women allow their partners to have other lovers when outside a negotiated radius from home (for a critical analysis of Brandt's pro-adultery discourse, see Rambukkana, 2015). As Frank and DeLamater (2010) indicated, this type of arrangement fits well with the professional conditions of the increasing number of people who travel for conferences, workshops, retreats, or business meetings. Michaels and

P. Johnson's (2015) words capture the contextual path of fluid relationships in its simplest form: "Relationships can open and close or have varying degrees and kinds of openness as circumstances demand" (p. 2). This idea of "varying degrees and kinds of openness" is related to the hybridity relational mode, to which I now turn.

The Hybridity Mode

Whereas the fluidity mode overcomes the mono/poly binary by describing how people shift from one pole to the other according to different variables, the hybridity mode entails the simultaneous coexistence, merging, or integration of mono/poly values or behaviors. The hybridity mode is equivalent to Brubaker's (2016) recombinatory form of the *trans of between*. In a relational context, individuals selectively blend elements of mono and poly identities or orientations, neither entirely belonging to one of them nor moving from one to the other. As Barker (2013) put it, "there are plural monogamies and non-monogamies which blend into each other and overlap" (p. 105). Pallotta-Chiarolli's (1995) offered a rationale for this mode:

> The "conflict" . . . between individuals' non-monogamous needs and desires, and the socially constructed and largely dysfunctional monogamous tradition, must be seen as a legitimate reason to develop new forms of relationships which synthesize elements of or transcend traditional marital alternatives. (p. 54)

In chapter 1, I framed the hybridity mode as a competence of relational freedom in terms of relational integration, or the ability to mindfully synthesize essential values of both monogamy and nonmonogamy in intimate relationships. As in the case of relational fluidity, the hybridity mode can manifest in several paths: the intrapersonal, relational, integrative, and subtle types of hybridity.

Intrapersonal Path to Relational Hybridity

One important type of the hybridity mode of transcending the mono/poly binary is what I call the intrapersonal path, which contemplates that most individuals can experience monogamous and nonmonogamous tendencies *at once*. In "The Song of Myself," Walt Whitman (1855/2007) famously wrote, "Very well then . . . I contradict myself. I am large . . . I contain multitudes" (p. 67)—and the image is pertinent when describing the often-conflicting complexity of human nature. Indeed, human beings contain a multiplicity of voices (beliefs, thoughts, feelings, desires, impulses, etc.), many of which can be at odds with each other. Whether one thinks of this inner diversity in psychological (Schwartz, 1995), archetypal (Hillman, 1975), or postmodern terms (Gergen, 1991), it seems unquestionable that each human individual is not a monolithic entity, but rather a dynamic, plural system shaped by many selves or subpersonalities. Another way to understand intrapersonal diversity is in terms of different human attributes (e.g., body, heart, mind, consciousness) and related intelligences (somatic, emotional, aesthetic, rational; see Ferrer, 2017; Gardner, 1993), whose developmental needs and forces might not be necessarily aligned at all times.

In a relational context, this intrapersonal diversity can manifest in multiple, conflicting thoughts and desires with regard to relationships. In a popular book on tantric polyamory, for example, Lessin (2006) claimed that most people contain an "Inner Monogamist" who desires the security of a stable relationship, and an "Inner Polyamorist" who wants sexual variety. Also, as discussed earlier, some people may want emotional but not sexual monogamy, while others are sexually monogamous but desire more than one deeply intimate emotional bond. As E. Anderson (2012) pointed out, in the same way that one can be homosexual regardless of one's self-description and actions, one can be nonmonogamous at heart (e.g., fantasizing about having many sexual partners) even if one does not acknowledge or act on those desires.

Disparities between inner desires and outer behaviors problematize standard notions of fidelity, additionally destabilizing the non/monogamy system. The following Zen story illustrates the issue of the significance of differences in inner perspectives:

> Two monks were on a pilgrimage. One day, they came to a deep river. At the edge of the river, a young woman sat weeping, because she was afraid to cross the river without help. She begged the two monks to help her. The younger monk turned his back. The members of their order were forbidden to touch a woman. But the older monk picked up the woman without a word and carried her across the river. He put her down on the far side and continued his journey. The younger monk came after him, scolding him and berating him for breaking his vows. He went on this way for a long time. Finally, at the end of the day the older monk turned to the younger one. "I only carried her across the river. You have been carrying her all day." (As cited by Gerrold, 1997, n.p.)

Although its traditional moral is a commendation for living in the present moment, the story is relevant to the present discussion. Imagine two husbands: the first has been fully devoted to his wife in both thought and behavior for decades, but on one occasion had a sexual encounter with another woman; the second has been sexually loyal to his partner throughout life, but unceasingly fantasizes having sex with other women. What if the second husband weekly (or daily) masturbates to an infinite number of women while watching porn? It might be reasonably asked, which of the two is more monogamous? For example, a wife reported the following about her husband's virtual affairs:

> He had affairs of the mind, and that to me is as much a violation as if he actually had a physical affair with someone . . . in one sense having an affair of the mind is worse than having an actual partner: My husband can, at any time,

have an "affair" without leaving the house or actually seeing another human being. (As cited in Haag, 2011, p. 198)

The bottom line is that the very idea of a mental affair "calls into question elemental definitions of marital fidelity" (Haag, p. 198)—and thus of both monogamy and nonmonogamy.

Although intermingling with the definitional path to relational fluidity, these examples also illustrate how people can be intrapersonally monogamous and nonmonogamous at once (e.g., in behavior vs. thought, or in sexual vs. emotional desire). In a modern Western relational context, a typical way in which this inner diversity becomes discernable is through tensions between desires and behaviors—tensions largely driven by both the complexity of human nature and cultural adherence to the mono/poly binary. If one embraces one's intrapersonal hybridity, however, that acceptance can help open doors to relational hybridity—that is, to crafting a relationship that is more nuanced, tailored to the plural needs of those involved, and arguably located outside the mono/poly binary. What this brief consideration of intrapersonal diversity strongly conveys is that human nature is too Protean to be satisfactorily captured or explained by mental binary oppositions; therefore, the intrapersonal path is one means of both understanding and cultivating relational hybridity.

Relational Path to Relational Hybridity

The relational path corresponds to situations where one member of a relationship is monogamous while the other has other sexual or romantic partners. In this "hybrid style of open relationship" (Sheff, 2014, p. 111), individual identities fall within the established mono/poly categories, but the relationship itself does not. To wit, the relationship as a whole is both monogamous and polyamorous, and neither—it is a *mono/poly* relationship (Taormino, 2008). This type of relationship is further complexified in the case of multipartnered, queer, mixed families where different members can be monogamous or polyamorous, either permanently or at different times (Pallotta-Chiarolli, 2010; Sheff, 2014).

Several of the already surveyed paths can impact the form of mono/poly relationships. For example, one can begin a relationship as mono but then shift to a poly relational style due to either pulls for personal growth (developmental path) or the falling in love with a person who awakens one's poly dispositions (interpersonal path). Conversely, one can begin a relationship as poly but eventually decide to monogamously commit to one's partner for developmental, definitional, or contextual reasons. Thus, mono/poly relationships can dynamically change over time, contingent on a multiplicity of factors related to the fluid nature of people's relational identity and evolution.

The various forms and challenges of mono/poly relationships have been widely discussed in the literature, and interested readers are encouraged to learn more through those highly informative works (e.g., Sheff, 2014; Taormino, 2008; Veaux & Rickert, 2014). The relational path offers a means of relational hybridity by deconstructing the assumption that both halves of the pairing must use the same relational mode—another powerful example of the hybridity mode of reexamining and evolving past the mono/poly dichotomy.

Integrative Path to Relational Hybridity

Arguably the most common way to hybridize mono/poly relational styles, the integrative path brings both mono and poly into a synthesis: two people are committed to each other as *primary partners* (e.g., living together, joining finances, having children) while maintaining various types of less significant sexual and/or emotional secondary or even tertiary bonds (see Sheff, 2014). Examples abound in Western culture, from early proposals of open marriages (Mazur, 1973; O'Neill & O'Neill, 1972) to the so-called new monogamy (T. Nelson, 2012, 2016) or monogamish partnerships (Savage, 2012), and from many open relationships (Labriola, 1999; Michaels & P. Johnson, 2015) to partnered nonmonogamy (Taormino, 2008) or hierarchical polyamory (Veaux & Rickert, 2014). This path can also include one person having two primary bonds, with those two primary partners either being independent from each other or forming a triadic relationship together (e.g., B. M. Foster & M. Foster, 1997). Even though bisexuality does not necessarily entail polyamory (Baumgartner, 2021), in the bisexual community such an integrative path often entails having partners from different biological sexes (Rust, 1996). In general, in the path of integration, people allow, support, or even encourage their partners to have sex with (at times selected) others, but can agree upon guidelines about the specific type of sexual contact with secondary partners (e.g., regarding exchanging sexual fluids) to "protect" or "make special" the primary relationship (e.g., R. Rubin, 2001; Taormino, 2008).

The classical argument for the value of this relational approach is that it fulfills the often-conflicting human needs for emotional constancy and sexual diversity (see chapter 1; E. Anderson, 2012; Ashkam, 1984; Brandon, 2010). Stressing its sexual benefits, for example, Taormino (2008) described how partnered nonmonogamy permits one member of a couple to fulfill sexual needs or fantasies their partner is not interested in, or (if the primary relationship is heterosexual) to explore sensuality or sexuality with a person of their own biological sex. Recently, this theorizing has received empirical support from Balzarini, Dharma, Muise et al.'s (2019) research, which showed that polyamorous people experience greater emotional nurturance with their primary partners and greater sexual eroticism with their secondary partners than individuals in monogamous relationships.

It is important to add, however, that for many people extradyadic sexual experimentation is not simply recreational, sex-centered, or just aimed at meeting emotional needs but rather central to identity construction, self-actu-alization, or psychospiritual growth (see chapter 3; Kingma, 1998; T. Moore, 1998). In this regard, Jamieson (2004) wrote, "In the majority of examples I came across practitioners of nonmonogamy were . . . achieving the stability of a couple while developing their identity through other sexual relationships" (p. 53). In particular, Overall (1988) argued, "A woman who freely takes on a second sexual relationship in addition to one she already has is likely to feel a comparable extension of her identity, or even a claiming or reclaiming of self" (p. 9). In an attachment theory context, one can regard the integrative path as allowing an exploration of diversity from the "secure haven" provided by the primary partnership (e.g., Conley, Ziegler et al., 2012),[4] as well as embodying the (mononormatively counterintuitive) principle that, in my own words, "with greater commitment comes greater freedom." In this vein, Taormino (2008) wrote that for many partnered nonmonogamous couples, the freedom to be with others grants them a "greater sense of security" (p. xx) in their relationship with their primary partners. Similarly, Sartorius (2004) argued that some forms of group marriage integrate commitment and sexual emancipation.

Although the path of integration has been understood as a prototypical polyamorous relationship (e.g., Heaphy et al., 2004), more recent work consid-ers integration to be a binary synthesis that re-situates monogamy and nonmo-nogamy in a continuum of relational possibilities (Pallotta-Chiarolli, 2010). It is important to note that the integrative path does not privilege hierarchical (i.e., involving primary and secondary bonds) over nonhierarchical polyamory (i.e., where no relationship is considered primary; see Duck-Chong, 2017). Even when people have multiple partners that are not ranked by importance, both mono and poly values (e.g., commitment and freedom) play equally fun-damental roles in most cases. A helpful way to envision this scenario is Barker's (2013) nonhierarchical model of a circle of connections—located concentrically in terms of degrees of closeness (and, I would add, commitment)—in which sexual relationships are not necessarily considered more important than non-sexual ones.

No matter how one understands this path, research shows that a new wave of cultural acceptance of both open marriages and relationships is underway. On the one hand, in her study of marriage trends in the United States, Haag (2011) concluded: "Marital nonmonogamy may be to the 21st century what premarital sex [and interracial marriage] was to the 20th: a behavior that shifts gradually from proscribed and limited, to tolerated and common" (p.

247). On the other hand, a recent study at Indiana University's Kinsey Institute revealed that in two national representative U.S. samples of over 8,500 single individuals, over 20% of people surveyed have had at least one open sexual relationship in their lives (Haupert et al., 2017).[5] In addition, as mentioned above, many poly relationships between primary partners tend to mimic central features of monogamous bonds (e.g., Finn, 2010; Finn & Malson, 2008; Jamieson, 2004). These and other factors (see chapters 2 and 3) lead me to include this approach within the hybridity mode of transbinary relationships.

Subtle Path to Relational Hybridity

An intriguing hybrid relational path entails the simultaneous relationships (or even marriage) with both physical person(s) and subtle beings that are nonphysical (e.g., imaginal, virtual, or spiritual). Longstanding in religious traditions and cultural storytelling, relationships with these subtle beings raise questions that may also apply to the more modern context of relationships through lucid dreaming, online avatars, or virtual reality equipment.

Although Western scientific naturalism remains understandably skeptical about the existence of subtle spiritual beings (see Ferrer, 2017), vast anthropological evidence documents people's sexual encounters with angels and the like, including the cross-cultural practice of *spirit marriage* (or spirit spouse) in which traditional shamans wed spirit helpers in dreams and other nonordinary states (Greenway, 2007; I. M. Lewis, 2003). In a celebrated account, religious historian Mircea Eliade (1964) recounted how a Goldi shaman (from Siberia) was initiated by a female *ayami* (helping spirit) who demanded that he regularly consummate their marriage sexually: "I sleep with her as with my own wife, but have no children" (as cited in Eliade, 1964, p. 73). Examples from other traditions include the West African Dagara's marriages and sexual encounters with the *kontomblé* ("little people"; Somé, 1999); consort marriage with Faery or otherworld entities in Celtic shamanism (Foxwood, 2007); mystery schools' rituals of divine conception in ancient Greece (Rigoglioso, 2009); spirit marriages in contemporary syncretic traditions such as Umbanda, Voodou, Makumba, or Santeria (Bramly, 1977/1994; C. L. Dow, 1997); and the practice of *Minghuen* or "spirit marriage" in China (S. Jordan, 1971). For the Dagara, Woolever (2010) pointed out, "Human marriage does not preclude spirit marriage. In fact, usually in a human marriage the husband and wife will each have a spirit partner and the spirit partners are married to each other in the otherworld" (p. 6).[6] As these examples illustrate, the cross-cultural incidence of this phenomenon is as striking to Westerners as it is uncontroversial for the people and cultures involved.

Bracketing the ontological status of purported subtle entities (for discussion, see Ferrer, 2017), entertaining the feasibility of sexual unions in subtle realms explodes the mono/poly framework in multiple directions. In the context of a dyadic relationship, one or both members could be (a) mono in the physical world and poly in subtle realms, (b) poly in the physical world and mono in subtle realms, (c) mono in both physical and subtle realms, or (d) poly in both physical and subtle realms.

These possibilities complexify the other surveyed paths to transbinary relationships. In the definitional path, for example, some people can consider intimate encounters with subtle beings as a breaking of their commitment to sexual or emotional fidelity while others may not (see following discussion). In the relational path, a person in a mono relationship with a poly partner may be actually "poly" in subtle or imaginal realms. In the contextual path, couples can make different arrangements regarding the types of sexual practices allowed in the physical and the various subtle milieus (dreaming, meditative–visionary, entheogenic, etc.). In the integrative path, a person could have a primary relationship and two secondary ones—the first with an embodied person and the second with a subtle being, or could have a primary relationship with a subtle being while engaging in multiple secondary partnerships with embodied persons. These examples can be multiplied endlessly.

These considerations have practical relevance for modern Western individuals, even secular people who may not believe in the ontological richness of subtle or spiritual realms. For instance, a Western psychology professor specialized in the study of dreams once told me that he and his wife had to discuss whether their monogamous vow extended to the dream world, where, being seasoned lucid dreamers as they were, both could willingly have sexual encounters with imaginal beings (for lucid dreaming, see Krippner et al., 2002; LaBerge & Rheingold, 1991). One might also ask here how different these affairs are—structurally, symbolically, and functionally—from the erotic–emotional encounters many have today in techno-imaginal realities through avatars or virtual reality equipment (e.g., MacWilliams, 2005; Maheu & Subotnik, 2001; Waskul et al., 2014). Pointing out the similarities between the spiritual and virtual worlds, Saraswati (2013) argued that the cyberspace allows for a fluid sexuality "that traverses various layers of 'reality,' that is, the virtual and the physical/actual/'real' worlds" (p. 588). As E. Anderson (2012) pointed out, cybersex "makes . . . physical monogamy a slippery definitional category because it calls into question what 'reality' is" (p. 79). Regardless of what one thinks about the ontological status of these encounters, no contemporary discussion of monogamy and nonmonogamy should ignore their experiential reality and practical impact on relationships. The subtle path opens a fascinating range of sexual–emotional encounters in reportedly nonphysical realms, including virtual reality, that drastically challenge the traditional ways in which most people have understood the mono/poly binary.

The Transcendence Mode

My discussion of the transcendence mode in intimate relationships closely follows Brubaker's (2016) types of *trans of beyond* in gender and racial identity: the neo-categorical path offers a new category beyond the binary (similar to *transgender* or *transracial*); the anti-categorical path rejects all relational categories; and, departing from Brubaker's framework, what I call the *trans-categorical path* seeks to overcome the human mind's dualistic conceptualizations.[7] In chapter 1, I associated this mode to the relational transcendence competence of relational freedom, understood as the capability to experience and enact intimate relationships beyond the mono/poly binary. Thus, what brings together the following paths is an explicit overcoming of all established "mono/poly" categories, radically undermining the very foundation of the non/monogamy system.

Neo-categorical Path to Relational Transcendence

This path is defined by the invention of a new term or semantic field that cannot be contained within the mono/poly categorical binary. In the same way that *transgender* can surpass both the gender binary and the gender continuum, new categories are used to overcome both the mono/poly binary and the non/monogamy system (Rambukkana, 2015; Willey, 2006). Such new terms can be variously used to convey an existential stance as well as a relational identity, orientation, or strategy (Klesse, 2014a; M. Robinson, 2013). Before offering my own thoughts on a new term for the space outside of or beyond the mono/poly binary, I review existing options.

To my knowledge, Western literature offers only four proposals with regard to terms for transbinary relational modes. First, Weitzman (2006) used the term *poly-fluid* to refer to individuals who are able to be both monogamous and polyamorous. Likewise, P. J. Benson (2008) coined the term *biamory* to refer to "the personality orientation in which a person can be content in either a monogamous or polyamorous relationship" (p. 322). Similarly, Turner (2019) recently proposed the term *ambiamory* (and *ambiamorous*) to refer to the capability of feeling happy in both monogamous and polyamorous relationships. Even if poly-fluid, biamorous, and ambiamorous people can freely choose between the two orientations, these accounts explicitly preserve the mono/poly categories and therefore remain close to the fluidity mode discussed above. Pallotta-Chiarolli's (2010) proposal of a border or "mestizaje identity that is multiple, fluid, beyond binaries and dualities" (p. 44) is more attuned to the neo-categorical approach discussed here.

Beyond these modern proposals, one might also consider non-Western categories here. For example, the Native American Awansa's *kiita* (long-term sexual partnerships outside marriage), *jiian kii* (married people's sexual–affectionate companions only taken after the birth of a couple's first child), or *ma'el qi* (spiritual bonds that can include sleeping together but not sex; Eagleshadow, 2016). Although adopting Indigenous terms for modern Western usages may be charged with cultural appropriation (Ziff & Rao, 1997), awareness of such cross-cultural understandings can provide tools to rethink relational identity on a more colorful canvas than that allowed by the white-and-black mono/poly landscape.

In my early work on this topic, I opted to leave the territory beyond the mono/poly binary unnamed (Ferrer, 2007), as an obvious pitfall of coining novel terms is that they can be reified, homogenized, or essentialized, thereby subverting their intended emancipatory power (Butler, 1997); however, I am persuaded by arguments advocating for the power of language to bring forth new psychosocial realities and ways of being (e.g., Brubaker, 2016; Hacking, 1986). For example, learning about the term *compersion* (as the opposite of jealousy) has helped many people to enact novel emotional realities beyond what they previously considered possible (see Deri, 2015; Wolfe, 2003). As Deri (2015) pointed out, "Having a word can force a reinterpretation of an experience within that context or even create its potential. Thus, I argue that learning the word compersion could increase the likelihood that it will occur" (p. 41). Similarly, speaking about *polyamory*, Sheff (2014) wrote, "People who were previously isolated in their desire to experience multiple partnerships talked about feeling as if a new world opened to them when they found out about the term" (p. 54; cf. Franceschi, 2006; Ritchie & Barker, 2006). As in the case of *bisexual*, *pansexual*, *transgender*, *queer*, and *polyamorous*, people whose identity does not fit within established relational categories can find solace, a sense of belonging, and a shared political identity capable of transformative social action in novel transbinary terms (cf. Castells, 2010).

Some obvious but problematic candidates for transbinary relational identities or styles are *metamory*, *transamory*, and *transgamy*. However, the term *metamour* is already used in the polyamory community to refer to one's partner's lovers (Ritchie & Barker, 2006; Sheff, 2014; Veaux & Rickert, 2014), and to identify oneself as *transamorous* or *transgamous* is not only verbally awkward, but may also evoke the sense of being "above" or "beyond" love and relationships, respectively.

While being mindful that some may prefer other terms or no terms whatsoever (see subsequent discussion), I have opted for the term *novogamy* (and *novogamous*) to characterize both the neo-categorical path to relational transcendence and the overall movement beyond the mono/poly binary. Beyond aesthetic considerations, the prefix *novo-* comes from the Latin *novus*, and in many languages (e.g., Portuguese, Italian, and Galician) *novo* simply means new.

Whatever term one may prefer, what matters is that the chosen term fulfills two vital roles. The new term should assist individuals who feel called to move beyond the mono/poly binary in gaining a new sense of relational identity and relational freedom. In addition, the chosen term should allow one to respond to the standard, and arguably oppressive question (especially for those who do not identify with the established categories), "Are you monogamous or polyamorous?" It is my hope that *novogamy* and *novogamous* offer these important supports. That said, not everybody may feel comfortable with this term or with using a new term at all—as the following two paths illustrate, some may prefer to do away with all categories entirely.

Anti-categorical Path to Relational Transcendence

Another path to moving beyond the mono/poly binary is through a sweeping stance against any form of relational categorization. This path is shaped by the perception of all categories as intrinsically limiting ideological traps or conceptual boxes; in other words, to identify oneself as, say, *novogamous* or *metamorous* may be seen as creating a new relational canon that suffocates sexual and relational autonomy. Reflecting on decades of feminist debate about what relational style (monogamy or nonmonogamy) is more patriarchal, S. Johnson's (1991) words captured this anti-categorical spirit:

> monogamy vs. non-monogamy had never been the real issue, . . . it had always been a ruse, distracting us from the truly revolutionary questions: How can we associate intimately with one another and be totally free—never compromising, never negotiating, always choosing independently what we want every moment? . . . What are the links between and among freedom, power, creativity, intimacy and integrity that bind them so closely that we can't have one without the others? . . . What would love look like in freedom? (p. 112)

Although positing freedom as the uncontroversial *summum bonum* in one's relational ethics is not without its problems (see chapter 5),[8] S. Johnson's account explicitly transcends the mono/poly binary without giving a specific name to her radical stance.

Among other possibilities, the anti-categorical path can manifest through the defense of radical relational fluidity and transgression—a kind of relational–sexual anarchy that challenges hierarchical distinctions between friends and partners, in which individuals are free to be whatever they want with whoever they want at any time and place without negotiations or compromises (e.g., Heckert, 2010; Heckert & Cleminson, 2011; Lano, 1995).[9] Swedish relationship anarchist Nordgren put it this way:

> I felt a need to put another piece on the table, so that the scale of possible relationship choices didn't just go between monogamous to polyamorous but had a third, outer point—relationship anarchy [which] says the gray scale between

love and friendship is so gray that we cannot draw a line, and thus we shouldn't institutionalize a difference between partners and nonpartners [as both monogamy and polyamory do]. (As cited in Anapol, 2010, p. 207)

Although this pathway could easily turn into a neo-liberal approach to intimate choices or a narcissistic "anything that pleases me goes" people can arguably engage relational–sexual anarchism in socially mindful ways—namely, by judiciously taking into account both systemic power relations possibly shaping one's perceived "free choices" and the impact of one's actions on others. As discussed in chapter 5, social awareness, mindfulness, and integrity (or their lack) are qualities that can be present in all relational styles: monogamy, nonmonogamy, polyamory, and novogamy. In any event, relational and sexual anarchy overcomes the mono/poly binary because it emphasizes "a radical commitment to people's freedom to determine the nature of their own sexual [and thus relational] practice" (Portwood-Stacer, 2010, p. 484) beyond attachment to any particular number of partners and, if more than one, without creating hierarchies among them.

Cross-cultural evidence is also helpful to illustrate the anti-categorical path. After researching the lived experience of people with multiple partners in Hong Kong, Ho (2006) concluded: "Very few would want to identify themselves as polyamorous or non-monogamous. For most of them, having multiple partnerships was just something they did; there was no need to assume a totalized identity as someone with an alternative lifestyle" (p. 560). Becoming aware of the culturally relative—and thus to a large extent arbitrary—nature of the mono/poly categories can also open grounds to overcome the binary in an anti-categorical fashion.

Finally, it is likely that the radical acceptance of relational freedom might eventually create a space where terms are no longer needed. This possibility receives support from the fact that younger generations—such as the so-called Generation Z (ages 15 to 23 in 2020)—are more uncomfortable than prior generations with forced gender binary categories (i.e., "man" and "woman") and less concerned with labeling particular gender identities (Pew Research Center, 2019), accepting more easily whatever names and pronouns someone tells them to use. In any event, the anti-categorical path transcends the mono/poly binary without creating or offering new terms of categories to describe the undertaking.

Trans-categorical Path to Relational Transcendence

This path offers a means to transcend binary relational thinking by shifting to transrational or nondual modes of cognition and being-in-the-world (e.g., T. Hart et al., 2000; Loy, 1987). The trans-categorical path can be illustrated by the notion of a *koan* (cf. Thurer, 2005), which is a rhetorical device used in

Japanese Zen Buddhism to trigger students' sudden awakening (*satori*)—that is, a direct apprehension of reality not filtered by the mind's conceptual categorizations (Heine, 2002). "What is the sound of one hand clapping?" and "What is your original face before your father and mother were born?" are among the well-known koans designed to force an intellectual impasse where the rational alternatives are wrong and an allegedly transrational response can emerge.

In this context, movement beyond the mono/poly alternatives can be engaged as an existential or living koan—a Zen-like path of the cultivation of transconceptual modes of thinking and being. In a trans-categorical context, the paradoxical issues raised by moving beyond the mono/poly binary cannot be entirely "solved" in the arena of formal (bivalent) logic, nor can they be addressed by newer or more encompassing relational categories or paradigms. Rather, paradoxes here become doorways to transconceptual ways of being by ineluctably (and, at times, humorously) highlighting the limits of logical–rational thinking, inviting individuals to expand their consciousness and enter the space of transrational modes of being and cognition (Ferrer, 2000, 2008). In other words, although paradoxes cannot be conceptually solved, they might be—like the Zen koans—realized or transcended in the realm of human action and experience. In the trans-categorical path, the movement beyond the mono/poly binary cannot be termed or conceptualized, but it can be lived.

Toward a Novogamous Society

Despite how personally and socially emancipatory CNMs have been in the context of Western mononormativity, it has become clear that—by defining itself in opposition to monogamy—nonmonogamy ultimately reinforces the non/monogamy system (Rambukkana, 2015; Willey, 2006). In this light, *the monogamist priority of exclusive unity above plurality and the nonmonogamist priority of inclusive plurality above unity can be seen as secret accomplices.*[10] In order to overcome the non/monogamy system and associated mono/poly binary, in this chapter I have mobilized the notion of the "'third' [as] that which questions binary thinking" (Garber, 1992, p. 11) through the discussion of three plural relational modes: fluidity, hybridity, and transcendence. These modes shape—and arguably develop—different components of what I have termed in this book *relational freedom*, that is, the capability to choose and transform one's relational style in dynamic, integrative, and transcending ways (see chapter 1). Mindful that some may prefer to avoid any categorization to refer to nonbinary or transbinary relational modes, I have nonetheless coined the term *novogamy* for existential (i.e., providing self-identity and belonging), enactive (i.e., the "bringing forth" of novel experiential realities), and communicative reasons.

In any event, considering the evolution of intimacy over the last decades (e.g., Beck & Beck-Gernsheim, 1995; Giddens, 1992; Haag, 2011; Stacey, 1996; Weeks, 2007; Witt, 2016), it is reasonable to expect that the twenty-first century will witness an even greater rise in sexual experimentation and relational diversification than the prior century. In particular, it is likely that many individuals will live relational identities beyond the mono/poly binary— for example, through fluidly moving between monogamy and nonmonogamy, hybridizing essential values of these relational styles, or enacting novel relational selves that may or may not be named or categorized.[11] Illustrating aspects of this emerging ethos, for example, Barker (2013) wrote, "Perhaps the emphasis should be on finding a style of relating which fits the people involved, rather than on searching for a relationship style to shoehorn people into" (p. 105). In this wider relational canvas, people may sequentially or cyclically practice monogamy and nonmonogamy, engaging these intimate styles according to different conditions, or (eventually) choosing one or another style as a permanent choice. These developments are to be considered optimistically, in the sense of addressing the marginalization of the growing number of individuals who can no longer tolerate the limited choice between monogamy and polyamory (e.g., Anapol, 2011; Cantor, 2014; Ferrer, 2007) and who may feel oppressed by the cultural pressure of having to choose between these categories (Barker & Iantaffi, 2019), both of which support and perpetuate arguably outdated social norms embedded in the non/monogamy system (Rambukkana, 2015; Willey, 2016).

Three recent studies provide evidence for aspects of this shift in the Unites States. First, a survey conducted by YouGove showed not only that a fifth of 997 U.S. respondents under age 30 have engaged in CNM but also that millennials see monogamy as existing in a spectrum rather than as a binary category (P. Moore, 2016; see also Morris, 2014). Second, Le Cunff (2018) also found support for a monogamy–nonmonogamy continuum using a self-designed Relationship Openness Scale (ROS) on a sample of 509 U.S. individuals identifying themselves as monogamous, polyamorous, or ambiamorous. The ROS measured respondents' degrees of openness toward both their own and their partners' sexual and romantic openness to others. Whereas polyamorous respondents naturally conveyed the greatest degrees of openness in all categories (Personal Sexual Openness, Personal Romantic Openness, Partner Sexual Openness, Partner Romantic Openness), "only 29.8% of respondents identifying as monogamous . . . scored zero on the overall Relationship Openness scale" (p. 4). Finally, a longitudinal study showed that the vast majority of children from polyamorous families report not being polyamorous, but feeling both free and open to be so in the future (Sheff, 2019). Although methodologically limited (i.e., convenience samples, nonvalidated scales), these studies pioneer the empirical exploration of transbinary intimate relationships and provide important foundations for future research.

Before closing this chapter, it is important to address one potential concern with regard to the transbinary modes of relationship discussed here. As Thurer (2005) pointed out concerning the overcoming of the gender binary, one potential drawback of these relational possibilities is that too much fluidity or hybridity may result in a lack of coherent identity and consequent psychological fragmentation. Nevertheless, relational identity is arguably not as essential to selfhood as gender, and transgender narratives have demonstrated that moving beyond established binaries can actually strengthen (vs. fragment) individuals' sense of authentic identity (e.g., Bornstein & Bergman, 2010). Building on Lynn Huffer's (2013) work and her own research on queer polyamorous women, K. L. Benson (2017, 2019) questioned not only the possibility but also the desirability of (the wildly diverse) poly and queer stable identities—as such stability can hinder the dynamic "becoming" of these individuals' subjectivities. Further, as Barker and Iantaffi (2019) observed, accepting one's fluidity can nurture self-compassion: "Recognizing that we are always—inevitably—a work in progress can be a relief which enables us to treat ourselves more kindly" (p. 217). Thus, by more fully embracing their inner diversity, complexity, and dynamism, people can foster their personal individuation—even if some (and socially oppressed groups in particular) may face psychological confusion and social stigma as they deviate from dominant mononormative structures (Conley, Moors et al., 2013; Grunt-Mejer & C. Campbell, 2016). As an increasing number of people seek and embrace relational freedom, it is my hope that Western social norms will evolve and be updated from their ancient roots to meet and match the needs of the current century, thus eliminating the potential social stigma.

In conclusion, I reiterate that my main aim in presenting novogamous or transbinary relational modes is to minimize the suffering of the growing number of individuals who feel excluded from—and thus oppressed by—the non/monogamy system and attendant mono/poly bipolarity. My hope is that this development not only expands the range of legitimate relational choices individuals can make but also advances scholarly discourse on contemporary relational styles and transformations of self-identity. To support these goals, the concluding chapter 5 discusses further the challenges and possibilities of relational freedom, as well as the impact of transcending the mono/poly binary for relational success standards and the very fate of romantic love.

Notes

1 Liberally using the term *poly* as a generic abbreviation for all types of CNM relationships (see Introduction, note 5), in this chapter I equate movement beyond the non/monogamy system with the overcoming of the mono/poly binary.

2   The question of whether monogamy and nonmonogamy (or polyamory) should be considered sexual or relational identities, orientations, dispositions, or choices has been widely debated in the literature (e.g., Barker, 2005; K. L. Benson, 2019; Klesse, 2014a, 2016; M. Robinson, 2013; Shannon & Willis, 2010). In this chapter, I opt to bracket a definitive answer to this question and leave open a plurality of interpretations (for discussion, see chapter 2).

3   Although developed independently, these three modes largely correspond to Brubaker's (2016) important categories and subcategories of *trans of between* and *trans of beyond*, devised to account for a variety of transbinary gender and racial identities. Brubaker's tripartite scheme also includes what he called *trans of migration*, in which individuals permanently shift from one gender or racial identity to another. The trans of migration is a category potentially included in novogamous relationships, where, at least in theory, one can permanently choose one or another relationship from a place of increased freedom.

4   Note that although the notion—originally put forward by Hazan and Shaver (1987)—that infant–caregiver dynamics influence adult romantic attachment styles seems uncontroversial (see Feeney & Noller, 1990, 2004; Hazan & Diamond, 2000), the overall validity of the attachment model to understand romantic relationships has been empirically refuted (against popular belief): not all romantic relationships are attachment relationships in that not everybody relies on their partners as a "safe haven" in times of distress or "secure base" for exploration (Fraley & Shaver, 2000). In addition, the entire literature on attachment and romantic relationships is limited by its mononormative focus on pair-bonding (see Brandon, 2010; Conley, Ziegler et al., 2012). For a helpful review of attachment theory in intimate relationships, see Brogaard (2015); and for a thorough historical analysis of the development of attachment theory, as well as of its shaky scientific foundations despite increasing popularity after the Second World War, see Vicedo (2013). In her extremely well-documented book, Vicedo argued that attachment theory's turning of maternal love into an innate biological drive, crucial for the well-being of both infants and society, both downgraded the moral value of motherhood and perpetuated the patriarchal relegation of women in the household.

5   Predictably, the surveys also revealed differences between genders and sexual orientations, with more men than women and more self-identified LGB than heterosexual people reporting greater engagement in CNM.

6   For most of these sources, I am indebted to Woolever's (2010) notable essay, "When God Had Sex: The Practice of Spirit Marriage in Ecstatic Spirituality."

7   In Brubaker's (2016) taxonomy, the third type of *trans of beyond* is called *postcategorical* and refers to the political account of a society in which individuals have transcended the gender or racial binary.

8   As R. Tarnas (personal communication, November 9, 2017) wrote in response to an earlier version of this chapter (Ferrer, 2018):

> I would argue that in relationships as in other spheres of life, freedom (as well as richness, depth, fullness, and other values) may actually be enhanced by the voluntary embrace of structures and commitments that would make an approach that

was "never compromising, never negotiating, always choosing independently what we want every moment" (S. Johnson, 1991, p. 112) seem painfully limiting and distorting. An analogy I would offer would be music, where the embrace of certain structures, such as a definite chordal structure in a composition, can free up and make possible forms of melodic beauty and emotional depth that could not be attained in a composition that was radically free of chordal structure.

Indeed, as I argue in chapter 5, relational freedom needs to be tempered by other considerations, and the enthroning of any single value in the enactment or assessment of intimate relationships is fraught with significant pitfalls and difficulties.

9 For a helpful discussion of the roots of contemporary sexual anarchic movements in the early twentieth-century thought of Havelock Ellis (1910), Emma Goldman (1917), and more radically, the German utopian Emil Rüdebusch (1903/04), see Schaupp (2009). Here Rüdebusch is credited for having articulated that self-realization should include sexual self-ownership, as well as for rejecting sexual monogamy, the ideology of romantic love, and the imposed connection between love and sexual desire. For an earlier account of the critique of monogamy in the works and lives of many turn-of-the-century anarchist and feminist thinkers, see Leeder (1996).

10 Here, I am paraphrasing Habermas (1992): "The metaphysical priority of unity above plurality and the contextualist priority of pluralism above unity are secret accomplices" (pp. 116–117).

11 Obviously, embodying novogamous identities will be easier for more socially privileged populations than for marginalized ones; for example, financially affluent, educated white men will most likely experience less social stigmatization than black men and women from lower socioeconomic status when deviating from mononormativity and transcending the mono/poly binary (see Block, 2008; Zimmerman, 2012). For further discussion, see chapter 5's section "Open Your Eyes to Social Privilege and Oppression—Your Own and Others."

Chapter 5

Relational Freedom and the Transformation of Intimate Relationships

This final chapter first offers a fuller presentation of the critical pluralistic approach animating this book's discussions on the transformation of intimate relationships.[1] Briefly, I argue that this approach provides the foundation for relational freedom by embracing all relationship styles (e.g., monogamy, nonmonogamy, and novogamy) while offering grounds for critical discernment within and among them. In the second section, I discuss the thorny question of the possibility of freedom in relationship style choice, in the context of the typology of sources of relational conditioning introduced in chapter 1. Whereas the exploration of evolutionary and biogenetic markers may not provide clear directions to enhancing one's relational freedom, more tangible work can be done at the historical, cultural, social, and biographical levels. In the context of this discussion, I also address the danger of overvaluing individual freedom over relational care and family or community values. The third section outlines a set of pragmatic criteria for relational success that I argue are more appropriate than the pervasive, monocentric standard of relationship longevity; in this regard, I submit for consideration the pertinence of emancipatory, healing, and transformational relationship standards in relation to both individuals and societies. In the concluding section, I consider the future of romance after the deconstruction of the belief in a single "soul mate," and propose that romantic love can stay perfectly alive—and perhaps even more freely flourish—outside patriarchal and monocentric dungeons.

Steps toward Relational Freedom

As I draw this book to a close, it is important to reiterate that I neither think of novogamy as superior to monogamy and nonmonogamy, nor seek to promote transbinary relational modes as most preferable or optimal for our times. In the same way that transgender or transracial identities are not respectively better or worse than identifying oneself as male or female or African American or Asian, novogamous identities or orientations are in principle not better or worse than monogamous and nonmonogamous ones. One might reasonably argue that the very notion of relational freedom and its attendant competences—relational integration, plasticity, autonomy, and transcendence (see chapter 1)—privilege novogamy, as these competences can be seen as transcending the mono/poly binary in various ways. However, the fact that relational freedom can include the temporary, indefinite, or retrospectively permanent adoption of both monogamy and nonmonogamy subverts in practice the elevation of novogamy as a superior relational choice. Understanding intimate relationships in terms of transbinary nomadic (i.e., movable over time) boundaries also dismantles generic hierarchical assessments of particular relationships styles and their mutually defining borders (Heckert, 2010; see also Barker, 2013). Indeed, one can follow any specific relationship style for the "right" or "wrong" reasons, and all relationship styles can become equally limiting ideologies; for a variety of reasons (e.g., ignorance, misinformation, cultural pressures), one can find oneself in a relational structure that is not personally beneficial or growthful. Thus, what can be termed "better" or "worse" is *not* any particular relational style but the extent to which that relational choice is attuned to one's dispositions, present developmental horizons, or, in some cases, sociopolitical contexts (e.g., M. Robinson, 2013).[2]

Once one rejects the spurious belief that relational styles can be assessed as superior or inferior to each other as wholes, a more nuanced evaluative gaze can be deployed. Relational styles—like cultures and human beings—are very likely to be both "higher" and "lower" in relation to one another, but *in different regards* (cf. McGrane, 1989) according to the particular individual and contextual variables. For example, given the poly emphasis on self-disclosure, communication, and sexual–emotional variety, it is understandable that some studies show nonmonogamous couples scoring higher than monogamous ones on certain measures, including intimacy (Conley, Ziegler et al., 2012; Morrison et al., 2013), emotional nurturance (with primary partners) and sexual eroticism (with secondary partners; Balzarini, Dharma, Muise et al., 2019), and sexual satisfaction (Conley & Moors, 2014; Conley et al., 2017).[3] Generally speaking, it is likely that having multiple romantic partners naturally enables people to fulfill a larger number of personal needs and desires than it is possible to when relating to a single person, which may in turn lead to greater sexual–emotional satisfaction (see Finkel et al., 2014; M. E. Mitchell et al., 2014; Moors, Matsick et al., 2017). Likewise, monogamy may offer a safer container than both nonmonogamy and most forms of novogamy for sexual–emotional healing (Brandon, 2016), as well as a less socially stigmatized family model for raising children (Otter, 2014; Pallotta-Chiarolli, 2010; Sheff, 2014). For some people, monogamy's sexual exclusivity can also evoke a sense of greater intimacy, sexual–emotional depth, and even sacredness (e.g., Masters, 2007). In sum, avoiding the so-called *holistic fallacy* (Benhabib, 2002), which in this context entails the claim that relational styles can be assessed as superior or inferior to each other as wholes, more individualized and contextually sensitive assessment approaches can be developed and used.[4]

It is vital that nonhierarchical accounts of relational styles be attended by a critical outlook able to offer qualitative distinctions—both within and among relational styles—in terms of not only social privilege but also a diversity of psychological, sociological, and spiritual markers (discussed here). Crucially, as Willey (2016) pointed out, a pluralistic account of relationship styles should also include the critique of compulsory or socially imposed monogamy's ideological mandates for healthy adult bonding (cf. E. Anderson, 2012; Emens, 2004). The critique of socially enforced monogamy, however, should include supporting the increasingly free, conscious choice of monogamy that becomes available for individuals as they achieve greater degrees of relational freedom. In this regard, Schippers (2019) wrote, "rejecting mononormativity can include sometimes *consciously* choosing monogamy rather than assuming it is the default unless otherwise specified" (p. 80). Barker et al. (2013) expressed a similar sentiment: "A politics of anti-mononormativity does not necessarily mean that a person must be in a multiple, or even an open, relationship: it is vital to differentiate between a rejection of monogamy and a critique of mononormativity" (p. 198). In addition, as Rambukkana (2015) has successfully argued, many types of privilege (e.g., heteronormative, patriarchal, sexist) can exist within both monogamous and nonmonogamous contexts—and the replacement of mononormativity with a new polyorthodoxy would not resolve those underlying issues of privilege. Instead of favoring a particular relationship model, what is needed is to understand "how intimacies can be variously privileged or oppressed in nuanced and intersecting ways [so that] we can start to formulate discursive alternatives to oppressive normativities in ways that actively seek to avoid reifying privilege" (p. 145). I think this position is exactly where one needs to stand in the modern West.

If anything can be regarded as "superior," then it might be relational freedom over relational "bondage" and narcissism. However, reaching for true relational freedom requires effort and diligence. As Derrida (1981) underlined, hierarchy is intrinsic to Western thinking and language, so no conceptual framework can fully avoid privileging a particular perspective; in Western discourse, to affirm or deny one thing implicitly denies or affirms, respectively, its opposite, polar, or alternate reality. While the existence of those culturally mediated, structural, unconscious forces cannot be denied, they certainly can be resisted and even overcome, as demonstrated by queer theory regarding sexual orientation, gender, and relational binaries, as well as other contemporary Western challenges to Derrida's arguably pessimistic verdict (e.g., Barker & Iantaffi, 2019; Brubaker, 2016; Garber, 1992; Hammack et al., 2019).[5] In addition, much can be learned from considering non-Western complementary accounts of binary opposites in which no polar reality is considered better than or superior to the other (e.g., Ani, 1994; Webb, 2012). Finally, I would argue that this hierarchical ethos can be overcome in human experience through an attitude of genuine openness to understand, respect, and be enriched by what is different. Freedom from relational narcissism (i.e., the consideration of one's relational choice as universally superior or optimal) may thus be an antidote to overcoming this conceptual paradox and enhancing relational freedom, while also relating more sympathetically with people adopting alternative relational orientations to one's own (see chapter 2).

On the Seeming (Im-)Possibility of Relational Freedom

In this book, I have placed considerable emphasis on the notion of relational freedom. For example, I have critiqued all types of relational normativity and identified several psychosocial forces (e.g., monopride/polyphobia, polypride/monophobia) driving relational style choices and leading to negative appreciations of alternate options. In addition, I have argued that the power to choose one or another relational structure in attunement with one's personal dispositions, developmental pulls, and sociopolitical junctures should be considered an advancement over the inability to do so. After all, who does not prefer to live in freedom rather than as a pawn of invisible forces and conditionings? Importantly, my advocacy for expanded relational choices should be sharply distinguished from a neo-liberal "cafeteria model" that commodifies intimate relationships or relationship types as menu options that one can narcissistically pick and choose (see Rambukkana, 2015; Schippers, 2020; Wilkinson, 2010). Further, as both MacKinnon (1987) and Illouz (2019) argued, to privilege freedom over justice or equality only empowers the socially advantaged. Thus, as argued here, the enhanced relational freedom I am after here is one that needs to be exercised with not only a caring sensitivity toward others and the world but also a commitment to eradicate social privilege and oppression. In short, relational freedom for all without social justice is a very dangerous oxymoron.

Unfortunately, the six levels of conditioning (i.e., evolutionary, biological, historical, cultural, social, and biographical) discussed in chapter 1 arguably make it quite challenging to not only *choose* one's relational style but also *know* with certainty whether such a choice is truly free. Moreover, these levels interact in complex and unconscious ways in human agency generally, and in each individual particularly; for example, biographical events can make a person more permeable to transgenerational traumas (e.g., A. Harris et al., 2017) and perhaps even collective or transpersonal complexes (e.g., Bache, 2000; Grof, 1985).

For this reason, as advanced in chapter 1, I believe relational freedom should be considered a *regulative principle*: In Habermas's (1973) "ideal speech situation," for example, all pertinent interlocutors are included, have equal voice, and are free to speak their honest opinion without deception, self-deception, or coercion. Although Habermas (2003) acknowledged that these ideal conditions are unachievable in practice, he persuasively argued that they offer a regulative orientation for actual discourses, in the sense that they can optimize full inclusion, noncoercion, and equality, as well as to help people avoid exclusions, manipulation, and self-deception.

In a similar fashion, even though *complete* transcendence of all the deep-seated evolutionary, historical, and sociocultural forces gripping relational freedom might be unattainable (for the time being?), I am convinced that every human being is capable of increasing both their awareness and freedom from those forces. As a regulative ideal, then, the concept of relational freedom can become a source of critical discernment, orientation, and even transformative self-exploration for one's intimate life. How can one distinguish freer from more coerced relational choices—especially in a cultural context in which monogamous values and ideals have been so deeply internalized? Although I do not have a definite answer to this critical question, I offer the following reflections as helpful in pursuing and optimizing the possibilities of relational freedom.

Learn from Evolutionary Psychology

To begin with, even though the *evolutionary level* affects all human beings in multifarious ways, and likely shapes a diversity of relational choices, the relevant findings of evolutionary psychology can be extremely illuminating. Once we expunge evolutionary psychology from its possible essentialist and patriarchal biases (see chapter 3, note, 3; Hrdy, 1997; Liesen, 2007), its emancipatory potential can be rescued and many of its insights put to good practical use. For example, such a study can raise one's awareness of the ample diversity of relational options evolutionarily engrained in human nature (e.g., Buss, 1994, 2006; Fisher, 2004, 2011; Gangestad & Simpson, 2000; Ryan & Jethá, 2010; D. E. Schmitt, 2005a, 2005b). Evolutionary psychology can also help people understand why their sexual libido toward their beloved partner(s) has decreased (or vanished) even as their love remains strong (E. Anderson, 2012; Buss, 1994; M. Robinson, 2009), as well as discern the archaic roots of sexual jealousy underlying and fueling some of their personal reactions (Buss, 2000a). This exploration of evolutionary factors can also lead to a more sensitive and compassionate attitude toward clandestine affairs (both one's own and one's partners') beyond the cultural knee-jerk reflex condemning these actions as moral failures, sexual compulsions, or even religious sins (cf. Barash & Lipton, 2009; Brandon, 2010)—or, at least, ensure that one's anger is one's own (vs. reactively parroting an unconscious cultural script). Importantly, reading the work of feminist evolutionists who debunk the myth of the sexually passive archaic female can empower contemporary women to be more assertive about who and what they want—and do not want—in their romantic and sexual lives (Hrdy, 1986, 1999). In sum, these and other insights from evolutionary psychology can shape individual and social conditions conducive to enhanced understanding and freedom in the intimate realm.

Take a Pass on the Search for Genetic Markers

Unfortunately, available and forthcoming research on the *biological level* is prey to a plethora of pitfalls and dilemmas. Imagine that the science of the future finds conclusive evidence about genetic or other biological markers for monogamous and nonmonogamous inclinations (e.g., those famously found in prairie and montane voles, respectively; see Z. Johnson & L. J. Young, 2015; K. A. Young et al., 2011; L. J. Young et al., 1999). Such biological evidence raises several (arguably nonempirical) interpretative quandaries, illustrated by the case of genetic markers. On the one hand, nonmonogamous indicators could be considered a genetic aberration to be eugenically modified through human genetic engineering.[6] (If such possibilities seem farfetched, see chapter 2's section "The Ideological Nature of the 'Mono–Poly Wars'") On the other hand, nonmonogamy could be thought of as a genetic adaptation to biosociocultural conditions where monogamy is no longer evolutionarily advantageous.[7] Perhaps more neutral accounts are conceivable in which those markers will be regarded as evolutionary possibilities expanding the sociocultural legitimacy of a greater range of human mating and relational options. Although scientific research might eventually shed further light upon these questions, observation is inevitably theory-laden one way or another (e.g., semantically, perceptually, technologically). No datum comes with its own interpretation, as classical postpositivist philosophers argued (Hanson, 1958; Kuhn, 1970) and contemporary philosophers of science have corroborated (e.g., Azzouni, 2004; H. Chang, 2005; Van Fraassen, 2008) while rejecting the relativistic connotations of the classical accounts (see Brewer & Lambert, 2001). Thus, I strongly suspect that a plurality of conflicting accounts—animated by theoretical biases and personal ideologies—will afflict these issues for many years to come. Moreover, even if one takes a positive view toward such markers, the information is not unequivocally useful to the task of attaining relational freedom, offering as it does the Janus-faced option of conducting (or making changes in) one's intimate life to match those markers, with the scientifically supported hope that relationships more aligned with one's "nature" will lead to greater happiness, or gaining a sense of personal empowerment for having overcome inherited or randomly mutated genetic dispositions.

Free Monogamy from Patriarchal Bonds

At the *historical–cultural level*, it is essential to critically ponder the probable shared origins of monogamy, private property, and patriarchy (e.g., Ryan & Jethá, 2010; Stearns, 2009) without falling into the genetic fallacy of condemning a practice due to its arguably tainted origins. In the tradition of critical theory (Geuss, 1981; Hoy & McCarthy, 1994), one of my aims in unveiling the ideological mechanisms fueling what I called the "mono–poly wars" has been precisely to raise awareness of these often-unconscious ideological systems, so that they can be more easily detected, consciously scrutinized, and gradually overcome (see chapter 2). One can carefully examine how socially imposed monogamy is currently *institutionalized* through mononormative ideologies (e.g., Barker & Langdridge, 2010b; Pieper & Bauer, 2005) and *internalized* as monopride/polyphobia. Likewise, people can also develop critical perspectives on how emergent polynormativities may become the other, equally problematic side of the same coin: reactions to monocentrism that have been ideologically internalized as polypride/monophobia. Given the cultural preponderance of monocentrism, it can be helpful to read critical analyses such as Kipnis's (2003) polemic against the U.S. cultural and institutional enforcement of monogamous marriage; Emens's (2004) meticulous account of how monogamy is systematically privileged in the U.S. legal system; or Bergstrand and Sinski's (2010) discussion of the cultural, institutional, therapeutic, and religious narratives legitimizing monogamy in Western culture. Although knowledge neither equals nor warrants freedom, it seems clear that the former can optimize the later. At least, these and other critical works (e.g., E. Anderson, 2012; Otter, 2014; Schechinger et al., 2018; Schippers, 2016, 2020; Tweedy, 2011) can help individuals become more aware of how some of their relational choices may have been imposed upon them by governments, institutions, social media, parents, and therapists in concealed but insidious ways (i.e., presented as the only, optimal, or "right" options).

Open Your Eyes to Social Privilege and Oppression—Your Own and Others'

At the interface of cultural and biographical factors, the *social level* of relational conditioning discussed in chapter 1 includes a legion of intersecting or interlocked social locations such as biological sex, gender, class, age, and race, which can also effectively influence one's capability to exercise relational freedom. For example, in the context of Western patriarchal mononormativity, straight and cisgender white men will most likely be less socially stigmatized when selecting a poly lifestyle than straight and cisgender white women, queer or trans women, and black or Latinx people in general (A. A. Alexander, 2019; Clardy, 2018; Pain, 2019; Sheff, 2005; C. N. Smith, 2017). Likewise, financially independent females will be more capable of freely opting for their relational style than females from lower socioeconomic backgrounds. As LeMoncheck (1997) pointed out, for example, "The sexual empowerment of a handful of promiscuous career women will have little or no practical meaning for those millions of women whose livelihoods continue to depend on the sexual and domestic demands of men" (p. 56). These examples can be easily multiplied but the point remains the same: whether independently or interdependently, social locations drastically impact the degree of relational freedom available to different populations.

The intersection of relational identity, gender identity, sexual orientation, race, and class is also at play in most popular relationship guides. On the one hand, many of these guides are informed by heteronormative monogamous values or targeted at sexually exclusive couples, which often leads to the neglect or devaluation of other relational alternatives (e.g., Love & J. Robinson, 2012; Masters, 2007; Neuman, 2001; Schnarch, 2009). On the other hand, most polyamory guides are written by and geared toward a white, middle-class, and educated readership, while ostensibly presenting universal polyamorous models that may not be sensitive to the relational conditions of other social groups (see Noël, 2006; Patterson, 2018; Petrella, 2007); thus, accessing these guides or benefiting from their advice will be harder for people with different racial, socioeconomic, and educational backgrounds than that target readership.

Despite what most popular self-help guides tell their readers, no amount of personal agency or psychotherapeutic work will either neutralize the monumental weight of structural inequality over individuals' relational freedom or transform the larger systems of privilege and oppression perpetuating such an inequality (cf. Haritaworn et al., 2006). However, steps can be taken to advance toward relational freedom at the social level. In particular, I find value in cultivating Schippers's (2020) "poly gaze" as a critical lens disclosing both mononormative and polynormative biases in the cultural narratives of what constitutes a "good" intimate life (e.g., films, music, television shows, journalism, social media). Importantly, according to Schippers, the poly gaze is not only a critical lens to read cultural products for their "hegemonic constructions of gender, race, class, nation, and sexuality" (p. 14) but also a transformational way to live in the world rooted in an ethics of mutual care that is oriented toward social justice. Framed this way, the poly gaze becomes an invaluable tool to discern and gradually dismantle sociocultural mechanisms of oppression preventing everybody—but especially marginal populations—from making freer relational choices.

In sum, scrutinizing the influence of these interacting structural forces in one's life is an important means to become aware of one's own social privilege and oppression; discern the additional challenges experienced by those outside the cultural "center" (white, male, cisgender, higher socioeconomic status); and start imagining strategic interventions aimed at maximizing relational freedom for both oneself *and* others. Bottom line: "the struggle is one," and striving toward personal relational freedom cannot be divorced from a commitment to gender, racial, class, and socioeconomic justice.

Inspect Formative Influences on Current Relationships and Relational Freedom

The other level whose exploration can more directly enhance one's relational freedom is the psychological or *biographical*. The three phases or elements outlined here can be undertaken simultaneously, either on one's own or with the support of a skillful counselor whose neutrality toward different relationship styles has been established (for discussions and resources, see Barker, 2017; Kisler & Lock, 2019; Orion, 2018; Schechinger et al., 2018; Weitzman, 2006; Weitzman et al., 2012). First, there is significant benefit to exploring one's unique early childhood conditions and challenges. These can include traumatic events like sexual or physical abuse, emotional neglect, and the quality of relationships with primary caregivers and siblings (e.g., rivalries and jealousy), among other possibilities. Second, an honest examination of the overall trajectory of one's sexual awakening, sexual experiences, intimate bonds, and romantic relationships can also be illuminating. And third, it is also helpful to inspect the ways—both negative and positive—that all those formative influences may still be shaping one's attachment system, intimate relationships, and relational style choices.

Although not all romantic relationships can be explained in terms of early childhood's attachment dynamics (see chapter 4, note 4), the influence of infant–caregiver relations on the nature of adult romantic bonds seems undeniable (Feeney & Noller, 2004; Hazan & Diamond, 2000; Numan, 2015; Numan & L. J. Young, 2016). In terms of negative effects, I suggest that suboptimal experiences in early childhood *do* have an impact on relational style choices, but that their particular outcome is so diverse that no generic correlation can be established between, say, secure or anxious attachment and one or another particular relational style. For example, while further empirical studies are necessary to explore possible connections between early attachment experiences and relational style propensities, available research strongly suggests no differences between the attachment styles of monogamous and nonmonogamous people (see chapter 2; Moors et al., 2015). Depending on diverse biographical and contextual variables, for example, fear of abandonment shaped by suboptimal childhood experiences could draw different people to "prefer" either monogamous or nonmonogamous lifestyles. Whereas monogamy can naturally feel like a safer (or the only safe) relational container for many people with this particular concern (e.g., Moors et al., 2015), others with similar anxieties may feel drawn to polyamorous relations as a way to avoid being left alone if their partner departs (as there will always be another person there for them). Although the latter point may be somewhat more valid for nonhierarchical forms of polyamory (i.e., with no primary partner), it seems evident that the particular ways in which biographical factors can condition or even "force" one's relational style should be individually assessed. In other words, relational choices cannot be generally linked to particular negative attachment experiences in childhood.

In terms of how positive or optimal childhood experiences and family dynamics can shape adult relational dispositions, the results are similar. Researchers have found that children's secure attachment style is optimized when expectant mothers are happy versus hesitant (W. B. Miller et al., 2009). However, as empirical studies found no significant differences in secure attachment between monogamous and nonmonogamous people (see Conley, Ziegler et al., 2012; Moors et al., 2015), no specific links between such early positive experiences and future relational choices can be safely made. In other words, a secure attachment can serve as a foundation for both stable monogamous commitments and for the nonmonogamous capability to hold that one's partner is sexually or romantically involved with another person without serious fears, jealousy, or anxieties (for an expanded discussion, see Fern, 2020).[8] Therefore, personal exploration of one's own biographical influences is critical, so that one's adult relational choices are made more freely, rather than as a reaction to the past.

Balance Individual Freedom with Collective Responsibility

Before closing this discussion, it is necessary to address an important objection to my positive assessment of individual relational freedom: the implied emphasis on autonomous individuation in relationships could be characterized as "the triumph of narcissism over family solidarity" (Stacey, 2011, p. 9). Similarly, although supporting the merits of enhanced self-determination, Cherlin (2009) warned about the negative impact on children of the serial monogamy model, whose current prevalence he understood as a byproduct of U.S. culture's greater allegiance to personal growth and freedom. Interestingly, Strassberg (2003) expressed similar concerns regarding polyamory, which she regarded as a "'self-ish' lifestyle that can in some instances expose children to feelings of betrayal and jealousy vis a vis their parents' new partners, to sexual molestation . . . to the loss of parental figures" (pp. 559–560). More recently, Regnerus (2017) critiqued modern individual sexual and relational freedoms as detrimental to marriage and families. While these and other authors sound the trumpets of concern, however, theirs is only half of the story.

With regard to concerns about the potential negative impact of nonmo-nogamy on children, several empirical studies show no differences in mental health and social adjustment between children with nonmonogamous parents and children with monogamous parents (Bevacqua, 2018; Hamdan et al., 2009; Pallotta-Chiarolli, 2006; Sheff, 2014). Furthermore, following the concerns about polyamory as a "selfish" lifestyle listed earlier, Strassberg (2003) immedi-ately added: "It is by no means clear that children of monogamous families do not experience similar traumas through adultery, divorce, incest . . . death and remarriage" (p. 560). So, it seems more likely that family rupture and trauma are the issue, rather than the particular relational style of the parents.

While the implications of emerging relational modes for family life are outside the scope of this book, the available evidence suggests that nontradi-tional lifestyles like polyamory can actually have a positive impact on families. Polyamorous lifestyles can potentially provide larger systems of financial, logis-tical, and emotional support for both parents and children (Conley, Ziegler et al., 2012; Pallotta-Chiarolli, 2010; Sheff, 2010, 2014). In this regard, in a longitudinal study of polyamorous families, the majority of children valued positively both the abundance and diversity of parental resources and role models provided by this relational model (Goldfeder & Sheff, 2013; Sheff, 2014).[9] As for parents, even though couples tend to reduce their CNM engage-ment during pregnancy and 6–12 months after giving birth (e.g., due to lack of time and energy, concerns with health risks, and decreased sexual libido), they also report benefits such as additional support from secondary partners and, in the case of women, expansion of identity beyond motherhood (Manley et al., 2018).

Alternative relational paradigms may also counter the current epidemics of broken families and single-parent households associated to the prevalent serial monogamy paradigm (Bergstrand & Sinski, 2010; Haag, 2011; Ryan & Jethá, 2010). In the words of a polyamorous mother: "Our kids are not experiencing the standard 'broken home'; instead, their experience is one of an expanding & loving tribe" (Kai, n.d., para 4). Thus, one can imagine a social world in which children are raised by multiple adults and parental separation may not have such a negative impact (for the present-day rise of multi-parenting, see Pallotta-Chiarolli, 2010; Sheff, 2014; Spanjer, 2015).[10] Even in a monogamous context, a greater presence of extended family and community members in child-rearing has been identified as advantageous for both children and couples: "In a world in which too many children suffer from a scarcity of caring adults in their lives, the perpetuation of an ideology [the exclusive nuclear family] that reinforces this lack of involvement can only be described as perverse" (A. H. Young, 1998, p. 555). As Bergstrand and Sinski (2010) pointed out, the isolated and privatized model of monogamous marriage may be one reason we no longer know how to "productively engage in the multiple parenting of children" (p. 153). Research has also found that having multiple attachment figures fulfilling different roles in different contexts is beneficial for children's adaptive development (Howes, 1999). Interestingly, cooperative raising of children by a wider range of care-takers than biological parents has been hypothesized as a major factor in the development of intersubjectivity in our hominid ancestors, as such conditions may have favored individuals better equipped to interpret other people's mental states and intentions (Hrdy, 2009); if so, multiple parenting would logically continue to encourage intersubjectivity. Indeed, the long-standing influence and sales success of Hillary Rodham Clinton's (1996) *It Takes a Village* suggests that many Westerners recognize the need for multiple parenting even if they do not know how to rediscover it on their own.[11] In any event, further research is imperative to gain a more informed picture of the short- and long-term impact of nonmonogamous and novogamous relational styles on children and families.

Finally, although the ability to exercise relational freedom is an important achievement, it should be obvious that such a competence must be balanced with a caring awareness and examination of the impact of one's choices on others—no matter how "right" or "truthful" a decision may feel for any individual. In other words, a mindful person may choose to postpone for some time the exercising of such freedom (e.g., moving from a monogamous to a polyamorous lifestyle, or vice versa, more attuned to her personal moment or disposition) due to a wide variety of reasons, such as the children's age, a partner with physical or mental health challenges, or social stigmatization, among others. To consider relational freedom *the* sacrosanct or privileged orientation in intimate decisions may not only be contextually insensitive but in some cases also result in selfish and uncompassionate behavior.

Be Open to Possibilities

To close this section, I would argue that the most judicious approach is to be open to all possibilities, and work to tease out one's own particular influences: some conditions may be mediating freedom, other coercing it, and still others somehow acting both ways simultaneously or at different developmental junctures. Clearly, some unconscious lenses can negatively condition one's relational freedom, while others might mediate or facilitate it. This is, after all, how some pro-monogamy authors have argued for the achievement of monogamy in the context of humanity's "natural" nonmonogamous desires (e.g., Barash & Lipton, 2009; Brandon, 2010). Thus, I propose that a more positive approach to hold engrained tendencies and conditioning forces may be to consider them as shaping a significant range of possibilities in which one can creatively participate, in order to contribute to the fulfillment of oneself, one's relationships, and humanity's evolving relational diversity. Furthermore, if one takes into consideration the admittedly speculative possibility of transpersonal (e.g., transgenerational, collective, karmic[12]) variables, then one could argue that certain particular conditions (e.g., cultural context, family dynamics, traumatic events) may be meaningful in terms of catalyzing the healing or transformation of not only individuals and family lineages (e.g., A. Harris et al., 2017) but also, some have argued, ethnic groups and even the entire human species (e.g., Bache, 2000; Grof, 1985). In any event, a thorough exploration of all the aforementioned avenues is both interesting and fruitful: individual conditions, ideally explored with the aid of a skilled and trusted therapist; collective conditions, explored as a family or community; and cultural conditions, explored as a society.

Judging from the fast-paced spreading of relational alternatives over the last few decades, especially in both adolescents and young adults (e.g., Freitas, 2013; Haag, 2011; L. Wade, 2017), it is likely that future generations will be able to achieve levels of relational freedom that are impossible for contemporary people. Relational freedom, however, is not the only standard with which to assess intimate relationships outside a mononormative context, and this book would not be complete without at least a brief discussion of other important criteria.

Beyond Longevity: New Criteria for Relational Success

In this section, I critically discuss relational longevity as monogamy's—and, due to mononormativity, Western culture's—central standard of success, and suggest a variety of alternative criteria. In this book, we have seen how mononormativity became psychologically internalized after centuries or millennia of social enforcement (Dabhoiwala, 2012; Herlihy, 1995; MacDonald, 1995). Through its adopted standards, this value system not only inhibits and marginalizes poly choices but also impacts the way even those choosing nonmonogamy think about the success or failure of intimate relationships. The two chief, interrelated standards of monogamy's relational success are sexual fidelity and the longevity of the exclusive bond. Although emotional fidelity is central to many nonmonogamies (e.g., Green et al., 2016; Wosick, 2012; Wosick-Correa, 2010), sexual fidelity is not at issue here because most of these alternative paradigms explicitly reject the need for sexual exclusivity as part of individual and relational fulfillment (e.g., Rodrigues, Lopes et al., 2017). However, a typical—even if empirically unfounded (see chapter 2)—criticism of polyamorous and CNM relations is that they do not last as much as monogamous ones (e.g., Regnerus, 2017). This belief can have practical negative consequences: when clients share about their poly relationships, many psychotherapists holding monogamous biases assume that such relationships cannot last (L. S. Jordan, 2018).

Interestingly, this longevity standard breathes with ease even in poly contexts. Over more than two decades, for example, sharing about my nonmonogamous lifestyle was invariably followed by questions about the length of my relationships. If short-term (in the questioner' eyes, that is), my relationships were consistently fashioned as failures, with a typical response being, "Ah, you see, nonmonogamy does not really work!" As Rust (1996) pointed out, "Relationships that do not conform to the traditional monogamous model are constructed as 'failed' relationships" (p. 131). Also, it is worth noting, when a monogamous relationship ends, very few question the system: its "failure" is typically attributed to other factors (e.g., personal handicaps, still not having found "The One"). In contrast, the ending of a polyamorous relationship is usually taken as an unequivocal proof that polyamory does not work (e.g., Carlström & Andersson, 2019; Patterson, 2018). In any case, the same common reaction occurred in audiences attending Barker's (2013) talks on nonmonogamy: when asking about how successful nonmonogamous relationships are, most people "meant whether or not such a relationship lasts over time" (p. 148). Even more poignantly, I have found, if I shared that my relationships had *not* lasted many years, the obvious implication was that there was "something wrong" with me— in some cases, the provided numerical data would also automatically eliminate me from being considered a potential, reliable partner. Strikingly, I obtained similar responses from both mono and poly individuals. Despite the increasing incidence of short-term serial monogamy today, the monogamous people I spoke with usually had higher standards for the length of a successful relationship.

Relational longevity is pursued by nonmonogamous people in not only hierarchical, but also nonhierarchical polyamory. In this regard, Samuels (2010) observed, "many more recent polyamorous discourses seem to assume that, in order to be considered as serious, such relationships will be long-term (or at least not terribly short-term)" (p. 212). This should not come as a surprise; after all, the long-term nature of sexual/emotional bonds is a key distinguishing feature between polyamory and "lesser" nonmonogamies such as promiscuity, swinging, or recreational sex (for critical discussions, see Klesse, 2006, 2007; Kőrösi, 2012; Noël, 2006). Hence, much research has focused on showing that polyamorous relations can persist as much as monogamous ones (e.g., Conley, Ziegler et al., 2012; Rubel & Bogaert, 2015; Wosick-Correa, 2010), and that introducing new partners can help dyadic relationships to last longer (e.g., Conley & Moors, 2014).[13] Whereas such research efforts are valuable and understandable—as they refute the common charge that polyamory is unsustainable or leads to the destruction of couples—they ironically perpetuate mononormative standards. As Michaels and P. Johnson (2015) pointed out, "Because the mononormative mindset still treats lifelong exclusivity as an ideal, even if few can attain it, the end of a relationship means one has fallen short of this ideal" (p. 74). Even if the longevity standard is considered a necessary mortgage paid by emerging relational paradigms to the received monogamous system (cf. Voegelin, 2000), in the rest of this section I argue that such a mortgage has already been paid off.

Although longevity can be desirable and growthful in many cases, I propose that it should not be the paramount—or even a central—benchmark of relational success, even less so outside a mononormative context. Since longevity has been the consciously promoted and unconsciously embedded relationship standard in the West for centuries, updating to new standards will require a sustained, collective effort. In this final section of the book, I humbly add my own contribution to the development of more appropriate criteria for overall relationship success.[14]

Overall Quality

Numerous scholars have suggested the overall quality of the relationship as a better standard for success (e.g., Barker, 2013; Deri, 2015; Rowan, 1995; Sheff, 2014). As for relationship quality, Rowan (1995) got to the heart of the matter:

> What does anybody mean by the word [failed] when they're talking about relationships? They mean the relationship ended. Which is very odd when you come to think of it. A meal is a failure because it doesn't taste nice, not because you ran out of food to eat, but a relationship can "fail" even if it's fun all the way through, because a meal isn't supposed to last forever and a relationship is if you're monogamous. But if you are not monogamous this just doesn't work anymore. (p. 18)

She added:

> I recommend that non-monogamous people abandon longevity as the sole measure of the success of a relationship, and instead turn back to quality (of which longevity may be a part, since more of a good thing is often good), which is good enough for meals, parties, and literary works. That way we can allow more than one of the relationships in our lives to be a success and we stand in no danger of having our successes re-written as failures the moment they are over. (p. 18)

In the same vein, Sheff (2014) wrote, "Simply staying together is not necessarily success—it is the tone of the relationship that determines the degree of success. . . . Success can be defined as meeting people's needs for specific period of time" (p. 277). Similarly, Barker (2013) observed, "The question of how long our relationship has lasted can overshadow the (perhaps more important) question of whether it is an enjoyable, nourishing, and positive aspect of our lives" (p. 151). Thus, more applicable than how long a relationship has lasted may be the question of relationship quality.

It is a simple matter to ask about relationship longevity; relationship quality assessment requires more nuanced and numerous inquiries along the following lines (listed here in past tense, though of course they can also be used to assess current relationships).

- How much love was experienced? Was this love limited to the relationship or also extended toward others and the world?
- To what degree were the personal needs (e.g., sexual, emotional, intellectual, spiritual, social) of all partners met in the relationship?
- Did friendship and mutual support successfully coexist with sex and romance?
- Were harmony, care, trust, respect, empathy, and kindness present even in conflicting moments or challenging situations?
- How mindfully was anger expressed and received? How were other "negative" emotions (e.g., annoyance, frustration, jealousy, shame, guilt, anxiety, fear, and despair) managed?
- How well and how fully were incompatibilities, disagreements, and conflicts addressed, resolved, or transcended?
- How much mindfulness, compassion, and forgiveness were exercised? In particular, how much were they offered in relation to oneself and one's partner(s)' perceived or self-perceived flaws, limitations, unhelpful patterns, and growing edges?
- How much sexual, sensuous, and emotional joy and delight characterized the relationship? Was sexuality an open soil conducive to mutual satisfaction, emotional bonding, vital regeneration, and ecstatic transcendence (as opposed to fraught with persistent challenges, conflicts, or frustrations)?
- To what extent were ego-transcendence (i.e., liberation from selfishness and egocentric concerns) and other spiritual qualities—such as inner peace, unconditional acceptance, generosity, and devotion—experienced in the relationship?

The list can go on, but that these examples illustrate the various ways intimate relationships can be assessed in relation to overall experiential qualities.

Healing, Transformative, and Emancipatory Power

In addition to relational quality and the satisfaction of personal needs (cf. Giddens, 1992), I propose that one should pay special attention to relationships' healing, transformative, and emancipatory power—despite how challenging a relationship is or might have been. Here, one could consider the degree of psychosomatic healing (e.g., from physical, emotional, or sexual trauma), personal development (e.g., emotional intelligence), sociopolitical emancipation (e.g., from patriarchal oppression), ecological awareness (e.g., living a more sustainable life), and spiritual transformation (e.g., enhanced presence, compassion, altruism) that a relationship catalyzed for all parties and the relationship's sphere of influence (e.g., friends, working partners, communities).

In this spirit, one can ask questions such as the following:

- To what extent is a relationship contributing to heal somatic dissociations, energetic blockages, sexual wounds, emotional conflicts, or cognitive ideologies and rigidities?
- Has a relationship fostered the growth of personal integrity and wholeness, individuation, sexual and emotional maturity, ethical behavior, and vocational development?
- To what extent did a relationship enhance sociopolitical awareness, empathy toward others (both human and nonhuman), and personal empowerment, to support becoming more effective culturally transformative agents?
- Has a relationship helped its members to become more aware of their own social privilege and oppression, as well as contributed to greater socioeconomic justice and equality?
- What have been the relationship's actual fruits in terms of not only possible biological progeny but also creative personal, social, and cultural projects carried out individually and/or as a relational unit?
- How effective is or has the relationship been in fostering ecological sustainability (see Barker, 2013)?
- To what degree did the relationship promote the emergence or growth of spiritual qualities such as mindfulness, compassion, generosity, and selflessness, as well as openness to previously unknown aspects or mysteries of life and the world?

In addition, letting go of the (empirically refutable) monocentric delusion of "unchanging romantic love" can also lead to an awareness of the continuing power of a relationship after it is no longer sexually and/or emotionally intimate. One might ask the following:

- How much friendship and love remain after an intimate relationship has ended?
- How has that love transformed in its postromantic phase?
- How much gratitude can one experience toward prior partners, even in those cases where aspects of the relationship or separation process were painful?

Assessment of Overall Relationship Quality and Healing/Transformative Power

These and similar questions can assist both laypeople and researchers in the development of more nuanced approaches to making qualitative distinctions within and among relationship styles. On the one hand, to assess relationship overall quality—in addition to standard measures such as the Intimacy Attitude Scale-Revised (IAS-R; Amidon et al., 1983) and the Relationship Assessment Scale (RAS; Hendrick et al., 1998)—researchers can develop qualitative studies shaped by the proposed parameters and use other relevant standardized tests. In the study of both particular relationships or different relationship styles, for example, researchers can apply the Spiritual Well-Being Scale (SWBS; Paloutzian et al., 2012), one or several of the many mindfulness scales available today (see Sauer et al., 2013), or sexual satisfaction and communication measures (see J. T. Parsons et al., 2012). On the other hand, to determine relationships' transformative power, researchers could carry out longitudinal studies (both on particular relationships and larger samples of people choosing different relationship styles), employing measures such as the Narcissism Personality Inventory (NPI; Raskin & Terry, 1988), the Spiritual Transformation Scale (STC; Cole et al., 2008), a combination of self-report and performance tests of emotional intelligence (see Brackett et al., 2006; Conte, 2005), or Body Awareness scales assessing embodied well-being, body image, and mind-body integration (see Mehling et al., 2009).[15] In other words, from the evaluative principles outlined in this section, applicable standards, rules, or tests to assess relational choices and practices could be selected or derived.

I firmly believe that we in the West are outgrowing and will gradually move beyond the monocentric obsession with relational longevity. In that process, it is likely that the preceding suggestions and similar orientations will become the widely accepted standards of relational success.

The Future of Romance

Before concluding this book, it is worth exploring what is left of the traditional concept of Western romance in nonmonogamous and novogamous intimate relationships. Generally, romantic love is understood as entailing reciprocal involuntary (and voluntary) passionate sexual feelings, desire for physical and emotional closeness, and irrational or even obsessive idealization between two persons (e.g., Branden, 2008; Karandashev, 2016; Solomon, 2006).[16] It has been conceptualized as having two phases: the state of being "in love" (i.e., persistent thinking about the other person, wanting to always be together, gazing into each other's eyes) and continuing romantic love (i.e., desiring to form an enduring "we" with whom to pool individual autonomy; see Nozick, 1989). Although it is demonstrably possible to be in love with more than one person (e.g., B. M. Foster & M. Foster, 1997; Sartorius, 2004), romantic love is usually considered to be dyadic, exclusive, and possessive (see Ben-Ze'ev & Goussinsky, 2008).

With regard to the dyadic and exclusive "requirement" of romantic love, as discussed in chapter 4, a central yardstick for intimacy in many contemporary nonmonogamous relationships is the feeling of being special for one's primary partner (Wosick, 2012). In other words, once free from egoic concerns, the sense of both feeling (even very) special to someone and regarding someone else (even very) special can perfectly subsist outside a monocentric context of sexual/emotional exclusivity. Furthermore, one can argue that nonmonogamous primary bonds require the rooting of love as deeply—and perhaps even deeper—than monogamous bonds, as such depth may be crucial to experience both one's own and one's partner's love toward others in a nonthreatening way. In other words, the deeper the love between two people, the more safely they may feel about both loving other people and supporting their partner's sexual/emotional openness to others. As Weaver and Woollard (2008) wrote in their lucid consideration of the value of both monogamy and nonmonogamy, "choosing to be nonmonogamous . . . displays faith in the strength of the relationship" (p. 521). Put more poetically, the more we surrender to the one, the more we can embrace the many—and the more we embrace the many, the more we may feel pull to surrender to the one. This perhaps counterintuitive dynamic can arguably shape a virtuous circle of mutual synergy between loving one and loving many. But there is more—as the evocative narratives described in Foster and Foster's (1997) *Three in Love* illustrate, romantic love can also dwell and expand beyond the confines of the dyadic couple.[17] However, I would argue that romance can also thrive outside of primary bonding; in a nonhierarchical polyamorous context, it is feasible that a well-predisposed person with a profound capability to love can experience a sense of genuine romanticism with many people without the need to focus a preferential love on one primary partner.

So, is there room for romanticism beyond monocentrism and its attendant Romantic Love Myth? Does romantic love survive the deconstruction of the belief in a single "soul mate" or "The One"? Can the spirit of romantic love be rescued from patriarchal and mononormative confinements? Is it possible to experience romantic passion beyond the delusions of monocentrism without falling into cynical attitudes toward love and intimate relationships? In short, how does romance look in a nonmonogamous or novogamous world?

These questions came insistently to life within me after I listened carefully to Tim Minchin's satiric song, "If I Didn't Have You." A polemical Australian composer and musician, Minchin is an outspoken fan of the so-called four horsemen of the New Atheism (Richard Dawkins, Daniel Dennett, Sam Harris, and Christopher Hitchens) and "has become something of a cult figure for atheists in the US" (Kellaway, 2013, para 11).[18] Even though "If I Didn't Have You" is written is a monocentric context ("I have just one life and just one love and, my love, that love is you," wrote Minchin in relation to his wife Sarah), the following lines illustrate the song's relentless deconstruction of some central assumptions of the Romantic Love Myth:

Yeah, yeah, if I didn't have you
. . .
Well I, really think that I would
Have somebody else

Someone else would do

Thus, even though Minchin stated that Sarah is her only love, the song's chorus stresses that such a love is entirely replaceable. In other words, she is the "The One" but not necessarily "The Only One." He continues:

Your love is one in a million
(One in a million)
You couldn't buy it at any price
(Can't buy love)

But of the 9 point 999 hundred thousand other loves
Statistically, some of them would be equally nice
(Equally nice)

Further, here Minchin indicates his conviction that other loves would be as fine as the love he currently enjoys with his wife Sarah. He adds:

. . .
But I'm just saying
I don't think you're special
I-I mean, I think you're special
But you fall within a bell curve
. . .
I mean I reckon it's pretty likely that if, for example
My first girlfriend, Jackie, hadn't dumped me
After I kissed Winston's ex-girlfriend Neah at Steph's party back in 1993
Enough variables would probably have been altered by the absence of that event

And in these lines, Minchin not only rejects the exclusive specialness of his love for his wife but also affirms the sheer arbitrariness of their being together. Therefore, he reiterates:

. . .
If I didn't have you
If I didn't have you
Someone else would do
Someone else would surely do

Commenting on the song, Minchin said: "It is a love song about how I chose to love her [Sarah]. It points out that the romantic worldview is wrong, that there is beauty in the reality behind the romance. I don't understand why people need more" (as cited in Kellaway, 2013, para. 33). He added, the "song is uncomfortable because it rubs your face in randomness, reminds you how arbitrary life is on a cosmic scale" (as cited in Kellaway, para. 34). I believe that both the song and Minchin's commentary accurately depict the deflation of romantic love characteristic of our postmodern, postromantic times (see Haag, 2011).

Whereas I consider the song's painstaking deconstruction of the Romantic Love Myth very important, I do not think that a relativistic devaluation of romantic love necessarily follows from such a move. On the one hand, the song's lyrics capture well the arguably vital, currently in-progress overcoming of the myth of finding an irreplaceable "The One" (for discussions, see Barker, 2013; Ben-Ze'ev & Goussinsky, 2008). On the other hand, as usually happens with the first waves of most emancipatory movements, Minchin's song goes arguably too far in the other direction: it renders romantic love as a purely arbitrary, accidental, inconspicuous affair infused with the meaninglessness of the most radical (and exhausted) forms of deconstructive postmodernism (e.g., Carr, 1992; Rosenau, 1992; Schiralli, 1999).

Bottom line: While the ideology of romantic love should be indeed forcefully critiqued (e.g., Ben-Ze'ev & Goussinsky, 2008; Kipnis, 2003), evolving past the Romantic Love Myth need not to weaken the amorous, passionate, ecstatic, and transcendent qualities of romance.[19] Likewise, rising above the delusional belief in the existence of a unique "soul mate" (among the 7.7 billion people currently populating the world) does not need to eradicate the extraordinary magic and romanticism one can feel with a single person—and which could be possibly extended to more than one person. As Brake (2018) argued, there can also be polyamorous weddings, rituals, and parties celebrating love and commitment in the presence of friends and family.

Thus, I propose, freedom from patriarchal (glass or golden) cages and monocentric strictures can and does coexist with genuine romantic feelings, a powerful evolutionary co-unfolding with one's partner(s), and even ego-transcendence and a sense of the sacred in intimate relationships. In other words, a freer essence of romantic love awaits beyond the promises, expectations, and delusions of the Romantic Love Myth from a bygone era. Once the deceptive spell of monocentric romance is dissolved, a different and more creative love can emerge—perhaps even a finer love that is meaningful, vibrant, and real beyond what one imagined to be possible.

In closing, in addition to advancing scholarly discourse on intimate relationships by identifying a middle path between ideological hierarchies and relativistic egalitarianisms, it is my hope that this book has promoted greater mutual understanding and respect among people choosing different relational styles, provided an expanded map of legitimate relational options, presented the first systematic exposition of transbinary or novogamous relationship modes, developed tools to explore and nurture relational freedom, and offered a transformed vision of intimate relationships and romantic love beyond limiting monocentric myths and delusions. These efforts are just baby steps in the exploration of the mostly uncharted territories that both unfold and are enacted beyond mononormative and polynormative lands, and I look forward to learning from others' intuitions and to witnessing what the future holds in store for intimate relationships. In this work, my efforts have been guided by an inner drive to foster conditions where human beings can more fully—and freely—express and receive embodied love, in all its forms. May it be so.

Notes

[1] For discussions of critical pluralism in philosophy and the social sciences, see Hoy and McCarthy (1994) and Regh and Bohman (2001).

[2] Weaver and Woollard (2008) expressed a similar sensibility in a different but complementary way:

> Monogamy is valuable when spouses choose to be monogamous because the marriage alone fulfils their sexual and emotional needs and they see the relationship as important enough to justify the [potential] sacrifices. The acceptance of monogamy is disvaluable if spouses choose to be monogamous due to jealousy, insecurity, or the desire to control each other. The rejection of monogamy is valuable when it springs from a realistic faith in the strength of the marriage and spouses' ability to fulfil their sophisticated sexual and emotional needs while sustaining the marriage. It is disvaluable when it springs from a lack of fulfilment within the relationship and a failure to value the marriage enough to protect it. (p. 521)

[3] As Balzarini, Dharma, Muise et al. (2019) acknowledged, however, these results are in conflict with prior research carried out by their own team (Balzarini, Dharma, Kohut, L. Campbell, Lehmiller et al., 2019) and other researchers (e.g., Mogilski et al., 2017), which showed no significant differences in relational quality between monogamous and nonmonogamous couples (see chapter 2). Further comparative research with larger and more representative samples is needed here; for example, Balzarini, Dharma, Muise et al.'s sample was composed of self-selected participants, which, as the researchers candidly admitted, could have biased the findings. In addition, as Conley et al. (2017) pointed out, it is important that these comparative studies distinguish among different CNM styles, such as open relationships, polyamory, and swinging; these researchers also suggested the possibility that those engaged in (socially marginalized) nonmonogamous relationships may feel more prone to describe more positively their relational experience than monogamous individuals. Another factor complicating the interpretation of these comparative findings is that monogamous and CNM individuals or couples may understand qualities such as

emotional nurturance and sexual satisfaction quite differently and in ways not fully captured by standardized measures or questionnaires.

4   Cf. Habermas: "One society may be superior to another with reference to the level of differentiation of its economic or administrative system, or with reference to technologies and legal institutions. But it does not follow that we are entitled to value this society more highly as a whole, as concrete totality, as a form of life" (cited in Dews, 1986, p. 169).

5   Derrida's work denounces, rejects, and dismantles the hierarchical structure of Western philosophical and scientific traditions. However, deconstruction proceeds by first reversing and then reinscribing the structure to make room for unstable meanings, ambiguity, difference, and undecidable concepts—not by overcoming it through dialectical moves or complementary accounts of binary poles (see also Derrida, 1982). In any event, Derrida's work should be appreciated as philosophically grounding contemporary challenges to the validity of binary hierarchical oppositions in both culture and human experience.

6   Human genetic engineering will most likely be practiced in the next centuries (Hawking, 2018), and the potential misuse of genetic engineering to alter (at birth or adulthood) the genetic dispositions of nonnormative populations (e.g., transgender, homosexual, queer, or polyamorous) by future conservative authoritarian regimes is as dystopic as it is terrifying. Unfortunately, the precedent of the Japanese government's unconsented sterilization of an estimated 25,000 people with disabilities under the Eugenics Protection Law (1946–1996) makes these scenarios more plausible (Yamaguchi, 2019). In addition, unless the science of the future develops some kind of genetic archeology or genealogy, the question of whether nonmonogamous genetic markers have increased in recent decades or centuries will remain unanswered. Since evolutionary psychology suggests the presence of multiple-mating strategies in our archaic past (e.g., Buss, 2006; D. E. Schmitt, 2005b), it is likely that those markers have been around for a very long time.

7   In an unpublished but relevant paper, for example, Boone (n.d.) speculated that the nonjealous (compersive) aspirations and behaviors characteristic of nonmonogamous relationships may be understood as an evolutionary adaptation (for now, by a minority population) to conditions in which community bonds have become more central than reproductive success for human survival, especially in light of overpopulation and resource scarcity. He asked: "In short, is polyamory flying in the face of accepted evolutionary logic, or is it rather spearheading human evolution—at least in the smaller context of human socio-sexual behavior—around its next adaptational curve?" (p. 6).

8   In this regard, future research exploring the relationship between jealousy, compersion, gender, and attachment styles in the context of different relationship paradigms should prove to be valuable to clarify these questions (e.g., Aumer et al., 2014; Mogilski et al., 2019; Szabrowicz, 2018). Future studies should also consider the impact of nuclear versus communal raising, the presence of other family members during childhood, the number of siblings and relational dynamics among them, parental favoritisms, unresolved trauma, and the role of jealousy in parents or family dynamics, among other possible factors. For example, researchers have

found correlations between differential parental affection toward siblings and their degree of jealousy in adult romantic relationships (Rauer & Volling, 2007).

9 My personal experience supports this finding: Although our household was not polyamorous in structure, I lived with eight other adults (of diverse sexual orientations and gender identities) in a Berkeley community house for about nine years (2005–2015). In 2010, a couple from the community had a baby who happily lived with us for the following five years. During that time, the parents often expressed their gratitude for the logistical and emotional support they received from other community members in raising their beautiful daughter. Further, when her parents told her that we all had to leave the house due the landlord's need to sell it (to pay for his medical bills), the five-year-old retorted: "Ah, okay, but we are all going to live together somewhere else, yes?" She continued, "Because I don't want to live by myself with just the two of you!" This anecdote imprinted in me the sense that, for kids who have experienced community life, the benefits of living with more adults (and, ideally, more children) is a no-brainer.

10 For helpful discussions on the different but related question of polyamorous marriage in particular and plural marriage in general, see Aviram and Leachman (2015) and Goldfeder (2017), respectively. In this regard, L. S. Anderson (2016) proposed the legalization of "open unions" or nonmonogamous marriages allowing two emotionally and financially committed adults to relinquish sexual exclusivity for a negotiated number of years, after which they could reaffirm the open agreement or enter a traditional marriage. More radically, Brake (2012, 2014) offered a sustained case for the extension of marital rights (e.g., tax benefits, shared health insurance and pension plans, bereavement leaves) to all caring relationships, including long-term friendships and committed polyamorous triads or groups (for discussions, see Brake, 2016; Klesse, 2016). The complex question of whether marriage should be in general regulated by democratic states, versus privatized through inclusive civil union policies, is problematized by a legion of cultural and contextual factors; for example, while the state regulation of marriage does at times constrain LGBTQ+ rights in some Western societies, it often protects women, girls, and children in Islamic nations (see Shrage, 2013). With Klesse (2016), however, my sense is that the most emancipatory path forward in the modern West is not to extend the scope of the socially privileged institution of marriage (why should married people have "special rights"?), but rather to implement legal and legislative reforms that secure basic rights and protections for all individuals and relationships.

11 The book, republished as a Tenth Anniversary Edition in 2006 (Clinton, 2006) and winner of a Grammy Award for Best Spoken Book Album in 1997, was published as picture book in 2017 (Clinton, 2017). It also spent 18 weeks on the *New York Times* Best Seller List during 1996 and had sold over 650,000 copies by 2000 (see Roberts, 2000).

12 While the mere mention of the word *karmic* in academic discourse is enough to discredit the reliability of any author or work, a genuine scientific spirit demands keeping one's mind open to the anomalous and the unknown. In this regard, before a priori dismissing karmic factors as absurd or impossible, readers may want to

carefully study Ian Stevenson's (1997) accumulation of over 2,500 documented cases of children from all over the world recalling previous lives and deaths, including in many cases accurate explanations for birthmarks as well as the exact names of both the dead person and close relatives (see Bering, 2013; Kaplan, 2010; for critiques, see Edwards, 1996; Ransom, 2015). Whether or not the possibility of previous lives and karma is substantiated, billions of people have included it in their spiritual understanding of human experience for millennia (see McClelland, 2010; Neufeldt, 1986), which implies a strong value for the human psyche even if only as a concept.

13 The latest effort comes from Hagemann (2018), who conducted an online survey on attendees of 17 alt.polycon conventions (1996–2008) reporting that "54% (22/41) of respondents with partners were in at least one relationship lasting over 21 years and 83% (34/41) of respondents with partners were in at least one relationship lasting over a decade" (p. 15).

14 I should reiterate here that, as with the rest of this book's proposals, I restrain the validity of these standards to modern Western culture (see chapter 2, note 9); it should be obvious that other cultures (e.g., Eastern, Amerindian, African) may naturally endorse different criteria, often emerging from their respective religious beliefs and behavioral codes. In addition, whereas I believe in the value of considering these cultural criteria in the context of almost any type of relationship, there may also be other relationship-style-specific criteria. For example, my critiqued standard of longevity is central to traditional, life-long monogamy; sexual fidelity is pertinent in the context of both life-long and serial monogamous vows; and some poly-specific standards of relational success include radical honesty (Klesse, 2006; Sheff, 2014; for critiques, see Finn, 2010; J. Zhu, 2018), the honoring of agreements regarding sexual boundaries (Sheff, 2014; Wosick, 2012), and the successful management of jealousy (Mint, 2010).

15 As with the study of how changes in personality affect life satisfaction (e.g., Boyce et al., 2013), controlling every possible variable beyond relationship impact that can influence personal transformation may prove to be an extremely challenging, if not impossible, task. Thus, while the use of empirical measures in methodologically rigorous designs is important, I believe that the power and possibility in assessing these novel standards of relational success lies in the skillful combination of quantitative and qualitative methodologies.

16 Romantic love has been variously discussed as an evolutionary drive like hunger and thirst (Fisher, 1992), an evolutionary adaptation facilitating long-time pair-bonding and cooperative breeding (Fletcher et al., 2015), a passionate longing for union with another (Hatfield & Rapson, 1993), an attachment bond (S. Johnson, 2013), an inventive modern idea or set of insights (Solomon, 2006), an ideology (Ben-Ze'ev & Goussinsky, 2008), a conscious choice shaped by a capitalist ethos (Illouz, 1997, 2012), an emotion (Brogaard, 2015), and a culturally constructed universal emotion (Karandashev, 2016), among others.

17 These and other accounts refute the still common practice of restricting romantic love to dyadic relationships (Soble, 1987) or the "'union' of two souls" (Solomon,

2006, p. 24). In this vein, T. H. Smith (2011) wrote, although not all couples love each other romantically, "romantic love . . . is the form of love appropriate to all and only couples" (p. 68). For a cogent critique of the "dyadic imaginary" (i.e., the ideology restricting romantic love to dyadic unions) from the perspective of bisexual experience, see Hidalgo et al. (2008).

[18] Interestingly, the cultural philosopher Jay Ogilvy, author of the countercultural classic *Multidimensional Man* (Ogilvy, 1977), wrote that the "new polytheism" (Ogilvy, 2013, p. 41) with which he characterized my participatory religious pluralism (Ferrer, 2002, 2008) represents not only a "spirituality that does justice to the multi-cultural condition of a globalized world" (p. 47) but also the best response to the criticisms of religion crafted by the so-called new atheists (Dawkins, 2006; Dennett, 2006; S. Harris, 2004; Hitchens, 2007). He wrote that this "newer, stronger pluralism . . . gives to the gods their sacred due, even as it widens the field for possible reverence" (p. 45). For other discussions of participatory pluralism, see Kripal (2003), Gleig and Boeving (2011), Duckworth (2014), and Ferrer (2017).

[19] Needless to say, these qualities can exist in intimate bonds eschewing both romance and sexuality. As both Wilkinson (2010) and Schippers (2020) argued, most poly narratives enthrone romantic–sexual connections as the most significant relationships one can have. A truly revolutionary polyamory, however, should shift the emphasis from having multiple romantic lovers to embracing many types of love and a larger commitment to others, the planet, and life itself (see also chapter 2; Barker et al., 2013; Cutas, 2018). Transbinary or novogamous relationships include and celebrate all these intimacy possibilities.

Coda

After Covid-19

As I bring this book to a close, the Balearic government has enforced new mobility restrictions (including a perimetral lockdown and 10:00 p.m. curfew) upon the citizens of Ibiza—that wondrous island in the Mediterranean where I recently moved to live closer to nature during these challenging times. It is February 2021, and the third wave of the Covid-19 pandemic crisis has fully arrived and will apparently be with us for many months to come. Both the need for "social" (physical) distancing and the understandable fears of contagion caused by the Covid-19 pandemic are certain to impact intimate relationships in general (including marriages and divorces) and nonmonogamous relational styles in particular.

As with the AIDS/HIV epidemic of the 1980s (Altman, 1986; LeMoncheck, 1997), I have no doubt that conservative religious and political sections will co-opt the present health threat to promote monocentric, polyphobic, and anti-promiscuity agendas. Stigma against nonmonogamous populations has already increased (see Madrigal-Borloz, 2020), as was also the case with gay men (and sexual minorities in general) in the wake of the AIDS crisis (see Engel, 2006; Waldby, 1996). In South Korea, the Protestant right is already scapegoating the LGBTQ+ community, in which nonmonogamy is common (see Moors et al., 2014), for the spreading of the Covid-19 virus (Klasto & Simpson, 2020; Sternlicht, 2020); in Fiji, radical evangelical Christians have blamed these populations for causing the pandemic (Anthony, 2020). This trend is unfortunately likely to increase as the pandemic stretches on.

Given the current state of affairs, it is not surprising that some voices have already proclaimed the Covid-19 crisis as heralding a return to sexually exclusive monogamy. For example, in "Covid-19, or the Triumph of Monogamy?" Aversa and Jannini (2020) wrote:

Sex between habitual partner[s] without symptoms, without suspected contacts, negative to the virus and living together from the beginning of the restrictions is to be considered safe and a real tool to stay connected and relieve
anxiety during forced cohabitation. On the contrary, new sex encounters with
non-habitual partners, where [the] distancing more than 6 feet rule applies,
making [*sic*] this practice a real challenge. For the single [person], practicing
autoerotism may represent the only way to maintain sexual health. (n.p.)

Although these guidelines may sound perfectly reasonable while no vaccine is
widely available, it is worth noting the potential polyphobia in the implicit association (in the article's title) of monogamy with safety and nonmonogamy with
unsafety. In the same way that a wife with a philandering husband engaging in
unprotected sex is more at risk of contracting a STI than a poly person whose
various lovers impeccably follow safe sex practices (Conley, Moors et al., 2013;
Conley et al., 2015; Swan & S. C. Thompson, 2016), a monogamous individual
whose partner takes public transportation or works at a hospital has arguably
greater chances of contracting Covid-19 than a nonmonogamous person whose
various lovers only leave their home to go to a nearby supermarket following
the recommended PPE safety measures. So, the degree of infection risk is not
in fact necessarily contingent on one's number of lovers (one vs. many) but on
the high-risk situations the people with whom one is physically intimate expose
themselves to. In addition, Aversa and Jannini failed to mention that nonmonogamous people can still interact in virtual ways (from love messages to online
parties to virtual sex) with multiple present or future partners (see Lehmiller et
al., 2020; Paul, 2020; Savage, 2020). As discussed in this book, nonmonogamy
can take different forms (sexual, emotional, nonphysical, etc.) and the mainstream linkage of nonmonogamy with sex is both problematic and ideological.
Indeed, some poly activists reported that the pandemic has put emotional connections front and center (e.g., G. Smith, 2020).

Whereas it is realistic to expect that the Covid-19 pandemic will pause
engagement in many of the relational pathways presented in this book (perhaps
even for quite some time), here I want to explain why I am confident that this
situation will be just temporary. To begin with, while no sexual (genital or
anal) contagion has been reported (though Covid-19 may spread via urine and
feces and has been found in men's semen; Li et al., 2020; Yeo et al., 2020), the
virus can be unquestionably transmitted via saliva and physical closeness; thus,
it would surely be irresponsible to organize or participate in sex parties, orgies,
and the like while no secure testing or vaccine has been widely applied (see Kale,
2020). As with STIs, some people may therefore adopt the practice of asking for
verbal reporting or even documentation of negative Covid-19 test results before
engaging in any kind of physical intimate contact (e.g., López, 2020a; N'diaye,
2020), even if regular testing can never guaranty total absence of risk (López,
2020b). As effective vaccines or immunotherapeutic drugs will soon become

widely available (see Buckland et al., 2020; Zimmer et al., 2021), I strongly suspect that such a practice will be relatively short-lived even if the residual effects of the pandemic may last up to two more years (K. A. Moore et al., 2020). To be sure, as with seasonal influenza, some people may avoid (or exert the appropriate caution when considering) physical closeness with potential intimate partners presenting symptoms related to the infection (e.g., cough, fever, runny nose). Once tests and vaccines are broadly available, however, I see no reason why the existence of Covid-19 would prevent people from (re)engaging in nonmonogamous lifestyles or physical intimacy with new people in general.

In addition, after months of social distancing, people may even experience a greater need for close physical and emotional contact than before. Times of uncertainty, fear, isolation, and sense of mortality are also known to lead to increased sexual urges, number of sexual partners, or even "risky" sexual activity—a phenomenon called "terror sex" in New York after 9/11 (Chiasson et al., 2005; E. Bell, 2017), and one that led conservative sex therapists to discourage nonnormative sexual practices (see Puar, 2007). On April 4, 2020, for example, *Wired UK* magazine reported not only rises in sales for Viagra, morning-after pills, condoms, and sex toys over the prior several weeks but also increased activity in dating websites, including one designed for people seeking extramarital affairs (Mellor, 2020; see also Smothers, 2020). Thus, although some studies have shown a decrease in sexual desire and activity among cohabitating couples during the pandemic (e.g., Karagöz et al., 2020; Schiavi et al., 2020), the tendency to search for future potential sexual partners even beyond established relationships appears to be on the rise.

In any case, although history never fully defines future events, its lessons are always worth considering. Even though the AIDS watershed decreased risky sexual practices in the male gay community, it did not do much to stop sexually promiscuous behavior while using condoms (e.g., Berkowitz, 2003; Escoffier, 2011), despite voices from within the gay movement urging this population to drop multipartnerism and return to sexual monogamy (e.g., Rotello, 1997). Further, it is important to remember that the spread and popularization of polyamory (and other CNMs) took place *after* the emergence of the AIDS epidemic. Thus, it is reasonable to expect that the new post-Covid-19 "normal" will include a continuation—and perhaps even an expansion—of the relational experimentation and diversification that have characterized the last few decades. One could even speculate that the so-called Great Pause created an opportunity for people to deeply reflect on what is not working in their intimate lives, including relational paradigms possibly adopted by default, and that the technologically facilitated nonphysical connections people nurtured (e.g., emotional, sexual-erotic, spiritual) could naturally turn into expanded physical connections as and when circumstances are favorable. In this light, one even wonders: Will Covid-19 be retrospectively seen as supporting and catalyzing a larger collective evolutionary impulse toward increased human interconnectivity? In any event, though I certainly possess no precognitive powers, I am convinced that the relational developments described in this book are unstoppable, and that no biological or sociopolitical force will irreversibly halt their growth.

Appendix I

Ten Theses on Relationships Styles

1. No relationship style—monogamy, nonmonogamy, or novogamy—is intrinsically superior or optimal as a whole.

2. All relationship styles can be "better" or "worse" in relation to one another in different regards—such as fostering greater intimacy, emotional healing, or social emancipation—contingent on the particular individual and contextual variables.

3. All relationship styles have "higher" and "lower" manifestations—from more mindful to more unconscious, from more life-enhancing to more fear-based, from more selfless to more selfish, and from more to less aware of social privilege and oppression.

4. Human beings are endowed with diverse personal dispositions, predisposing people to thrive in the context of different relationship styles.

5. Developmental and sociopolitical conditions can call individuals to engage in different relationship styles at various junctures of their lives, with no identifiable universal or paradigmatic linear sequence.

6. People can follow a specific relationship style for the "right" or "wrong" reasons—for example, from a place of freedom, knowledge, and attunement to their needs and dispositions; or due to psychocultural conditioning, social coercion, ignorance, or personal fears or deficits.

7. All relationship styles can become equally limiting ideologies when adopted in a situation of ignorance or social imposition, or when maintained as universally superior or optimal (i.e., relational narcissism).

8. The non/monogamy system and attendant mono/poly binary can be transcended in three interconnected modes, which together comprise what I term *novogamy*: fluid movement between monogamy and nonmonogamy, hybridization of the essential values of these relational styles, and enaction of novel transbinary relational styles/selves that may or may not be named or categorized.

9. To seek or achieve greater freedom in relationship style choice does not privilege novogamy over other styles, because novogamy can include

the temporary, indefinite, or retrospectively permanent adoption of both monogamy and nonmonogamy.

10. Ultimately, the most important tasks in relationship choice are to "know thyself," be truthful to oneself and others, trust and be open to life's callings, and live the type of relationship that is more attuned to one's evolving potentials while being mindful of the impact of one's relational actions on others in contexts of social privilege and oppression.

Appendix II

The Alpha Male versus the Omega Man

It is likely that the ongoing evolution of gender and intimate relationships will gradually transform not only human sexuality but also sexual identity. I leave the task of discussing such changes in the female gender for discerning women attuned to the spirit of the times, as well as for the relevant transgender people in the case of nonbinary gender identities. Here I focus on exploring one possible shift in male sexual identity: the movement from the traditional Alpha Male to what I name the *Omega Man*—not to be confused with the so-called Omega Male, often described as a kind, sweet man lacking self-esteem, initiative, or ability. In contrast, as I conceive it, the Omega Man is a confident, creative, and sexually potent person who is often successful professionally or finds himself in leadership positions, even if he tends to stay behind the scenes and not emphasize his own talents or accomplishments.

Before proceeding, a few caveats. The following descriptions of the Alpha Male and the Omega Man are *prototypical* or *archetypal*. In other words, in order to clearly differentiate these sexual identity roles, the following account is blatantly essentializing and will not therefore capture the lived reality of most modern Western males. As should be obvious, "to be Alpha" or "to be Omega" is not an either/or affair: whereas some men are very Alpha and others very Omega, most contemporary men are hybrids who combine Alpha and Omega qualities in various degrees and fashions.

In addition, my account is deliberately polarizing and polemical. Perhaps due to my own personal dispositions, I tend to cast the Omega Man in a far more favorable light than the Alpha Male; however, there may be situations where Alpha qualities might be useful, for example, the ability to make a noncooperative decision in a critical situation calling for immediate action, or even taking certain romantic or sexual initiatives. Thus, although I believe that many Alpha sexual attitudes and behaviors are obsolete, not constructive, and should be thus overcome, the following controversy should not be read as an absolute critique of the Alpha or an unconditional vindication of the Omega.

In contrast, as alluded before, my sense is that many integrated men (both present and future) might well be shaped by a selective blend of Alpha and Omega qualities, as well as enjoy the ability and freedom to flow between such modes of masculinity depending on what is most appropriate in each situation.

Finally, it is important to stress that I write as not only a white, middle-class, cisgender, and mostly heterosexual male but also a self-identified Omega Man with some Alpha qualities (e.g., I tend be the "life of the party," can be self-centered at times, and my ego still inflates a bit from social recognition). Also, unless otherwise stated, the following account seeks to reflect traditional heterosexual relationships between cisgender men and women. In any event, it should be obvious that my particular sexual identity and social location bias this essay, and that a more complete or balanced picture of these sexual identities should incorporate other perspectives. For example, embracing Omega qualities may not only look quite different for other ethnic and social groups but also be far more challenging to enact in social contexts that stigmatize Omega traits as effeminate, weak, or not belonging to "real" men. That said, I trust that this somewhat playful polemic raises awareness of these two male sexual roles, as well as contributes to the ongoing transformation of both male sexual identity and gender relations.

- Alpha Males instinctively seek to conquer females and dominate males in the context of power over relationships. Omega Men foster the cultivation of harmonious relationships with and among males and females in the context of mutually empowering relationships.
- In social interactions, Alpha Males are like the Sun: their dazzling brightness eclipses the light of all other stars in the sky. Omega Men are like the Moon: their subtle glow allows the beauty of all other observable stars to be appreciated.
- Alpha Males build their confidence through ranking highly in social/sexual hierarchies and seeking constant approval. Omega Men are confident men who neither accept social/sexual hierarchies nor need social recognition to bolster their egos.
- Alpha Males are usually unapologetic and believe themselves to be always right. Omega Men sincerely apologize when they "screw up" and gracefully express gratitude when shown to be wrong.
- Regardless of sexual orientation, Alpha Males display conventional "masculine" traits in their social self-presentation; however, the "suave" Alpha Male (prevalent in New Age circles) is a gentle and even "feminine" man who uses these qualities to perpetuate Alpha supremacy. Omega Men often combine "masculine" and "feminine" qualities and can easily be socially scanned as gay, even when they are heterosexually inclined.
- If self-identified as heterosexual, Alpha Males tend to be homophobic, speaking and acting in ways that do not leave any room for questioning their sexual orientation (regardless of their inner desires). Omega Men are often "queer straight men" who appreciate all sexual orientations; they

can also be openly bisexual, homosexual, metrosexual, omnisexual, or pansexual.

- Alpha Males treat women as their possession: no other man should approach "their" mates with a sexual or romantic interest and less without their explicit permission—with this attitude being displayed at times even toward ex-partners. Omega Men treat women as autonomous agents with the right and power to act freely without having to be accountable to their sexual mates or romantic partners.

- Alpha Males are strongly driven to have progeny (ideally sons) to socially prove their virility, propagate their genetic seed, and continue their patriarchal family legacy. They usually do not get too involved in raising children (except to inculcate Alpha traits) and can easily leave their mates to procreate with other women. Omega Men may want to have children but are not normally compelled to do so, as they understand that there are many ways to materialize their primary creative energy. If they become parents, they consciously choose to do so to foster the constructive evolution of humanity, fully supporting the individuation of their children beyond their own belief systems.

- Alpha Males use their own well-being as a primary reference for the success of intimate relationships: if they are not enjoying a relationship or do not feel it is (egotistically) beneficial for them, they walk away. New Age Alpha Males insidiously disguise this modus operandi through (pseudo)spiritual tenets such as "living your truth" or "following your bliss." Omega Men are able to make decisions based on the well-being of a wider ecosystem of relationships that includes their partners and larger community; they understand how living one's truth entails the negotiations and compromises that inevitably arise when relating to other whole persons whose truths may be different.

- If self-identified as monogamous, Alpha Males tend to display mate-guarding behavior, feeling uncomfortable about their partners' male friendships (especially if the friend is new or attractive) and jealous of their partners' general interactions with other men, who are often perceived as potential competitors. If Alpha Males cheat, they often feel entitled to do so (because they are "real" men, after all) as they shamelessly apply the typical patriarchal double standard that simultaneously forbids the same behavior in women. Monogamous Omega Men support their partners' interactions, friendships, and affective connections with other men. They do not usually have sex with other women, out of either their commitment to sexual exclusivity or the understanding that they would naturally have to tell their partners and accept that they too could then have sex with other men.

- If self-identified as polyamorous, Alpha Males (mis-)use poly rhetoric to build a harem of women whose intimate contact with other males they monitor and control—a phenomenon that Sheff (2006) aptly called *poly-hegemonic masculinity*. Polyamorous Omega Men fully respect the autonomy and freedom of their mates, not just tolerating but supporting and even celebrating women's loving and sexual connections with others.

- Alpha Males approach sexual encounters as conquests aimed at boosting their confidence, providing self-centered pleasure, and sexually "hooking" females; their perception that they can and do sexually please women is thus essential, and they tend to fall into depression if their sexual power or talents are questioned. Omega Men approach sexual interactions as creative encounters with the Other and the mystery of Eros as it spontaneously flows through and between sexual partners; if a sexual relationship does not fully work out, they are genuinely open to receive constructive feedback and understand that sexual chemistry does not need to spark with everybody.
- Alpha Males are sexually potent men whose force tends to dominate, subjugate, control, or even violate women's psychological and energetic boundaries. This tendency eventually creates or reinforces women's impulse toward the energetic "castration" of men (i.e., blocking the full reception of their instinctive energy), as well as inner blocks and conflicts in women who are minimally emancipated from patriarchy and thus feel uneasy submitting to men's self-centered desires. Omega Men are sexually potent men whose force offers a respectful and assuring presence that allows women to fearlessly "surrender" to sexual pleasure without risk of physical or psychological harm, as well as to open to and fully receive (nonaggressive or degrading) strong male energy without fears or conflicts.
- Alpha Males tend to connect with their inner animal's instinctive sexuality in rampant and often unconscious ways, which often leads to the (gross or subtle) tendencies to harass or dominate women described above. Omega Men, even if honoring the "possession" codes of the instinctive world, tend to display a sexuality free of aggression (unless playful or mutually agreed upon), in a context of love and respect for their partners, and normally accompanied by the presence of the heart and consciousness (except in possible intentional explorations of purely Dionysian [i.e., unrestrained] sexuality).
- Alpha Males have a phallus (as a symbol of virility and patriarchal power over others). Omega Men have penises (as an organ of fertility and pleasurably shared power).
- For Alpha Males, erection is imperative and the lack of phallic arousal during sex is automatically translated as a "failure." Omega Men fully trust their bodies, appreciating the many passionate and tender forms of connection that can emerge with both an erect and a languid penis.
- Alpha Males display a genitally centered sexuality where penetration and orgasm are essential elements. Omega Men enjoy a full-body sexuality that can take many different forms and is usually free from orgasm compulsion.
- Alpha Males typically self-identify as having a large phallus and do not miss any opportunity to boast about their endowment. Omega Men have penises of miscellaneous sizes and understand that, except in some rare and extreme cases (penises too small or too large to be practical for penetrative sex), size does not really matter.
- Put succinctly, if somewhat crudely, Alpha Males are fuckers, while Omega Men are lovers (which does not mean that Omega Men cannot provide a "good fuck").

Although this appendix is the most acerbic part of this book, I mean no disrespect to men who identify themselves as Alpha Males, as that is the main male social identity valued in the dominant Western culture. It is my hope that this book—and this hopefully somewhat humorous appendix—will help support the creation of an updated male identity more appropriate for the twenty-first century. That said, I firmly believe there are things that need to be said with certain force (always valued by Alpha Males) and, above all, without ever losing the sense of humor, both in relation to the subject matter and to ourselves.

Abbasi, I. S., & Alghamdi, N. G. (2017). When flirting turns into infidelity: The Facebook dilemma. *The American Journal of Family Therapy, 45*(1), 1–14.

Abbasi, I. S., & Alghamdi, N. G. (2018).The pursuit of romantic alternatives online: Social media friends as potential alternatives. *Journal of Sex & Marital Therapy, 44*(1), 16–28.

Adam, B. D. (2010). Relationship innovation in male couples. In M. Barker & D. Langdridge (Eds.), *Understanding non-monogamies* (pp. 55–69). Routledge.

Adamopoulou, E. (2013). New facts on infidelity. *Economic Letters, 121*(3), 458–462.

Agger, B. (2013). *Critical social theories* (3rd ed.). Oxford University Press.

Ainsworth, M. D. S., Blehar, M. C., Waters, E., & Wall, S. (1978). *Patterns of attachment: A psychological study of the strange situation.* Lawrence Erlbaum.

Alexander, A. A. (2019). "We don't do that!" Consensual non-monogamy in HBO's *Insecure. Journal of Black Sexuality and Relationships, 6*(2), 1–16.

Alexander, R. D. (1987). *The biology of moral systems.* Aldine de Grutyer.

Al-Krenawi, A., & Kanat-Maymon, Y. (2015). Psychological symptomatology, self-esteem and life satisfactions on women from polygamous and monogamous marriages in Syria. *International Social Work, 60*(1), 196–201.

Allen, E. S., & Baucom, D. H. (2006). Dating, marital, and hypothetical extradyadic involvements: How do they compare? *The Journal of Sex Research, 43*(4), 307–317.

Allen, N. B., Lewinsohn, P. M., & Seeley, J. R. (1998). Prenatal and perinatal influences for psychopathology in childhood and adolescence. *Developmental Psychopathology, 10*(3), 513–529.

Allyn, D. (2000). *Make love, not war: The sexual revolution, an unfettered history.* Routledge.

Altman, D. (1986). *AIDS in the mind of America: The social, political, and psychological impact of a new epidemic.* Anchor.

Amato, P. R. (2001). Children of divorce in the 1990s: An update of the Amato and Keith (1991) meta-analysis. *Journal of Family Psychology, 15*(3), 355–370.

Amato, P. R. (2010). Research on divorce: Continuing trends and new developments. *Journal of Marriage and Family, 72*(3), 650–666.

Amato, P. R. (2014). The consequences of divorce for adults and children: An update. *Journal of Marriage and the Family, 62*(4), 1269–1287.

Amato, P. R., & Previti, D. (2003). People's reasons for divorcing: Gender, social class, the life course, and adjustment. *Journal of Family Issues, 24*(5), 602–626.

Amidon, E., Kumar, V. K., & Treadwell, T. (1983). Measurement of intimacy attitudes: The intimacy attitude scale—revised. *Journal of Personality Assessment, 47*(6), 635–639.

Anapol, D. (1997). *Polyamory: The new love without limits. Secrets of sustainable intimate relationships.* IntiNet Resource Center.

Anapol, D. (1998). *Compersion: Meditations on using jealousy as a path to unconditional love* [eBook]. IntiNet Resource Center.

Anapol, D. (2004). A glimpse of harmony. In S. Anderlini-D'Onofrio (Ed.), *Plural loves: Designs for bi and poly living* (pp. 109–119). Harrington Park Press.

Anapol, D. (2010). *Polyamory in the 21st century: Love and intimacy with multiple partners.* Rowman & Littlefield.

Anapol, D. (2011, July). Beyond polyamory. *Psychology Today.* https://www.psychologytoday.com/blog/love-without-limits/201107/beyond-polyamory

Anderlini-D'Onofrio, S. (2004a). Polyamory. In J. Eadie (Ed.), *Sexuality: The essential glossary* (pp. 164–165). Arnold.

Anderlini-D'Onofrio, S. (2004b). Plural loves: By and poly utopias for a new millennium. In S. Anderlini-D'Onofrio (Ed.), *Plural loves: Designs for by and poly living* (pp. 1–6). Harrington Park Press.

Anderlini-D'Onofrio, S. (2010). *Gaia and the new politics of love: Notes for a poly planet.* North Atlantic Books.

Anderlini-D'Onofrio, S., & Hagamen, L. (Eds.). (2015) *Ecosexuality: When nature inspires the arts of love.* CreateSpace Independent Publishing Platform.

Andersen, K. (2012, October 19). *"Polyamory": The next civil rights movement.* Life Site News. https://www.lifesitenews.com/news/polyamory-the-next-civil-rights-movement

Anderson, E. (2012). *The monogamy gap: Men, love, and the reality of cheating.* Oxford University Press.

Anderson, K. G. (2006). How well does paternity confidence match actual paternity? Evidence from worldwide nonpaternity rates. *Current Anthropology, 47*(3), 513–518.

Anderson, L. S. (2016). Marriage, monogamy, and affairs: Reassessing intimate relationships in light of growing acceptance of consensual non-monogamy. *Washington and Lee Journal of Civil Rights and Social Justice, 22*(1), 3–47.

Andersson, C. (2015). A genealogy of serial monogamy: Regulations of intimacy in twentieth-century Sweden. *Journal of Family History, 40*(2), 195–207.

Angell, M. (2016). Why to be a parent? Review of A. Gopnik, *The gardener and the carpenter: What the new science of child development tells us about the relationship between parents and children. The New York Review of Books, 63*(17), 8, 10.

Ani, M. (1994). *Yurugu: An Afrocentric critique of European thought and behavior.* Africa World Press.

Anthony, K. (2020, October 12). *Fiji activist says sexual minorities blamed for COVID-19.* Pacific Beat. ABC Radio Australia. https://www.abc.net.au/radio-australia/programs/pacificbeat/fiji-lgbti/12753444

Apostolou, M., & Wang, Y. (2020). The challenges of keeping an intimate relationship: An evolutionary examination. *Evolutionary Psychology, 18*(3). https://doi: 10.1177/1474704920953526

Apt, C., & Hurlbert, D. F. (1994). The sexual attitudes, behavior, and relationships of women with histrionic personality disorder. *Journal of Sex and Marital Therapy, 20*(2), 125–133.

Aral, S. O., & Leichliter, J. S. (2010). Non-monogamy: Risk factor for STI transmission and acquisition and determinant for STI spread in populations. *Sexually Transmitted Infections, 86*(3), 29–36.

Archer, C., Ephraim, L., & Maxwell, L. (2013a). Introduction: Politics on the terrain of second nature. In C. Archer, L. Ephraim, & L. Maxwell (Eds.), *Second nature: Rethinking the natural through politics* (pp. 1–25). Fordham University Press.

Archer, C., Ephraim, L., & Maxwell, L. (Eds.). (2013b). *Second nature: Rethinking the natural through politics*. Fordham University Press.

Areshidze, G. (2017). Taking religion seriously? Habermas on religious translation and cooperative learning in post-secular society. *American Political Science Review, 111*(4), 724–737.

Arkowitz, H., & Lilienfeld, S. O. (2013, March 1). Is divorce bad for children? The breakup may be painful, but most kids adjust well over time. *Scientific American.* https://www.scientificamerican.com/article/is-divorce-bad-for-children/?redirect=1

Ashkam, J. (1984). *Identity and stability in marriage.* Cambridge University Press.

Atkins, D. C., Baucom, D. H., & Jacobson, N. S. (2001). Understanding infidelity: Correlates in a national random sample. *Journal of Family Psychology, 15*(4), 735–749.

Atkins, D. C., Yi, J., Baucom, D. H., & Christensen, A. (2005). Infidelity in couples seeking marital therapy. *Journal of Family Psychology, 19*(3), 470–473.

Atwood, J. D. (2005). Cyber-affairs. "What's the big deal?" Therapeutic considerations. *Journal of Couple and Relationship Therapy, 4*(2–3), 117–134.

Aumer, K., Bellew, W., Ito, B., Hatfield, E., & Heck, R. (2014). The happy green eyed monogamist: Role of jealousy and compersion in monogamous and non-traditional relationships. *Electronic Journal of Human Sexuality, 17*(28). http://www.ejhs.org/volume17/happy.html

Aversa, A., & Jannini, E. A. (2020). COVID-19, or the triumph of monogamy? *Minerva Endocrinologica, 45.* https://doi.org/10.23736/S0391-1977.20.03207-1

Aviram, H., & Leachman, G. (2015). The future of polyamorous marriage: Lessons from the marriage equality struggle. *Harvard Journal of Law and Gender, 38,* 269–336.

Azzouni, J. (2004). Theory, observation, and scientific realism. *British Journal for the Philosophy of Science, 55*(3), 371–392.

Bachc, C. M. (2000). *Dark night, early dawn: Steps to a deep ecology of mind.* State University of New York Press.

Bachmann, C. F. (2018). *Polyamory as a feminist practice: How loving many can liberate the female* body [Unpublished manuscript]. https://www.academia.edu/40652240/Polyamory_as_a_Feminist_Practice_How_Loving_Many_can_Liberate_the_Female_Body

Baker, B. (2017, March 9). The biggest threat facing middle-age men isn't smoking or obesity. It's loneliness. *Boston Glove.* https://www.bostonglobe.com/magazine/201

7/03/09/the-biggest-threat-facing-middle-age-men-isn-smoking-obesity-loneliness/k6 saC9FnnHQCUbf5mJ8okL/story.html

Baker, R., & Bellis, M. A. (1995). *Human sperm competition: Copulation, masturbation and infidelity*. Chapman and Hall.

Balstrup, S. K. (2012). *To believe in love: The religious significance of the romantic love myth in Western modernity* [Unpublished bachelor of arts thesis, University of Sydney].

Balter, M. (2015). Can epigenetics explain homosexuality puzzle? Study in twin brothers finds a link between DNA methylation and sexual orientation. *Science, 350*(6257), 148.

Balzarini, R. N., Schumlich, E. J., Kohut, T., & Campbell, L. (2018). Dimming the "halo" around monogamy: Re-assessing stigma surrounding consensually non-monogamous romantic relationships as a function of personal relationship orientation. *Frontiers in Psychology, 9*(984). https://doi.org/10.3389/fpsyg.2018.00894

Balzarini, R. N., Dharma, C., Kohut, T., Campbell, L., Holmes, B. M., Lehmiller, J. J., & Harman, J. J. (2019). Demographic comparison of American individuals in polyamorous and monogamous relationships. *The Journal of Sex Research, 56*(6), 681–694.

Balzarini, R. N., Dharma, C., Kohut, T., Campbell, L., Lehmiller, J. J., & Harman, J. J., & Holmes, B. M. (2019). Comparing relationship quality across different types of romantic partners in polyamorous and monogamous relationships. *Archives of Sexual Behavior, 48*(6), 1749–1767.

Balzarini, R. N., Dharma, C., Muise, A., & Kohut (2019). Eroticism versus nurturance: How eroticism and nurturance differs in polyamorous and monogamous relationships. *Social Psychology, 50*(3), 185–200.

Balzarini, R. N., McDonald, J. N., Kohut, T., Lehmiller, J. J., Holmes, B. M., & Harman, J. (2020). Compersion: When jealousy-inducing situations don't (just) induce jealousy. *Archives of Sexual Behavior*. https://doi.org/10.31234/osf.io/k3tzf

Bamberger, J. (1974). The myth of matriarchy: Why men rule in primitive society. In M. Z. Rosaldo & L. Lamphere (Eds.), *Women, culture, and society* (pp. 263–280). Stanford University Press.

Barash, D. P., & Lipton, J. E. (2001). *The myth of monogamy: Fidelity and infidelity in animals and people*. Henry Holt & Co.

Barash, D. P., & Lipton, J. E. (2009). *Strange bedfellows: The surprising connection between sex, evolution, and monogamy*. Bellevue Literary Press.

Barber, N. (2002). *The science of romance: Secrets of the sexual brain*. Prometheus Books.

Barker, M. (2005). This is my partner, and this is my . . . partner's partner: Constructing a polyamorous identity in a monogamous world. *Journal of Constructivist Psychology, 18*(1), 75–88.

Barker, M., Heckert, J., & Wilkinson, E. (2013). Queering polyamory: From one love to many loves and back again. In T. Sanger & Y. Taylor (Eds.), *Mapping intimacies: Relations, exchanges, affects* (pp. 190–208). Palgrave Macmillan.

Barker, M., & Langdridge, D. (Eds.). (2010a). *Understanding non-monogamies*. Routledge.

Barker, M., & Langdridge, D. (2010b). Whatever happened to non-monogamies? Critical reflections on recent research and practice. *Sexualities, 13*(6), 748–772.

Barker, M., & Ritchie, A. (2007). Hot bi babes and feminist families: Polyamorous women speak out. *Lesbian & Gay Psychology Review, 8*(2), 141–151.

Barker, M.-J. (2013). *Rewriting the rules: An integrative guide to love, sex and relationships.* Routledge.

Barker, M.-J. (2017). *Good practice across the counselling professions 001: Gender, sexual, and relationship diversity (GSRD).* British Association for Counselling and Psychotherapy.

Barker, M.-J., & Iantaffi, A. (2019). *Life isn't binary: On being both, beyond, and in-between.* Jessica Kingsley Publishers.

Barkow, J. (Ed.). (2006). *Missing the revolution: Darwinism for social scientists.* Oxford University Press.

Bates, L. (2016). *Everyday sexism: The project that inspired a worldwide movement.* Thomas Dunne Press.

Bauch, C. T., & McElreath, R. (2016). Disease dynamics and costly punishment can foster socially imposed monogamy. *Nature Communications, 7*(11219). https://doi.org/10.1038/ncomms11219

Bauman, Z. (2003). *Liquid love: On the fragility of human relationships.* Polity Press.

Baumeister, R. F. (1988). Masochism as escape from self. *Journal of Sex Research, 25*(1), 28–59.

Baumeister, R. F. (2000). Gender differences in erotic plasticity: The female sex drive as socially flexible and responsive. *Psychological Bulletin, 126*(3), 347–374.

Baumeister, R. F., & Bratslavsky, E. (1999). Passion, intimacy, and time: Passionate love as a function of change in intimacy. *Personality and Social Psychology Review, 3*(1), 49–67.

Baumeister, R. F., Smart, L., & Boden, J. M. (1996). Relation of threatened egotism to violence and aggression: The dark side of high self-esteem. *Psychological Review, 103*(1), 5–33.

Baumgartner, R. (2021). "I think that I'm not a relationship person": Bisexual women's accounts of (internalised) binegativity in non-monogamous relationships narratives. In E. Maliepaard & R. Baumgartner (Eds.), *Bisexuality in Europe: Sexual citizenship, romantic relationships, and bi+ identities* (pp. 115–130). Routledge.

Beck, U., & Beck-Gernsheim, E. (1995). *The normal chaos of love.* Polity.

Beckerman, S., & Valentine, P. (Eds.). (2002). *Cultures of multiple fathers: The theory and practice of partible paternity in lowland South America.* University of Florida Press.

Beggan, J. K. (2021). *The dilemma of coalition instability in consensual nonmonogamy: Three against two against one.* Rowman & Littlefield.

Bell, L. (2017). *The "other" in 9/11 literature: If you see something, say something.* Palgrave Macmillan.

Bell, R. (2007). *Sex God: Exploring the endless connections between sexuality and spirituality.* HarperCollins.

Bengston, V. L. (2001). Beyond the nuclear family: Increasing the importance of multi-generational bonds. *Journal of Marriage and Family, 63*(1), 1–16.

Benhabib, S. (2002). *The claims of culture: Equality and diversity in the global era.* Princeton University Press.

Benjamin, J. (1988). *The bonds of love: Psychoanalysis, feminism, and the problem of domination*. Pantheon Books.

Benson, K. L. (2017). Tensions of subjectivity: The instability of queer polyamorous identity and community. *Sexualities, 20*(1–2), 24–40.

Benson, K. L. (2019). Margins of identity: Queer polyamorous women's navigation of identity. In B. L. Simula, J. E. Sumerau, & A. Miller (Eds.), *Expanding the rainbow: Exploring the relationships of bi+, polyamorous, kinky, ace, intersex, and trans people* (pp. 95–105). Brill Sense.

Benson, P. J. (2008). *The polyamory handbook*. Author House.

Ben-Ze'ev, A., & Brunning, L. (2018). How complex is your love? The case of romantic compromises and polyamory. *Journal for the Theory of Social Behaviour, 48*(1), 98–116.

Ben-Ze'ev, A., & Goussinsky, R. (2008). *In the name of love: Romantic ideology and its victims*. Oxford University Press.

Berger, B. (2017). *The family in the modern age: More than a lifestyle choice*. Routledge.

Berger, M. T., & Guidroz, K. (2009). (Eds.). *The intersectional approach: Transforming the academy through race, class, and gender*. The University of North Carolina Press.

Bergstrand, C. R., & Sinski, J. B. (2010). *Swinging in America: Love, sex, and marriage in the 21st century*. Praeger.

Bering, J. (2013, November 2). Ian Stevenson's case for the afterlife: Are we "skeptics" really just cynics? *Scientific American*. https://blogs.scientificamerican.com/bering -in-mind/ian-stevensone28099s-case-for-the-afterlife-are-we-e28098skepticse28099-r eally-just-cynics/

Berkowitz, R. (2003). *Stayin' alive: The invention of safe sex*. Westview Press.

Berman, M. I., & Frazier, P. A. (2005). Relationship power and betrayal experience as predictors of reactions to infidelity. *Personality and Social Psychology Bulleting, 31*(12), 1617–1627.

Betzig, L. (1989). Causes of conjugal dissolution: A cross-cultural study. *Current Anthropology, 30*(5), 654–676.

Betzig, L. (1992). Roman monogamy. *Ethology and Sociobiology, 13*(5–6), 351–383.

Betzig, L. (1995). Medieval monogamy. *Journal of Family History, 20*(2), 181–216.

Betzig, L. L. (1986). *Despotism and differential reproduction: A Darwinian view of history*. Aldine de Gruyter.

Bevacqua, J. (2018). Adding to the rainbow of diversity: Caring for children of polyamorous families. *Journal of Pediatric Health Care, 32*(5), 490–493.

Bhattacharyya, G. (1998). *Tales of dark-skinned women*. UCL Press.

Bickford, J., Barton, S. E., & Mandalia, S. (2007). Chronic genital herpes and disclosure . . . The influence of stigma. *International Journal of STD and AIDS, 18*(9), 589–592.

Birnbaum, G. E., Reis, H. T., Mikulincer, M., Gillath, O., & Orpaz, A. (2006). When sex is more than sex: Attachment orientations, sexual experience, and relationship quality. *Journal of Personality and Social Psychology, 91*(5), 929–943.

Block, J. (2008). *Open: Love, sex and life in an open marriage*. Seal Press.

Blow, A. J., & Hartnett, K. (2005). Infidelity in committed relationships II: A substantive review. *Journal of Marital and Family Therapy, 31*(2), 217–233.

Blumer, M. L. C., Haym, C., Zimmerman, K., & Prouty, A. (2014). What's one got to do with it? Considering monogamous privilege. *Family Therapy Magazine, 13*(2), 28–33.

Bogaert, A. F. (2015). Asexuality: What it is and why it matters. *The Journal of Sex Research, 52*(4), 362–379.

Bonello, K. (2009). Gay monogamy and extra-dyadic sex: A critical review of the theoretical and empirical literature. *Counselling Psychology Review, 24*(3–4), 51–65.

Boone, D. (n.d.). *Non-jealousy in polyamorous relationships: Countering evolution, or driving it forward?* [Unpublished manuscript]. https://www.academia.edu/19579836/Non-jealousy_in_Polyamorous_Relationships_Countering_Evolution_or_Driving_it_Forward

Borgerhoff Mulder, M. (2009). Serial monogamy as polygyny or polyandry? Marriage in the Tanzanian Pimbwe. *Human Nature, 20*(2), 130–150.

Bornstein, K., & Bergman, S. B. (Eds.). (2010). *Gender outlaws: The next generation.* Seal Press.

Bowlby, J. (1969). *Attachment and loss: Vol. 1. Attachment.* Basic Books.

Boyarin, D. (1995). Body politic among the brides of Christ: Paul and the origins of Christian sexual renunciation. In G. L. Gimbush & W. S. Lowe (Eds.), *Asceticism* (pp. 459–478). Oxford University Press.

Boyce, C. J., Wood, A. W., & Powdthavee, N. (2013). Is personality fixed? Personality changes as much as "variable" economic factors and more strongly predicts changes to life satisfaction. *Social Indicators Research, 111*(1), 287–305.

Brackett, M. A., Rivers, S. E., Shiffman, S., Lerner, N., & Salovey, P. (2006). Relating emotional abilities to social functioning: A comparison of self-report and performance measures of emotional intelligence. *Journal of Personality and Social Psychology, 91*(4), 780–795.

Bradbury, T. N., & Karney, B. R. (2014). (Eds.). *Intimate relationships* (2nd ed.). W.W. Norton & Company.

Braida, N. (2021). Plurisexualities and consensual non-monogamies: Challenging normativities in Italy. In E. Maliepaard & R. Baumgartner (Eds.), *Bisexuality in Europe: Sexual citizenship, romantic relationships, and bi+ identities* (pp. 131–145). Routledge.

Brake, E. (2012). *Minimizing marriage: Marriage, morality, and the law.* Oxford University Press.

Brake, E. (2014). Recognizing care: The case for friendship and polyamory. *Syracuse Law and Civic Engagement Forum, 1*(1). http://slace.syr.edu/issue-1-2013-14-on-equality/recognizing-care-the-case-for-friendship-and-polyamory/

Brake, E. (Ed.). (2016). *After marriage: Rethinking marital relationships.* Oxford University Press.

Brake, E. (2018). Do subversive weddings challenge amatonormativity? Polyamorous weddings and romantic love ideals. *Analyze: Journal of Gender and Feminist Studies, 11*, 61–84.

Bramly, S. (1994). *Macumba: The teachings of Maria-José, mother of the gods* (Trans. M Bogin). City Lights Books. (Original work published 1977)

Branden, N. (2008). *The psychology of romantic love: Romantic love in an anti-romantic age.* Jeremy P. Tarcher/Penguin.

Brandon, M. (2010). *Monogamy: The untold story.* Praeger.

Brandon, M. (2016). Monogamy and nonmonogamy: Evolutionary considerations and treatment challenges. *Sexual Medicine Reviews, 4*(4), 343–352.

Brandt, J. (2002). *The 50-mile rule: Your guide to infidelity and extramarital etiquette.* Ten Speed.

Brecher, B. (2012). The family and neoliberalism: Time to revive a critique. *Ethics and Social Welfare, 6*(2), 157–167.

Brennan, J., & Jaworski, J. (2015). *Markets without limits: Moral virtues and commercial interests.* Routledge.

Brewer, W. F., & Lambert, B. L. (2001). The theory-ladenness of observation and the theory-ladenness of the rest of the scientific process. *Philosophy of Science, 68*(3), 176–186.

Brewis, A., & Meyer, M. (2005). Marital coitus across the life course. *Journal of Biosocial Science, 37*(4), 499–518.

Bricker, M. E., & Horne, S. E. (2007). Gay men in long-term relationships: The impact of monogamy and non-monogamy on relational health. *Journal of Couple & Relationship Therapy, 6*(4), 27–47.

Brizendine, L. (2006). *The female brain.* Broadway Books.

Brogaard, B. (2015). *On romantic love: Simple truths about a complex emotion.* Oxford University Press.

Brotto, L. A., & Yule, M. (2016). Asexuality: Sexual orientation, paraphilia, sexual dysfunction, or none of the above? *Archives of Sexual Behavior, 46*(3), 619–627.

Brown, J. (2019). *Grounded spirituality.* Enrealment Press.

Brown, J. (2020). "Non-monogamy is the hardest thing to disclose": Expressions of gender, sexuality, and relationships on the university campus. *Women's Studies Journal, 34*(1/2), 107–115.

Brown, R. P., Baughman, K., & Carvallo, M. (2018). Culture, masculine honor, and violence toward women. *Personality and Social Psychology Bulletin, 44*(4), 538–549.

Brubaker, R. (2016). *Trans: Gender and race in an age of unsettled identities.* Princeton University Press.

Brunning, L. (2016). The distinctiveness of polyamory. *Journal of Applied Philosophy, 33*(3), 1–19.

Buckland, M. S., Galloway, J. B., Fhogartaigh, C. N., Meredith, L., Provine, N. M., Bloor, S., Ogbe, A., Zelek, W. M., Smielewska, A., Yakovleva, A., Mann, T., Bergamaschi, L., Turner, L., Mescia, F., Toonen, E. J. M., Hackstein, C-P., Akther, H. D., Vieira, V. A., Ceron-Gutierrez, L. et al. (2020). Treatment of COVID-19 with remdesivir in the absence of humoral immunity: A case report. *Nature Communications, 11*, 6385. https://doi.org/10.1038/s41467-020-19761-2

Buddhaghosa, B. (1976). *The path of purification (Visuddhimagga, 2 Vol.)* (Bhikkhu Nyanamoli, Trans.). Shambhala.

Budgeon, S. (2008). Couple culture and the production of singleness. *Sexualities, 11*(3), 301–316.

Burchell, J. L., & Ward, J. (2011). Sex drive, attachment style, relationship status and previous infidelity as predictors of sex differences in romantic jealousy. *Personality and Individual Differences, 51*(5), 657–661.

Burgess, E. W., & Locke, H. J. (1945). *The family: From institution to companionship.* American Book.

Burleigh, T. J., & Rubel, A. N. (2020). Counting polyamorists who count: Prevalence and definitions of an under-researched form of consensual nonmonogamy. *Sexualities, 23*(1–2), 3–27.

Burrus, V. (2004). *The sex lives of the saints: An erotics of ancient hagiography.* University of Pennsylvania Press.

Bushell, R., & Sheldon, P. J. (Eds.). (2009). *Wellness and tourism: Mind, body, spirit, place.* Cognizant.

Buss, D. M. (1994). *The evolution of desire: Strategies of human mating.* Basic Books.

Buss, D. M. (2000a). *The dangerous passion: Why jealousy is as necessary as love or sex.* Free Press.

Buss, D. M. (2000b). Desires in human mating. *Annals of the New York Academy of Sciences, 907*(1), 39–49.

Buss, D. M. (2006). Strategies of human mating. *Psychological Topics, 15*(2), 239–260.

Buss, D. M., & Malamuth, N. (Eds.). (1996). *Sex, power, conflict: Evolutionary and feminist perspectives.* Oxford University Press.

Buss, D. M., & Shackelford, T. K. (1997). Susceptibility to infidelity in the first year of marriage. *Journal of Research in Personality, 31*(2), 193–221.

Buss, D. M., & Schmitt, D. E. (1993). Sexual strategies theory: An evolutionary perspective on human mating. *Psychological Review, 100*(2), 204–232.

Butler, J. (1997). Imitation and gender subordination. In L. Nicholson (Ed.), *The second wave: A reader in feminist theory* (pp. 300–315). Routledge.

Butler, J. (2004). *Undoing gender.* Routledge.

Butzer, B., & Campbell, L. (2008). Adult attachment, sexual satisfaction, and relationship satisfaction: A study of married couples. *Personal Relationships, 15*(1), 141–154.

Buunk, B. P., & Dijkstra, P. (2004). Men, women, and infidelity: Sex differences in extradyadic sex and jealousy. In J. Duncombe, K. Harrison, G. Allen, & D. Marsden (Eds.), *The state of affairs: Explorations in infidelity and commitment* (pp. 103–120). Lawrence Erlbaum Associates.

Buunk, A. P., Massar, K., & Dijkstra, P. (2007). A social cognitive evolutionary approach to jealousy: The automatic evaluation of one's romantic rivals. In J. P. Forgas, M. G. Haselton, & W. von Hippel (Eds.), *Sydney symposium of social psychology. Evolution and the social mind: Evolutionary psychology and social cognition* (pp. 213–228). Routledge/Taylor & Francis Group.

Byers, E. S. (2005). Relationship satisfaction and sexual satisfaction: A longitudinal study of individuals in long-term relationships. *Journal of Sex Research, 42*(2), 113–118.

Cabezón, J. I. (2017). *Sexuality in classical South Asian Buddhism.* Wisdom Publications.

Callis, A. S. (2014). Bisexual, pansexual, queer: Non-binary identities and the sexual borderlands. *Sexualities, 17*(1–2), 63–80.

Campbell, A. (2012). The study of sex differences: Feminism and biology. *Zeitschrift für Psychologie, 220*(2), 137–143.

Campbell, K., & Wright, D. W. (2010). Marriage today: Exploring the incongruence between Americans' beliefs and practices. *Journal of Comparative Family Studies, 41*(3), 329–345.

Cantor, S. (2014). *Between monogamy and polyamory.* https://betweenandbeyondblog.wordpress.com/2014/08/14/between-monogamy-polyamory-2/

Carastathis, A. (2016). *Intersectionality: Origins, contestations, horizons.* University of Nebraska Press.

Cardoso, D. (2018). Celos, género y comunidad. In S. Cendral (Ed.), *(h)amor³: Celos y culpas* (pp. 239–249). Continta Me Tienes.

Carey, M. (2013, October 16). *Is polyamory a choice?* Slate. https://slate.com/human-interest/2013/10/is-polyamory-a-choice.htmls

Carlström, C., & Andersson, C. (2019). Living outside protocol: Polyamorous orientations, bodies, and queer temporalities. *Sexuality & Culture, 23*(4), 1315–1331.

Carnes, P., Delmonico, D. L., & Griffin, E. (2007). *In the shadows of the net: Breaking free of compulsive online sexual behavior.* Hazelden.

Carr, K. L. (1992). *The banalization of nihilism: Twentieth-century responses to meaninglessness.* State University of New York Press.

Carter, C. S., & Perkeybile, A. M. (2018). The monogamy paradox: What do love and sex have to do with it. *Frontiers in Ecology and Evolution, 6*(202). https://doi.org/10.3389/fevo.2018.00202

Castells, M. (2010). *The power of identity* (2nd. ed.). Wiley-Blackwell.

Chalmers, H. (2019). Is monogamy morally permissible? *The Journal of Value Inquiry, 53*(2), 225–241.

Chambliss, K. (2017). *Jealousy survival guide: How to feel safe, happy, and secure in an open relationship* [eBook]. (E. Sheff, Ed.). Loving Without Boundaries.

Chang, H. (2005). A case for old-fashioned observability, and a reconstructive empiricism. *Philosophy of Science, 72*(5), 876–887.

Chang, R. S., & McCristal Culp, Jr., J. (2002). After intersectionality. *UMKC Law Review, 71*(2), 485–491.

Chapais, B. (2010). The deep structure of human society: Primate origins and evolution. In P. M. Kappeler & J. B. Silk (Eds.), *Mind the gap: Tracing the origins of human universals* (pp. 19–51). Springer.

Chapais, B. (2013). Monogamy, strongly bounded groups, and the evolution of human social structure. *Evolutionary Anthropology, 22*(2), 52–65.

Charles, M. (2002). Monogamy and its discontents: On winning the Oedipal war. *American Journal of Psychoanalysis, 62*(2), 119–143.

Charny, I. W. (1992). *Existential/dialectical marital therapy: Breaking the secret code of marital therapy.* Brunner Mazel.

Charny, I. W., & Asinelli-Tal, S. (2004). Study of "sex-less" (sex avoidant) young couples. *Journal Family Psychotherapy, 16* (1/2) 197–218.

Chasin, C. J. (2019). Asexuality and the re/construction of sexual orientation. In B. L. Simula, J. E. Sumerau, & A. Miller (Eds.), *Expanding the rainbow: Exploring the relationships of bi+, polyamorous, kinky, ace, intersex, and trans people* (pp. 209–219). Brill Sense.

Cheng, S., & Powell, B. (2015). Measurement, methods, and divergent parents: Reassessing the effects of same-sex parents. *Social Science Research, 52*, 615–626.

Cherlin, A. (2009). *The marriage-go-round: The state of marriage and the family in America today.* Alfred A. Knopf.

Chiasson, M. A., Hirshfield, S., Humberstone, M., DiFilippi, J., Koblin, B. A., & Reimen, R. H. (2005). Increased high risk sexual behavior after September 11 in men who have sex with men: An Internet survey. *Archives of Sexual Behavior, 34*(5), 527–535.

Chivers, M., Rieger, G., Latty, E., & Bailey, J. M. (2004). A sex difference in the specificity of sexual arousal. *Psychological Science, 15*(11), 736–744.

Chodorow, N. (1978). *The reproduction of mothering: Psychoanalysis and the sociology of gender.* University of California Press.

Chopel, G. (1992). *Tibetan arts of love: Sex, orgasm, and spiritual healing* (J. Hopkins & D. Y. Yuthok, Trans). Snow Lion Publications.

Christopher, F. S., & Sprecher, S. (2004). Sexuality in marriage, dating, and other relationships: A decade review. *Journal of Marriage and Family, 62*(4), 999–1017.

Cianci, R., & Gambrel, P. (2003). Maslow's hierarchy of needs: Does it apply in a collectivist culture? *Journal of Applied Management and Entrepreneurship, 8*(2), 143–161

Citci, S. H. (2014). The rise of monogamy. *SERIEs, 5*, 377–397. https://doi.org/10.1007/s13209-014-0113-y

Clanton, G. (2006) Jealousy and envy. In J. E. Stets & J. H. Turner (Eds.), *Handbook of the sociology of emotions* (pp. 410–442). Springer.

Clardy, J. L. (2018). "I don't want to be a playa no more": An exploration of the denigrating effects of "player" as a stereotype against African American polyamorous men. *Analyze: Journal of Gender and Feminist Studies, 11*, 38–60.

Clinton, H. R. (1996). *It takes a village: And other lessons children teach us.* Simon & Schuster.

Clinton, H. R. (2006). *It takes a village: And other lessons children teach us* (Tenth Year Anniversary Edition). Simon & Schuster.

Clinton, H. R. (2017). *It takes a village: And other lessons children teach us* (Illustrated by Marla Frazee). Simon & Schuster.

Cohen, P. N. (2012). *Family inequality: 200 researchers respond to Regnerus paper.* https://familyinequality.wordpress.com/2012/06/29/200-researchers-respond-to-regnerus-paper/

Cohen, P. N. (2016). Multiple-decrement life table estimates of divorce rates. *Open Science Framework.* https://osf.io/zber3/

Cohen, P. N. (2018). *The family: Diversity, inequality, and social change* (2nd ed.). W. W. Norton & Company.

Cole, B. S., Hopkins, C. M., Tisak, J., Steel, J. L., & Carr, B. I. (2008). Assessing spiritual growth and spiritual decline following a diagnosis of cancer: Reliability and validity of the spiritual transformation scale. *Psycho-Oncology, 17*(2), 112–121.

Collins, L. (1999). Emotional adultery: Cybersex and commitment. *Social Theory and Practice, 25*(2), 243–270.

Collins, P. H. (2019). *Intersectionality as critical social theory*. Duke University Press.

Collins, P. H., & Bilge, S. (2016). *Intersectionality*. Polity Press.

Collins, S. (1998). *Nirvana and other Buddhist felicities*. Cambridge University Press.

Confer, J. C., Easton, J. A., Fleischman, D. S., Goetz, C. D., Lewis, D. M., Perilloux, C., & Buss, D. M. (2010). Evolutionary psychology: Controversies, questions, prospects, and limitations. *American Psychologist, 65*(2), 110–126.

Conkey, M. W., & Tringham, R. E. (1998). Archaeology and the goddess: Exploring the contours of feminist archeology. In D. C. Stanton & A. J. Stewart (Eds.), *Feminism in the academy* (pp. 199–247). The University of Michigan Press.

Conley, T. D., Matsick, J. L., Moors, A. C., Ziegler, A., & Rubin, J. D. (2015). Re-examining the effectiveness of monogamy as an STI-preventive strategy. *Preventive Medicine, 78*, 23–28.

Conley, T. D., & Moors, A. C. (2014). More oxygen please! How polyamorous relationship strategies may oxygenate marriage. *Psychological Inquiry, 25*(1), 56–63.

Conley, T. D., Moors, A. C., Matsick, J. L., & Ziegler, A. (2013). The fewer the merrier? Assessing stigma surrounding consensually non-monogamous romantic relationships. *Analyses of Social Issues and Public Policy, 13*(1), 1–30.

Conley, T. D., Moors, A. C., & Ziegler, A., & Karathanasis, C. (2012). Unfaithful individuals are less likely to practice safer sex than openly non-monogamous individuals. *The Journal of Sexual Medicine, 9*(6), 1559–1565.

Conley, T. D., Piemonte, J. L., Gusakova, S., & Rubin, J. D. (2017). Sexual satisfaction among individuals in monogamous and consensually non-monogamous relationships. *Journal of Social and Personal Relationships, 35*(4), 509–531.

Conley, T. D., Ziegler, A., & Moors, A. C. (2013). Backlash from the bedroom: Stigma mediates gender differences in acceptance of casual sex offers. *Psychology of Women Quarterly, 37*(3) 392–407.

Conley, T. D., Ziegler, A., Moors, A. C., Matsick, J. L., & Valentine, B. A. (2012). A critical examination of popular assumptions about the benefits and outcomes of monogamous relationships. *Personality and Social Psychology Review, 17*(2), 124–141.

Conner, R. P., & Sparks, D. H. (2004). *Queering Creole spiritual traditions: Lesbian, gay, bisexual, and transgender participation in African-inspired traditions in the Americas*. Harrington.

Conte, J. M. (2005). A review and critique of emotional intelligence measures. *Journal of Organizational Behavior, 26*(4), 433–440.

Coontz, S. (2005). *Marriage, a history: How love conquered marriage*. Viking Penguin.

Cooper, A., & Sportolari, L. (1997). Romance in cyberspace: Understanding online attraction. *Journal of Sex Education and Therapy, 22*(1), 7–14.

Copen, C. E., Leichliter, J. S., Spicknall, I. H., & Aral, S. O. (2019). STI risk reduction strategies among US adolescents and adults with multiple opposite-sex partners or perceived partner non-monogamy, 2011–2017. *Sexually Transmitted Diseases*. https //doi.org/10.1097/OLQ.0000000000001067

Copulsky, D. (2016). Asexual polyamory: Potential challenges and benefits. *Journal of Positive Psychology, 2*, 11–15.

Cott, N. F. (2002). *Public vows: A history of marriage and the nation*. Harvard University Press.

Cowell, E. B. (Ed.). (1895). *The Jataka or stories of the Buddha's former births, Vol II* (W. H. D. Rouse, Trans.). The University Press.

Cox II, D. (2009). Sacred sexuality and conservative American Christianity: Probing the boundaries. In A. Moore & C. Zuccarini (Eds.), *Persons and sexuality: Interdisciplinary reflections* (pp. 53–64). Inter-Disciplinary Press.

Cramer, R. J., Langhinrichsen-Rohling, J., Kaniuka, A. R., Wilsey, C. N., Mennicke, A., Wright, S., Montanaro, E., Bowling, J., & Heron, K. E. (2020). Preferences in information processing, marginalized identity, and non-monogamy: Understanding factors in suicide-related behavior among members of the alternative sexual community. *International Journal of Environmental Research and Public Health, 17*(3233). https://doi:10.3390/ijerph17093233

Crawford, M., & Popp, D. (2003). Sexual double standards: A review and methodological critique of two decades of research. *Journal of Sex Research, 40*(1), 13–26.

Creenshaw, K. (1989). Demarginalizing the intersection of race and sex: A black feminist critique of antidiscriminatory doctrine, feminist theory and antiracist politics. *University of Chicago Legal Forum, 1*(8), 139–167.

Cruz, J. (2016). A utilitarian defense of non-monogamy. *Polymath: An Interdisciplinary Arts and Sciences Journal, 6*(2), 46–52.

Cutas, D. (2018). Editorial: On love [Monograph: Analyzing love]. *Analyze: Journal of Gender and Feminist Studies, 11*, 5–15.

Dabhoiwala, F. (2012). *The origins of sex: A history of the first sexual revolution.* Oxford University Press.

Daly, M., Wilson, M., & Weghorst, S. J. (1982). Male sexual jealousy. *Ethology and Sociobiology, 3*(1), 11–27.

Daly, S. J. (2021). Bisexual women and monogamy. In E. Maliepaard & R. Baumgartner (Eds.), *Bisexuality in Europe: Sexual citizenship, romantic relationships, and bi+ identities* (pp. 100–114). Routledge.

Davenport, B., & Scott, S. J. (2018). *Mindful relationship habits: 25 practices for couples to enhance intimacy, nurture closeness, and grow a deeper connection.* Oldtown Publishing.

Dawkins, R. (1978). *The selfish gene.* Oxford University Press.

Dawkins, R. (2006). *The God delusion.* Houghton Mifflin.

Dawson, S. J., Suschinsky, K. D., & Lalumière, M. L. (2013). Habituation of sexual responses in men and women: A test of the preparation hypothesis of women's genital responses. *Journal of Sexual Medicine, 10*(4), 990–1000.

de la Croix, D., & Mariani, F. (2015). From polygyny to serial monogamy: A unified theory of marriage institutions. *Review of Economic Studies, 82*(2), 565–607.

de Lauretis, T. (1991). Queer theory: Lesbian and gay sexualities: An introduction. *differences: A Journal of Feminist Cultural Studies, 3*(2), iii–xviii.

de Munck, V. C., & Kronenfeld, D. B. (2016). Romantic love in the United States: Applying cultural models theory and methods. *SAGE Open, 6*(1), 1–17.

de Sousa, R. (2017). Love, jealousy, and compersion. In C. Grau & A. Smuts (Eds.), *The Oxford handbook of philosophy of love.* Oxford University Press. https://10.1093/oxfordhb/9780199395729.013.30

Debrot, A., Stellar, J. E., MacDonald, G., Keltner, D., & Impett, E. A. (2020). Is touch in romantic relationships universally beneficial for psychological well-being? The role of attachment avoidance. *Personality and Social Psychology Bulletin*. Online first publication. https://doi.org/10.1177/0146167220977709

Del Giudice, M., Gangestad, S. W., & Kaplan, H. S. (2015). Life history theory and evolutionary psychology. In D. Buss (Ed.), *The handbook of evolutionary psychology. Vol. 1: Foundations* (pp. 88–114). John Wiley & Sons.

DeLamater, J. D., & Hyde, J. S. (1998). Essentialism vs. social constructivism in the study of human sexuality. *The Journal of Sex Research, 35*(1), 10–18.

Dennett, D. (2006). *Breaking the spell: Religion as a natural phenomenon*. Viking.

DePaulo, B. (2006). *Singled out: How singles are stereotyped, stigmatized, and ignored, and still live happily ever after*. St. Martin's Press.

Deri, J. (2015). *Love's refraction: Jealousy and compersión in queer women's polyamorous relationships*. University of Toronto Press.

Derrida, J. (1981). *Positions* (A. Bass, Trans.). University of Chicago Press.

Derrida, J. (1982). *Margins of philosophy*. University of Chicago Press.

Dessein, B., & Teng, G. (Eds.). (2016). *Text, history, and philosophy: Abhidharma across Buddhist scholastic traditions*. Brill.

DeSteno, D., Barlett, M. Y., Braverman, J., & Salovey, P. (2002). Sex differences in jealousy: Evolutionary mechanism or artifact of measurement. *Journal of Personality and Social Psychology, 83*(3), 1103–1116.

DeSteno, D., Valdesolo, P., & Barlett, M. Y. (2006). Jealousy and the threatened self: Getting to the heart of the green-eyed monster. *Journal of Personality and Social Psychology, 91*(4), 626–641.

Dews, P. (Ed.). (1986). *Autonomy and solidarity: Interviews with Jürgen Habermas*. New Left Books.

Diamond, L. M. (2013). Sexuality in relationships. In J. A. Simpson & L. Campbell (Eds.), *The Oxford handbook of close relationships* (pp. 589–614). Oxford University Press.

DiBello, A. M., Rodriguez, L. M., Hadden, B. W., & Neighbors, C. (2015). The green eyed monster in the bottle: Relationship contingent self-esteem, romantic jealousy, and alcohol–related problems. *Addictive Behaviors, 49*, 52–58.

Diener, E., & Seligman, M. E. P. (2002). Very happy people. *Psychological Science, 13*(1), 81–84.

Dietrich, D. M., & Schuett, J. M. (2013). Culture of honor and attitudes toward intimate partner violence in Latinos. *SAGE Open* (April-June), 1–11. https://doi.org/10.1177/2158244013489685

Donnelly, D., & Burgess, E. (2008). The decision to remain in an involuntarily celibate relationship. *Journal of Marriage and Family, 70*(2), 519–535.

Döring, N. (2002). Studying online-love and cyber-romance. In B. Batinic, U.-D. Reips, & M. Bosnjak (Eds.), *Online social sciences* (pp. 333–356). Hogrefe & Huber Publishers.

Dow, C. L. (1997). *Sarava!: Afro-Brazilian magick*. Llewellyn.

Dow, M. M., & Eff, E. A. (2013). When one wife is enough: A cross-cultural study of the determinants of monogamy. *Journal of Social, Evolutionary, and Cultural Psychology, 73*(3), 211–238.

Duck-Chong, L. (2017). Non-hierarchical polyamory: Stepping off the relationship escalator. *Archer* (June 20). https://archermagazine.com.au/2017/06/non-hierarchical-polyamory/

Duckworth, D. (2014). How nonsectarian is "nonsectarian"?: Jorge Ferrer's religious pluralist alternative to Tibetan Buddhist inclusivism. *Sophia, 53*(3), 339–348.

Duffy, A., Dawson, D. L., & das Nair, R. (2016). Pornography addictions in adults: A systematic review of definitions and reported impact. *The Journal of Sexual Medicine, 13*(5), 760–777.

Duma, U. (2009). *Jealousy and compersion in close relationships: Coping styles by relationship types* [Diploma Thesis, Johannes Gutenberg University Mainz]. GRIN Verlag.

Eagle, M. (2007). Attachment and sexuality. In D. Diamond, S. J. Blatt, & J. D. Lichtenberg (Eds.), *Attachment and Sexuality* (pp. 27–78). Taylor & Francis.

Eagleshadow, P. P. (2016). *The fourteen love relationships of the Awansa-Ta'pish.* https://freelovecommunity.wordpress.com/2016/03/

Eagly, A. H., & Wood, W. (2013). Feminism and evolutionary psychology: Moving forward. *Sex Roles: A Journal of Research, 69*(9–10), 549–556.

Easton, D. (2010). Making friends with jealousy: Therapy with polyamorous clients. In M. Barker & D. Langdridge (Eds.), *Understanding non-monogamies* (pp. 207–211). Routledge.

Easton, D., & Liszt, C. (1997). *The ethical slut: A guide to infinite sexual possibilities.* Greenery Press.

Ebersohn, S., & Bouwer, A. C. (2015). A bio-ecological interpretation of relationships challenges in the context of the reconstituted family. *South African Journal of Education, 35*(2), 1–11.

Eda, H. (2013). Intimate agency: A radical sexual revolution. In N. de Haro García & M.-A. Tseliou (Eds.), *Gender and love: Interdisciplinary perspectives* (2nd ed., pp. 13–20). Brill.

Edelstein, S. (2011). *Sex and the spiritual teacher: Why it happens, when it's a problem, and what we all can do.* Wisdom Publications.

Edwards, P. (1996). *Reincarnation: A critical examination.* Prometheus Books.

Eisbruger, C. L. (2006). Secularization, religiosity, and the United States. *Indiana Journal of Global Legal Studies, 13*(2), 445–472.

Eliade, M. (1964). *Shamanism: Archaic techniques of ecstasy* (W. R. Trask, Trans.). Bollingen.

Eliens, J. H. (2009). *The spirituality of sex.* Praeger.

Elizabeth, A. (2013). Challenging the binary: Sexual identity that is not duality. *Journal of Bisexuality, 13*(3), 329–337.

Eller, C. (2000). *The myth of matriarchal prehistory: Why an invented past won't give women a future.* Beacon Press.

Ellsworth, R. M. (2011). The human that never evolved: A review of Christopher Ryan and Caclida Jethá, *Sex and dawn: How we mate, how we stray, and what it means for modern sexuality. Evolutionary Psychology, 9*(3), 325–335.

Emens, E. (2004). Monogamy's law: Compulsory monogamy and polyamorous existence. *New York University Review of Law and Social Change, 29*(2), 277–376.

Enciso Domínguez, G. (2018). La gran pregunta de los celos: Comprendiendo el poliamor. In S. Cendral (Ed.), *(h)amor³: Celos y culpas* (pp. 151–173). Continta Me Tienes.

Engel, J. (2006). *The epidemic: A global history of AIDS.* Smithsonian Books/Collins.

Engler, J. (2003). Being somebody and being nobody: A reexamination of the understanding of self in psychoanalysis and Buddhism. In J. D. Safran (Ed.), *Psychoanalysis and Buddhism: An unfolding dialogue* (pp. 37–100). Wisdom Publications.

Epstein, M. (2007). *Psychotherapy without the self: A Buddhist perspective*. Yale University Press.

Erber, R., & Erber, M. (2017). *Intimate relationships: Issues, theories, and research* (3rd. ed.). Routledge.

Erickson, A. L. (2005). The marital economy in comparative perspective. In M. Ågren & A.L. Erickson (Eds.), *The marital economy in Scandinavia and Britain, 1400–1900* (pp. 3–20). Ashgate.

Escoffier, J. (2011). Sex, safety, and the trauma of AIDS. *Women's Studies Quarterly, 39*(1/2), 129–138.

Essau, C. A., Sasagawa, S., Lewinsohn, P. M., & Rohde, P. (2018). The impact of pre- and perinatal factors on psychopathology in adulthood. *Journal of Affective Disorders, 236*, 52–59.

Eyler, D. R., & Baridon, A. P. (1992, May 1). More than just friends: Learn how to harness your workplace productively outside the bedroom. *Psychology Today*. https://www.psychologytoday.com/us/articles/199205/more-just-friends?page=5

Fagan, P. F., & Churchill, A. (2012). *The effects of divorce on children*. Research Synthesis. Marriage & Religion Research Institute. https://downloads.frc.org/EF/EF12A22.pdf

Fairbrother, N., Hart, T. A., & Fairbrother, M. (2019). Open relationship prevalence, characteristics, and correlates in a nationally representative sample of Canadian adults. *Journal of Sex Research, 56*(6), 695–704.

Farrel, B., & Farrel, P. (2006). *Red-hot monogamy: Making your marriage sizzle*. Harvest House Publishers.

Faure, B. (1998). *The red thread: Buddhist approaches to sexuality*. Princeton University Press.

Faure, B. (2003). *The power of denial: Buddhism, purity, and gender*. Princeton University Press.

Faure, B. (2009). *Unmasking Buddhism*. Wiley-Blackwell.

Fay, B. (1987). *Critical social science: Liberation and its limits*. Cornell University Press.

Fay, B. (1996). *Contemporary philosophy of social science: A multicultural approach*. Blackwell.

Faye, G. (2014). *Sex and deviance*. Arktos Media Ltd.

Feeney, J. A., & Noller, P. (1990). Attachment style as a predictor of adult romantic relationships. *Journal of Personality and Social Psychology, 58*(2), 281–291.

Feeney, J. A., & Noller, P. (2004). Attachment and sexuality in close relationships. In J. H. Harvey, A. Wenzel, & S. Sprecher (Eds.), *Handbook of sexuality in close relationships* (pp. 183–201). Erlbaum.

Fenigstein, A., & Peltz, R. (2002). Distress over the infidelity of a child's spouse: A crucial test of evolutionary and socialization hypotheses. *Personal Relationships, 9*(3), 301–312.

Fennell, J. (2018). "It's all about the journey": Skepticism and spirituality in the BDSM subculture. *Sociological Forum, 33*(4), 1045–1067.

Fern, J. (with E. Rickert & N. Samaran). (2020). *Polysecure: Attachment, trauma and consensual nonmonogamy*. Thorntree Press.

Ferrer, J. N. (2000). Transpersonal knowledge: A participatory approach to transpersonal phenomena. In T. Hart, P. Nelson, & K. Puhakka (Eds.), *Transpersonal knowing: Exploring the horizon of consciousness* (pp. 213–252). State University of New York Press.

Ferrer, J. N. (2002). *Revisioning transpersonal theory: A participatory vision of human spirituality*. State University of New York Press.

Ferrer, J. N. (2006). What's the opposite of jealousy? Questioning the Buddhist allegiance to monogamy. *Tricycle: The Buddhist Review* (Summer), 83–85.

Ferrer, J. N. (2007). Monogamy, polyamory, and beyond. *Tikkun: Culture, Spirituality, Politics, 22*(1), 37–43, 60–62.

Ferrer, J. N. (2008). Spiritual knowing as participatory enaction: An answer to the question of religious pluralism. In J. N. Ferrer & J. H. Sherman (Eds.), *The participatory turn: Spirituality, mysticism, religious studies* (pp. 135–169). State University of New York Press.

Ferrer, J. N. (2017). *Participation and the mystery: Transpersonal essays on psychology, education, and the mystery*. State University of New York Press.

Ferrer, J. N. (2018). Beyond the non/monogamy system: Fluidity, hybridity, and transcendence in intimate relationships. *Psychology and Sexuality, 9*(1), 3–20.

Fincham, F. D., & May, R. W. (2017). Infidelity in romantic relationships. *Current Opinion in Psychology, 13*, 70–74.

Finkel, E. J., Cheung, E. O., Emery, L. F., Craswell, K. L., & Larson, G. M. (2015). The suffocation model: Why marriage in America is becoming an all-or-nothing institution. *Current Directions in Psychological Science, 24*(3), 238–244.

Finkel, E. J., Hui, C. M., Carswell, K. L., & Larson, G. M. (2014). The suffocation of marriage: Climbing Mount Maslow without enough oxygen. *Psychological Inquiry, 25*(1), 1–41.

Finlay, S.-J., & Clarke, V. (2003). "A marriage of inconvenience?" Feminist perspectives on marriage. *Feminism & Psychology, 13*(4), 415–420.

Finn, M. (2010). Conditions of freedom in practices of non-monogamous commitment. In M. Barker & D. Langdridge (Eds.), *Understanding non-monogamies* (pp. 225–236). Routledge.

Finn, M., & Malson, H. (2008). Speaking of home truth: (Re)productions of dyadic-containment in non-monogamous relationships. *British Journal of Sociology, 47*(3), 519–533.

Firestein, B. A. (1996). (Ed.). *Bisexuality: The psychology and politics of an invisible minority* SAGE.

Fischer, T. F. C., De Graaf, P. M., & Kalmijn, M. (2005). Friendly and antagonistic contact between former spouses after divorce: Patterns and determinants. *Journal of Family Issues, 26*(8), 1131–1163.

Fisher, H. (1992). *Anatomy of love: A natural history of mating, marriage, and why we stray*. Ballantine.

Fisher, H. (2004). *Why we love: The nature and chemistry of romantic love*. Henry Holt & Co.

Fisher, H. E. (2011). Serial monogamy and clandestine adultery: Evolution and consequences of the dual human reproductive strategy. In S. C. Roberts (Ed.), *Applied evolutionary psychology* (pp. 93–111). Oxford University Press.

Fleckenstein, J., & Cox II, D. (2015). The association of an open relationship orientation with health and happiness in a sample of older US adults. *Sexual and Relationship Therapy, 30*(1), 94–116.

Fleisher, R. M., & Foss-Morgan, R. (2016). *The sexless marriage: Rescuing a sexless marriage and making it all it can be using this empowering integrative approach.* Basic Health Publications.

Fletcher, G. O., Simpson, J. A., Campbell, L., & Overall, N. C. (2015). Pair-bonding, romantic love, and evolution: The curious case of *Homo Sapiens. Perspectives on Psychological Science, 10*(1), 20–36.

Foley, L., & Fraser, J. (1998). A research note on post-dating relationships: The social embeddedness of redefining romantic couplings. *Sociological Perspectives, 41*(1), 209–219.

Foster, B. M., & Foster, M. (1997). *Three in love: Ménages à trois from ancient to modern times.* Harper Collins.

Foster, J. D. (2016). Serial monogamy. In C. L. Shehan (Ed.), *The Wiley Blackwell encyclopedia of family studies* (Vol. 3) (pp. 1739–1741). Wiley-Blackwell.

Foxwood, O. (2007). *The faery teachings.* Stewart Books.

Fraley, R. C., & Davis, K. E. (1997). Attachment formation and transfer in young adults' close friendships and romantic relationships. *Personal Relationships, 4*(2), 131–144.

Fraley, R. C., Roisman, G. I., Booth-LaForce, C., Owen, M. T., & Holland, A. S. (2013). Interpersonal and genetic origins of adult attachment styles: A longitudinal study from infancy to early adulthood. *Journal of Personality and Social Psychology, 104*(5), 817–838.

Fraley, R. C., & Shaver, P. R. (2000). Adult romantic attachment: Theoretical developments, emerging controversies, and unanswered questions. *Review of General Psychology, 4*(2), 132–154.

Franceschi, G. J. (2006). *Women maintaining a consensually non-monogamous relationship: A qualitative investigation* (Publication No. 3199398) [Doctoral dissertation, Aliant International University]. ProQuest Dissertations and Theses Global.

Frank, E., Anderson, C., & Rubinstein, D. (1978). Frequency of sexual dysfunctions in normal couples. *New England Journal of Medicine, 299*(3), 111–115.

Frank, K., & DeLamater, J. (2010). Deconstructing monogamy: Boundaries, identities, and fluidities across relationships. In M. Barker & D. Langdridge (Eds.), *Understanding non-monogamies* (pp. 9–22). Routledge.

Freitas, D. (2013). *The end of sex: How hookup culture is leaving a generation unhappy, sexually unfulfilled, and confused about intimacy.* Basic Books.

Freud, S. (1955). Some neurotic mechanisms in jealousy, paranoia, and homosexuality. In J. Strachey (Ed. and Trans.), *The standard edition of the complete works of Sigmund Freud* (Vol. 18, pp. 223–232). Hogarth Press. (Original work published 1922)

Fuchs, E. (1983). *Sexual desire and love: Origins and history of the Christian ethics of sexuality and marriage* (M. Daigle, Trans.). Seabury Press.

Fuller, R. C. (2001). *Spiritual but not religious: Understanding unchurched America*. Oxford University Press.

Fuller, R. C. (2008). *Spirituality in the flesh: Bodily sources of religious experiences*. Oxford University Press.

Fuss, D. (1991). Inside/out. In D. Fuss (Ed.), *Inside/out: Lesbian theories, gay theories* (pp. 1–10). Routledge.

Gahran, A. (2017). *Stepping off the relationship escalator: Uncommon love and life*. Off the Escalator Enterprises.

Gangestad, S. W., & Simpson, J. A. (2000). The evolution of human mating: Trade-offs and strategic pluralism. *Behavior and Brain Sciences, 23*(4), 573–644.

Garber, M. (1992). *Vested interests: Cross-dressing and cultural anxiety*. Routledge.

Garcia, J. R., Reiber, C., Massey, S. G., & Merriwether, A. M. (2012). Sexual hookup culture: A review. *Review of General Psychology, 16*(2), 161–176.

Gardner, H. (1993). *Frames of mind: The theory of multiple intelligences*. Basic (Original work published 1983).

Garner, C., Person, M., Goddard, C., Patridge, A., & Bixby, T. (2019). Satisfaction in consensual nonmonogamy. *The Family Journal, 27*(2), 115–121.

Gergen, K. (1991). *The saturated self: Dilemmas of identity in contemporary life*. Basic Books.

Germino, D. (2019, May 23). *How to find joy in other's good fortune: Turning jealousy into inspiration*. Medium. https://medium.com/@dgermino/how-to-find-joy-in-others-good-fortune-8995eb5529a4

Gerrold, D. (1997). *Zen and the art of whatever*. http://www.taoism.net/articles/zenart.htm

Geuss, R. (1981). *The idea of a critical theory: Habermas and the Frankfurt school*. Cambridge University Press.

Giddens, A. (1992). *The transformation of intimacy: Sexuality, love, and eroticism in modern societies*. Stanford University Press.

Gimbutas, M. (1989). *The language of the goddess*. Thames & Hudson.

Gleig, A., & Boeving, N. G. (2009). Spiritual democracy: Beyond consciousness and culture. *Tikkun: Culture, Spirituality, Politics* (May/June), 64–68.

Goetz, A. T., Shackelford, T. K., Romero, G. A., Kaighobadi, F., & Miner, E. J. (2008). Punishment, proprietariness, and paternity: Men's violence against women from an evolutionary perspective. *Aggression and Violent Behavior, 13*(6), 481–489.

Goldfeder, M. (2017). *Legalizing plural marriage: The next frontier in family law*. (Brandeis Series on Gender, Culture, Religion, and Law). Brandeis University Press.

Goldfeder, M., & Sheff, E. (2013). Children of polyamorous families: A first empirical look. *Journal of Law and Social Deviance, 5*(1), 150–243.

Goldman, E. (1917). *Anarchism and other essays*. Mother Earth Publishing.

Goldstein, A., & Brandon, M. (2004). *Reclaiming desire: 4 keys to finding your lost libido*. St. Martin Press.

Goodman, C. (2009). *Consequences of compassion: An interpretation and defense of Buddhist Ethics*. Oxford University Press.

Gopaldas, A. (2013). Intersectionality 101. *Journal of Public Policy & Marketing, 32*(Special Issue), 90–94.

Goss, R. E. (2004). Proleptic sexual love: God's promiscuity reflected in Christian polyamory. *Theology and Sexuality, 11*(1), 52–63.

Gould, E. D., Moav, O., & Simhon, A. (2008). The mystery of monogamy. *American Economic Review, 98*(1), 333–357.

Green, A. I., Valleriani, J., & Adam, B. (2016). Marital monogamy as ideal and practice: The detraditionalization thesis in contemporary marriages. *Journal of Marriage and Family, 78*(2), 416–430.

Greenberg, S. (2019). Divine kink: A consideration of the evidence of BDSM as spiritual ritual. *International Journal of Transpersonal Studies, 38*(1), 220–235.

Greenway, C. (2007). Spirit. In O. Espin & J. B. Nickoloff (Eds.), *An introductory dictionary to theology and religious studies* (pp. 1315–1316). Liturgical Press.

Grof, S. (1985). *Beyond the brain: Birth, death, and transcendence in psychotherapy.* State University of New York Press.

Grunt-Mejer, K., & Campbell, C. (2016). Around consensual nonmonogamies: Assessing attitudes toward nonexclusive relationships. *Journal of Sex Research, 53*(1), 45–53.

Gusmano, B. (2018). Coming out through an intersectional perspective: Narratives of bisexuality and polyamory in Italy. *Journal of Bisexuality, 18*(1), 15–34.

Haag, P. (2011). *Marriage confidential: Love in a post-romantic age.* HarperCollins.

Habermas, J. (1973). *Theory and practice* (J. Viertel, Trans.). Beacon.

Habermas, J. (1992). *Postmetaphysical thinking: Philosophical essays* (W. M. Hohengarten, Trans.). The MIT Press.

Habermas, J. (2002). *Religion and rationality*. Polity Press.

Habermas, J. (2003). *Truth and justification* (B. Fultner, Trans.). The MIT Press.

Habermas, J. (2008). Secularism's crisis of faith: Notes on post-secular society. *New Perspectives Quarterly, 25*(4), 17–29.

Hacking, I. (1986). Making up people. In T. C. Heller & C. Brooke-Rose (Eds.), *Reconstructing individualism: Autonomy, individuality, and the self in Western thought* (pp. 222–236). Stanford University Press.

Hagemann, I. K. (2018). *Exploring pioneers in polyamory: alt.polycon attendance, current relationship status, and current identities.* https://archive.org/details/Exploring_Pi oneers_in_Polyamory___alt.polycon

Hall, S. (1992). The West and the rest: Discourse and power. In S. Hall & B. Gieben (Eds.), *Formations of modernity* (pp. 275–331). Polity Press.

Halpern, E. L. (1999). If love is so wonderful, what's so scary about MORE? *Journal of Lesbian Studies, 3*(1/2), 157–164.

Hamdan, S., Auerbach, J., & Apter, A. (2009). Polygamy and mental health of adolescents. *European Child and Adolescent Psychiatry, 18*(12), 755–760.

Hammack, P. L., Frost, D. M., & Hughes, S. D. (2019). Queer intimacies: A new paradigm for the study of relationship diversity. *The Journal of Sex Research, 56*(4–5), 556–592.

Hancock, A.-M. (2016). *Intersectionality: An intellectual history.* Oxford University Press.

Hanegraaff, W. J. (1998). *New Age religion and Western culture. Esotericism in the mirror of secular thought.* State University of New York Press.

Hanson, N. R. (1958). *Patterns of discovery: An inquiry into the conceptual foundations of science.* Cambridge University Press.

Harden, K. P., Carlson, M. D., Kretsch, N., Corbin, W. R., & Fromme, K. (2015). Childhood sexual abuse and impulsive personality traits: Mixed evidence for moderation by DRD4 genotype. *Journal of Research in Personality, 55*, 30–40.

Haritaworn, J., Lin, C. J., & Klesse, C. (2006). Poly/logue: A critical introduction to polyamory. *Sexualities, 9*(5), 515–529.

Harrington, L. (2016). *Sacred kink: The eightfold paths of BDSM and beyond*. Mystic Productions.

Harris, A., Kalb, M., & Klebanoff, S. (Eds.). (2017). *Demons in the consulting room: Echoes of genocide, slavery, and extreme trauma in psychoanalytic practice*. Routledge.

Harris, C. R. (2003). Factors associated with jealousy over real and imaginary infidelity: An examination of the sexual cognitive and evolutionary psychology perspectives. *Psychology of Women Quarterly, 27*(4), 319–329.

Harris, C. R., & Darby, R. S. (2010). Jealousy in adulthood. In S. L. Hart & M. Legerstee (Eds.), *Handbook of jealousy: Theory, research, and multidisciplinary approaches* (pp. 547–571). Wiley-Blackwell.

Harris, S. (2004). *The end of faith: Religion, terror, and the future of religion*. W. W. Norton.

Hart, S. L. (2010). The ontogenesis of jealousy in the first year of life: A theory of jealousy as a biologically-based dimension of temperament. In S. L. Hart & M. Legerstee (Eds.), *Handbook of jealousy: Theory, research, and multidisciplinary approaches* (pp. 57–82). Wiley-Blackwell.

Hart, S. L., & Legerstee, M. (Eds.). (2010). *Handbook of jealousy: Theory, research, and multidisciplinary approaches*. Wiley-Blackwell.

Hart, T., Nelson, P., & Puhakka, K. (Eds.). (2000). *Transpersonal knowing: Exploring the horizon of consciousness*. State University of New York Press.

Harvey, P. (1995). *The selfless mind: Personality, consciousness and nirvana in early Buddhism*. Curzon.

Harvey, P. (2000). *An introduction to Buddhist ethics: Foundations, values, and issues*. Cambridge University Press.

Haslam, K. R. (2005–2013). *Polyamory collection*. Kinsey Institute. https://kinseyinstitute.org/pdf/HaslamFindingAid.pdf

Hatfield, E., & Rapson, R. L. (1993). *Love, sex, and intimacy: Their psychology, biology, and history*. HarperCollins.

Hatfield, E., Traupmann, J., & Sprecher, S. (1984). Older women's perceptions of their intimate relationships. *Journal of Social and Clinical Psychology, 2*(2), 108–124.

Haupert, M. L., Gesselman, A. N., Moors, A. C., Fisher, H. E., & Garcia, J. R. (2017). Prevalence of experiences with consensual nonmonogamous relationships: Findings from two national samples of single Americans. *Journal of Sex and Marital Therapy, 43*(5), 424–440.

Havelock, E. (1910). *Studies in the psychology of sex. Vol. VI: Sex in relation to society*. F. A. Davis.

Havighurst, R. J. (1972). *Developmental tasks and education*. David McKay (Original work published 1948).

Hawkes, R., & Lacey, C. (2019). "The future of sex": Intermedial desire between fembot fantasies and sexbot technologies. *The Journal of Popular Culture, 52*(1), 98–116.

Hawking, S. (2018). *Brief answers to the big questions.* Bantam Books.

Hazan, C., & Diamond, L. M. (2000). The place of attachment in human mating. *Review of General Psychology, 4*(2), 186–204.

Hazan, C., & Shaver, P. (1987). Romantic love conceptualized as an attachment process. *Journal of Personality and Social Psychology, 52*(3), 511–524.

Heaphy, B., Donovan, C., & Weeks, J. (2004). A different affair? Openness and non-monogamy in same sex relationships. In J. Duncombe, K. Harrison, G. Allen, & D. Marsden (Eds.), *The state of affairs: Explorations in infidelity and commitment* (pp. 167–186). Erlbaum.

Heckert, J. (2010). Love without borders? Intimacy, identity, and the state of compulsory monogamy. In M. Barker & D. Langdridge (Eds.), *Understanding non-monogamies* (pp. 255–266). Routledge.

Heckert, J., & Cleminson, R. (Eds.). (2011). *Anarchism and sexuality: Ethics, relationships and power.* Routledge.

Hehman, J. A., & Salmon, C. A. (2019). Sex-specific developmental effects of father absence on casual sexual behavior and life history strategy. *Evolutionary Psychological Science, 5*(1), 121–130

Heine, S. (2002). *Opening a mountain: Koans of the Zen masters.* Oxford University Press.

Heinemann, I. (2018). Selling the nuclear family: Social order, gender and consumption in magazine advertising in the U.S. since World War II. *Cosmo: Comparative Studies in Modernism, 12,* 25–41.

Heinlin, K., & Heinlin, R. (2004). *The sex and love handbook: Polyamory! Bisexuality! Swingers! Spirituality! (and even) monogamy! A Practical optimistic relationship guide.* Do Things Records & Publishing.

Hekma, G., & Giami, A. (Eds.). (2014). *Sexual revolutions.* Palgrave MacMillan.

Helm, B. (2010). *Love, friendship, and the self: Intimate identification and the sociality of persons.* Oxford University Press.

Hemovich, V., & Crano, W. D. (2009). Family structure and adolescent drug use: An exploration of single-parent families. *Substance Use & Misuse, 44*(14), 2099–2113.

Hendrick, S. S., Dicke, A., & Hendrick, C. (1998). The Relationship Assessment Scale. *Journal of Social and Personal Relationships, 15*(1), 137–142.

Henrich, J., Boyd, R., & Richerson, P. J. (2012). The puzzle of monogamous marriage. *Philosophical Transactions of the Royal Society B: Biological Sciences, 367*(1589), 657–669.

Herlihy, D. (1995). Biology and human history: The triumph of monogamy. *Journal of Interdisciplinary History, 25*(4), 571–583.

Hertlein, K. M., & Piercy, F. P. (2006). Internet infidelity: A critical review of the literature. *The Family Journal, 14*(4), 366–371.

Hidalgo, D. A., Barber, K., & Hunter, E. (2008). The dyadic imaginary: Troubling the perception of love as dyadic. *Journal of Bisexuality, 7*(3/4), 171–189.

Hillman, J. (1975). *Re-visioning psychology.* Harper & Row.

Hirsch, J. S., Meneses, S., Thompson, B., Negroni, M., Pelcastre, B., & del Rio, C. (2007). The inevitability of infidelity: Sexual reputation, social geographies, and marital HIV risk in rural Mexico. *American Journal of Public Health, 97*(6), 986–996.

Hitchens, C. (2007). *God is not great: How religion poisons everything.* Twelve.

Hite, S. (1991). *The Hite report on love, passion, and emotional violence.* Optima.

Ho, P. S. Y. (2006). The (charmed) circle game: Reflections on sexual hierarchy through multiple sexual relationships. *Sexualities, 9*(5), 547–564.

Hogenboom, M. (2016, June 23). *Polyamorous relationships may be the future of love.* BBC. http://www.bbc.com/future/story/20160623-polyamorous-relationships-may-be-the-future-of-love

Houtman, D., & Aupers, S. (2007). The spread of post-Christian spirituality in 14 Western countries, 1981–2000. *Journal for the Scientific Study of Religion, 46*(3), 305–320.

Howard, R., Marshall, P., Grazer, B. (Producers), & Howard, R. (Director). (2005). *Cinderella man.* United States/Canada: Miramax Films.

Howes, C. (1999). Attachment relationships in the context of multiple caregivers. In J. Cassidy & P. R. Shaver (Eds.), *Handbook of attachment: Theory, research, and clinical applications* (pp. 671–687). Guilford.

Hoy, D. C., & McCarthy, T. (1994). *Critical theory.* Blackwell.

Hrdy, S. B. (1986). Empathy, polyandry, and the myth of the coy female. In R. Bleier (Ed.), *Feminist approaches to science* (pp. 119–146). Pergamon Press.

Hrdy, S. B. (1997). Raising Darwin's consciousness: Female sexuality and the prehominid origins of patriarchy. *Human Nature, 8*(1), 1–49.

Hrdy, S. B. (1999). *The woman that never evolved: With a new preface.* Harvard University Press.

Hrdy, S. B. (2009). *Mother and others: The evolutionary origins of mutual understanding.* Belknap/Harvard.

Huffer, L. (2013). *Are the lips a grave? A queer feminist on the ethics of sex.* Columbia University Press.

Hupka, R. B., & Ryan, J. M. (1990). The cultural contribution to jealousy: Cross-cultural aggression in sexual jealousy situations. *Behavior Science Research, 24*(1–4), 51–71.

Hutzler, K. T., Giuliano, T. A., Herselman, J. R., & Johnson, S. M. (2016). Three's a crowd: Public awareness and (mis)perceptions of polyamory. *Psychology & Sexuality, 7*(2), 69–87.

Hypatia from Space (2018). *Compersion: Polyamory beyond jealousy* [eBook]. Independently published.

Illouz, E. (1997). *Romantic utopia: Love and the cultural contradictions of capitalism.* University of California Press.

Illouz, E. (2012). *Why love hurts: A sociological explanation.* Polity Press.

Illouz, E. (2019). *The end of love: A sociology of negative emotions.* Oxford University Press.

Irwin, A. C. (1991). *Eros toward the world: Paul Tillich and the theology of the erotic.* Fortress Press.

Isler, K., & van Schaik, C. P. (2012). How our ancestors broke through the gray ceiling: Comparative evidence for cooperative breeding in early Homo. *Current Anthropology, 53*(6), 453–465.

Jackson, S., & Scott, S. (2004). The personal is still political: Heterosexuality, feminism, and monogamy. *Feminism and Psychology, 14*(1), 151–157.

Jacobson, C., & Burton, L. (2011). *Modern polygamy in the United States: Historical, cultural, and legal issues.* Oxford University Press.

James, G. W., & Moore, L. (2006). *Spirited: Affirming the soul and Black gay/lesbian identity.* RedBone.

James, W. H. (1981). The honeymoon effect on marital coitus. *The Journal of Sex Research, 17*(2), 114–123.

Jamieson, L. (1998). *Intimacy: Personal relationships in modern societies.* Polity.

Jamieson, L. (2004). Intimacy, negotiated nonmonogamy, and the limits of the couple. In J. Duncombe, K. Harrison, G. Allen, & D. Marsden (Eds.), *The state of affairs: Explorations in infidelity and commitment* (pp. 35–57). Lawrence Erlbaum Associates.

Jayatilleke, K. N. A. (1980). *Early Buddhist theory of knowledge.* Motilal Banarsidass.

Jenkins, C. S. I. (2015). Modal monogamy. *Ergo: An Open Access Journal of Philosophy, 2*(8), 175–194.

Jenkins, C. S. I. (2017). *What love is: And what it could be.* Basic Books.

Johnson, H. (2012). When feminism meets evolutionary psychology: The enduring legacy of Margo Wilson. *Homicide Studies, 16*(4), 332–345.

Johnson, H., Ollus, N., & Nevala, S. (2008). *Violence against women: An international perspective.* Springer.

Johnson, M. P., & Leslie, L. (1982). Couple involvement and network structure: A test of the dyadic withdrawal hypothesis. *Social Psychology Quarterly, 45*(1), 34–43.

Johnson, S. (1991). *The ship that sailed into the living room: Sex and intimacy reconsidered.* Wildfire Books.

Johnson, S. (2013). *The love sense: The revolutionary new science of romantic relationships.* Little, Brown and Company.

Johnson, S. M., Giuliano, T. A., Herselman, J. R., & Hutzler, K. T. (2015). Development of a brief measure of attitudes towards polyamory. *Psychology & Sexuality, 6*(4), 325–339.

Johnson, Z., & Young, L. J. (2015). Neurobiological mechanisms of social attachment and pair bonding. *Current Opinion in Behavioral Sciences, 3*, 38–44.

Jokela, M., Rotkirch, A., Rickard, I. J., Pettay, J., & Lummaa, V. (2010). Serial monogamy increases reproductive success in men but not in women. *Behavioral Ecology, 21*(5), 906–912.

Jones, A. (2019). Sex is not a problem: The erasure of pleasure in sexual science research. *Sexualities, 22*(4), 643–668.

Jones, C. (2010). Lying, cheating, and virtual relationships. *Global Virtue Ethics Review, 6*(1), 3–12.

Jordan, L. S. (2018). "My mind kept creeping back . . . this relationship can't last": Developing self-awareness of monogamous bias. *Journal of Feminist Family Therapy, 30*(2), 109–127.

Jordan, L. S., Grogan, C., Muruthi, B., & Bermúdez, J. M. (2017). Polyamory: Experiences of power from without, from within, and in between, *Journal of Couple & Relationship Therapy, 16*(1), 1–19.

Jordan, S. (1971). Two forms of spirit marriage in rural Taiwan. *Bijdragen tot de Taal-, Land- en Volkenkunde, 127*(1), 181–189.

Josephs, L. (2018). *The dynamics of infidelity: Applying relationship science to psychotherapy practice*. American Psychological Association.

Käär, P., Jokela, J., Merilä, J., Helle, T., & Kojola, I. (1998). Sexual conflict and remarriage in preindustrial human populations: Causes and fitness consequences. *Evolution and Human Behavior, 19*(3), 139–151.

Kai (n.d.). *16 surprising things I learned in 4 years of ethical non-monogamy*. The Free Love Diaries. http://freelovediaries.com/16-surprising-relationship-perspectives-gai ned-4-years-ethical-non-monogamy/

Kaldera, R. (2005). *Pagan polyamory: Becoming a tribe of hearts*. Llewellyn Publications.

Kale, K. (2020, March 11). Hands off! Sex parties and the spread of coronavirus. *The Guardian*. https://www.theguardian.com/lifeandstyle/shortcuts/2020/mar/11/hands-o ff-can-orgies-survive-in-the-age-of-coronavirus

Kalmijn, M. (2003). Friendship networks over the life course: A test of the dyadic withdrawal hypothesis using survey data on couples. *Social Networks, 25*(3), 231–249.

Kanazawa, S., & Still, M. C. (1999). Why monogamy? *Social Forces, 78*(1), 25–50.

Kane, P. (2010). *The monogamy challenge: Creating and keeping intimacy*. Relationship Transformations Press.

Kaplan, M. (2010, February 8). Reincarnation: The cabinet of Dr. Stevenson. Why has no one looked at the evidence for reincarnation? *Psychology Today*. https://www.psychologytoday.com/intl/blog/bozo-sapiens/201002/reincarnation-the-cabinet-dr -stevenson

Karagöz, M. A., Gül, A., Borg, C., Erihan, I. B., Uslu, M., Ezer, M., Erbağci, Çatak, B., & Bağcıoğlu, M. (2020). Influence of COVID-19 pandemic on sexuality: A cross-sectional study among couples in Turkey. *International Journal of Impotence Research*. https://doi.org/10.1038/s41443-020-00378-4

Karandashev, V. (2016). *Romantic love in cultural contexts*. Springer International Publishing AG.

Kean, J. (2015). A stunning plurality: Unraveling hetero- and mononormativities through HBO's *Big Love*. *Sexualities, 18*(5/6), 698–713.

Kean, J. (2017). Relationship structure, relationship texture: Case studies in non/monogamies research. *Cultural Studies Review, 23*(1), 18–35.

Kellaway, K. (2013, September 28). Interview. Tim Minchin: "I really don't like to upsetting people." *The Guardian*. https://www.theguardian.com/stage/2013/sep/28/ tim-minchin-interview-matilda-jesus

Kelly, J. B. (2000). Children's adjustment in conflicted marriage and divorce: A decade review of research. *Journal of the American Academy of Children and Adolescent Psychiatry, 39*(8), 963–973.

Kelly, J. B., & Emery, R. (2003). Children's adjustment following divorce: Risk and resilience perspectives. *Family Relations, 52*(4), 352–362.

Kerista Commune (1984). *Polyfidelity: Sex in the Kerista commune and other related theories on how to solve world's problems*. Performing Arts Social Society.

Kern, S. (1992). *The culture of love: Victorians to moderns*. Harvard University Press.

King, M. (2009). *Postsecularism: The hidden challenge to extremism*. James Clarke.

Kingma, R. D. (1998). *The future of love: The power of the soul in intimate relationships*. Broadway Books.

Kinsey, A., Pomeroy, W., Martin, C., & Gebhard, P. (1953). *Sexual behavior in the human female*. WB Saunders.

Kipnis, L. (1998). Adultery. *Critical Inquiry, 24*(2), 289–327.

Kipnis, L. (2001, October 14). Love in the 21st century; against love. *The New York Times Magazine*. https://www.nytimes.com/2001/10/14/magazine/love-in-the-21st-century-against-love.html

Kipnis, L. (2003). *Against love: A polemic*. Pantheon Books.

Kirsch, J. (2004). *God against the Gods: The history of the war between monotheism and polytheism*. Viking Compass.

Kisler, T. S., & Lock, L. (2019). Honoring the voices of polyamorous clients: Recommendations for couple and family therapists. *Journal of Feminist Family Therapy, 31*(1), 40–58.

Klasto, S.-P., & Simpson, A. C. (2020, May 15). *Gay Korea: Homophobia sparked by Seoul coronavirus cluster driven by Protestant right*. The Conversation. https://theconversation.com/gay-korea-homophobia-sparked-by-seoul-coronavirus-cluster-driven-by-protestant-right-138491

Kleinplatz, P. J., Ménard, A. D., Paquet, M.-P., Paradis, N., Campbell, M., Zuccarino, D., & Mehak, L. (2009). The components of optimal sexuality: A portrait of "great sex." *The Canadian Journal of Human Sexuality, 18*(1–2), 1–14.

Klesse, C. (2005). Bisexual women, non-monogamy and differentialist anti-promiscuity discourses. *Sexualities, 8*(4), 445–464.

Klesse, C. (2006). Polyamory and its 'others': Contesting the terms of non-monogamy. *Sexualities, 9*(5), 565–583.

Klesse, C. (2007). *The spectrum of promiscuity: Gay male bisexual non-monogamies and polyamories*. Routledge.

Klesse, C. (2014a). Polyamory: Intimate practice, identity, or sexual orientation? *Sexualities, 17*(1/2), 81–99.

Klesse, C. (2014b). Poly economics—Capitalism, class, and polyamory. *International Journal of Politics, Culture, and Society, 27*, 203–220.

Klesse, C. (2016). Marriage, law and polyamory. Rebutting mononormativity with sexual orientation discourse? *Oñati Socio-Legal Series, 6*(6), 1348–1376.

Klusmann, D. (2002). Sexual motivation and the duration of partnership. *Archives of Sexual Behavior, 31*(3), 275–287.

Kohut, T., Fisher, W. A., & Campbell, L. (2017). Perceived effects of pornography on the couple relationship: Initial findings of open-ended, participant-informed, "bottom-up" research. *Archives of Sexual Behavior, 46*(2), 585–602.

Kolesar, A. E. A., & Pardo, S. (2019). The religious and philosophical characteristics in a consensually nonmonogamous sample. *International Journal of Transpersonal Studies, 38*(1), 99–117.

Kolmes, K., & Witherspoon, R. G. (2012). Sexual orientation microaggressions in everyday life: Expanding our conversations about sexual diversity: Part I & II. *Independent Practitioner* (Summer), 96–101.

Koltko-Rivera, M. E. (2006). Rediscovering the later version of Maslow's hierarchy of needs: Self–transcendence and opportunities for theory, research, and unification. *Review of General Psychology, 10*(4), 302–317.

Kőrösi, M. (2012). *Transformative potential or social exclusion? The case of polyamory* [Unpublished manuscript]. Liszt Academy of Music, Budapest, Hungary.

Kreider, R. M., & Ellis, R. (2011). Number, timing, and duration of marriages and divorces: 2009. *Household Economic Studies* (May), 1–23. U.S. Department of Commerce/U.S. Census Bureau.

Kripal, J. J. (2003). In the spirit of Hermes: Reflections on the work of Jorge N. Ferrer. *Tikkun: Culture, Spirituality, Politics, 18*(2), 67–70.

Krippner, S., Bogzaran, F., & de Carvalho, A. P. (2002). *Extraordinary dreams and how to work with them.* State University of New York Press.

Kristjánsson, K. (2002). *Justifying emotions: Pride and jealousy.* Routledge.

Kuhn, T. (1970). *The structure of scientific revolutions* (2nd ed.). University of Chicago Press.

Kurdek, L. A. (1988). Relationship quality of gay and lesbian cohabitating couples. *Journal of Homosexuality, 15*(3–4), 93–118.

Kurdek, L. A., & Schmitt, J. P. (1986). Relationship quality of gay men in closed or open relationships. *Journal of Homosexuality, 12*(2), 85–99.

Kurtz, S. (2006). Polyamory would destroy monogamous marriage. In M. E. Williams (Ed.), *Sex* (pp. 173–180). (Opposing Viewpoints Series). Greenhaven Press.

Kutob, R. M., Yuan, N. P., Wertheim, B. C., Sbarra, D. A., Loucks, E. B., Nassir, R., Bareh, G., Kim, M. M., Snetselaar, L. G., & Thomson, C. A. (2017). Relationship between marital transitions, health behaviors, and health indicators of post-menopausal women: Results from the Women's Health Initiative. *Journal of Women's Health, 26*(4), 313–320.

LaBerge, S., & Rheingold, H. (1991). *Exploring the world of lucid dreaming.* Ballantine.

Labriola, K. (1999). Models of open relationships. *Journal of Lesbian Studies, 3*(1/2), 217–225.

Labriola, K. (2013). *The jealousy workbook: Exercises and insights for managing open relationships.* Greenery Press.

Lagerlöf, N.-P. (2010). Pacifying monogamy. *Journal of Economic Growth, 15*(3), 235–262.

Lano, K. (1995). Friends can't be lovers: The paradox of monogamy. In K. Lano & P. Claire (Eds.), *Breaking the barriers of desire: New approaches to multiple relationships* (pp. 107–112). Five Leaves Publications.

Lansford, J. E. (2009). Parental divorce and children's adjustment. *Perspectives on Psychological Science, 4*(2), 140–152.

LaSala, M. C. (2004). Monogamy of the heart: Extradyadic sex and gay male couples. *Journal of Gay & Lesbian Social Services, 17*(3), 1–24.

Lawson, A. (1988). *Adultery: An analysis of love and betrayal.* Basic Books.

Le Cunff, A.-L. (2018). Non-monogamy: Measuring degrees of sexual and romantic exclusivity in relationships. *Sexuality & Gender Studies, 26*(2), 41–47.

Lee, B. H., & O'Sullivan, L. F. (2019). Walk the line: How successful are efforts to maintain monogamy in intimate relationships. *Archives of Sexual Behavior, 48*(6), 1735–1748.

Lee, E. M., Klement, K. R., Ambler, J. K., Loewald, T., Comber, E. M., Hanson, S. A., Pruitt, B., & Sagarin, B. J. (2016). Altered states of consciousness during an extreme ritual. *PLoS One, 11*(5). https://doi.org/10.1371/journal.pone.0153126

Lee, J. D., & Craft, E. A. (2002). Protecting one's self from a stigmatized disease... once one has it. *Deviant Behavior, 23*(3), 267–299.

Leeder, E. (1996). Let our mothers show the way. In H. J. Ehrlich (Ed.), *Reinventing anarchy, again* (pp. 142–148). AK Press.

Leeker, O., & Carlozzi, A. (2014). Effects of sex, sexual orientation, infidelity expectations, and love on distress related to emotional and sexual infidelity. *Journal of Marital and Family Therapy, 40*(1), 68–91.

Lehmiller, J. J. (2015). A comparison of sexual health history and practices among monogamous and consensually nonmonogamous sexual partners. *Journal of Sexual Medicine, 12*(10), 2022–2028.

Lehmiller, J. J., Garcia, J. R., Gesselman, A. N., & Mark, K. P. (2020). Less sex, but more sexual diversity: Changes in sexual behavior during the COVID-19 coronavirus pandemic. *Leisure Sciences: An Interdisciplinary Journal.* https://doi.org/10.1080/0 1490400.2020.1774016

Leighton, T. D. (2012). *Faces of compassion: Classic bodhisattva archetypes and their modern expression.* Wisdom.

LeMoncheck, L. (1997). *Loose women, lecherous men: A feminist philosophy of sex.* Oxford University Press.

Lerum, H. (forthcoming). From revolutionary to evolutionary: Evolutionary psychology rhetoric in four guides to polyamorous relationships. *Science as Culture.*

Lessin, J. K. (2006). *Polyamory many loves: The poly tantric lifestyle—A personal account.* AuthorHouse. 1995

Levine, A., & Heller, R. (2010). *Attached: The new science of adult attachment and how it can help you find—and keep—love.* TarcherPerigee.

Levine, E. C., Herbenick, D., Martinez, O., Fu, T.-C., & Dodge, B. (2018). Open relationships, nonconsensual nonmonogamy, and monogamy among U.S. adults: Findings from the 2012 National Survey of Sexual Health and Behavior. *Archives of Sexual Behavior, 47*(15), 1439–1450.

Levine, S., & Levine, A. (1995). *Embracing the beloved: Relationship as a path of awakening.* Doubleday.

Levine, S. B. (2017). A little deeper, please. *Archives of Sexual Behavior, 46*(3), 639–642.

Levy, D., Prause, N., & Finn, P. (2014). The emperor has no clothes: A review of the "pornography addiction" model. *Current Sexual Health Reports, 6*(2), 94–105.

Lewis, I. M. (2003). *Ecstatic religion: A study shamanism and spirit possession* (3rd ed.). Routledge.

Lewis, J. (2001). *The end of marriage? Individuation and intimate relations.* Edward Elgar.

Li, D., Jin, M., Bao, P., Zhao, W., & Zhang, S. (2020). Clinical characteristics and results of semen tests among men with coronavirus disease 2019. *JAMA Network Open, 3*(5):e208292. https://doi:10.1001/jamanetworkopen.2020.8292

Liesen, L. T. (2007). Women, behavior, and evolution: Understanding the debate between feminist evolutionists and evolutionary psychologists. *Politics and the Life Sciences, 26*(1), 51–70.

Lim, M. M., Bielsky, I. F., & Young, L. J. (2005). Neuropeptides and the social brain: Potential rodent models of autism. *International Journal of Developmental Neuroscience, 23*(2–3), 235–243.

Litschi, A., Gordon, D., Porter, A., Regnerus, M., Ryngaert, J., & Sarangaya, L. (2014). *Relationships in America*. The Austin Institute for the Study of Family and Culture. https://relationshipsinamerica.com/

Liu, C. (2000). A theory of marital sexual life. *Journal of Marriage and the Family, 62*(2), 363–374.

Loevinger, J. (1976). *Ego Development*. Jossey-Bass.

Long, A. (1997). The one or the many: The great goddess revisited. *Feminist Theology, 5*(15), 13–29.

López, C. (2020, September 16). Dating isn't any safer if you're tested regularly for the coronavirus, according to an expert. *Business Insider*. https://www.businessinsider.com/geting-tested-regularly-for-coronavirus-doesnt-make-dating-safer-2020-9

López, C. (2020, October 8). What's like to be polyamorous and non-monogamous during a pandemic. *Business Insider*. https://www.businessinsider.in/science/health/news/what-its-like-to-be-polyamorous-and-non-monogamous-during-a-pandemic/articleshow/78558339.cms

Loue, S. (2006). *Sexual partnering, sexual practices, and health*. Springer.

Love, P., & Robinson, J. (2012). *Hot monogamy: Essential steps to more passionate, intimate lovemaking*. Plume.

Loy, D. (1987). The clôture of deconstruction: A Mahāyāna critique of Derrida. *International Philosophical Quarterly, 27*(1), 59–80.

Loy, D. (2000). *Lack and transcendence: The problem of death and life in psychotherapy, existentialism, and Buddhism*. Humanities Press.

Lukas, D., & Clutton-Brock, T. H. (2013). The evolution of social monogamy in mammals. *Science, 341*(6145), 526–530.

MacDonald, K. (1990). Mechanisms of sexual egalitarianism in Western Europe. *Ethology and Sociobiology, 11*(3), 195–237.

MacDonald, K. B. (1995). The establishment and maintenance of socially imposed monogamy in Western Europe. *Politics and the Life Sciences, 14*(1), 3–23.

Macfarlane, A. J. (1986). Love and capitalism. *The Cambridge Journal of Anthropology, 11*(2), 22–29.

MacKinnon, C. (1987). *Feminism unmodified: Discourses on life and law*. Cambridge University Press.

MacWilliams, M. (2005) Digital Waco: Branch Davidian virtual communities after the Waco tragedy. In M. Højsgaard & M. Warburg (Eds.), *Religion in cyberspace* (pp. 180–198). Routledge.

Madison, A. (2017). *Ashley Madison: An unauthorized autobiography*. Friesen Press.

Madrigal-Borloz, V. (2020, July 28). Violence and discrimination based on sexual orientation and gender diversity during the coronavirus disease (Covid-19) pandemic. *United Nations General Assembly, Seventy-Fifth Session*. https://undocs.org/A/75/258

Maheu, M. M., & Subotnik, R. (2001). *Infidelity on the Internet: Virtual relationships and real betrayal*. Sourcebooks.

Malkemus, S. A., & Romero, M. T. (2012). Sexuality as a transformational path: Exploring the holistic dimensions of human vitality. *International Journal of Transpersonal Studies, 31*(2), 33–41.

Manley, M. H., Diamond, L. M., & van Anders, S. M. (2015). Polyamory, monoamory, and sexual fluidity: A longitudinal study of identity and sexual trajectories. *Psychology of Sexual Orientation and Gender Diversity, 2*(2), 168–80.

Manley, M. H., Legge, M. M., Flanders, C. E., Goldberg, A. E., & Ross, L. E. (2018). Consensual non-monogamy in pregnancy and parenthood: Experiences of bisexual and plurisexual women with different-gender partners. *Journal of Sex and Marital Therapy, 44*(8), 721–736.

Mark, K., Rosenkrantz, D., & Kerner, I. (2014). Bi"ing into monogamy: Attitudes toward monogamy in a sample of bisexual-identified adults. *Psychology of Sexual Orientation and Gender Diversity, 1*(3), 263–269.

Mark, K. P., Janssen, E., & Milhausen, R. R. (2011). Infidelity in heterosexual couples: Demographic, interpersonal, and personality-related predictors of extradyadic sex. *Archives of Sexual Behavior, 40*(5), 971–982.

Marks, M. J., Young, T. M., & Zaikman, Y. (2017). The sexual double standard in the real world: Evaluations of sexually active friends and acquaintances. *Social Psychology, 50*(2), 67–79.

Marlowe, F. W. (2000). Paternal investment and the human mating system. *Behavioural Processes, 51*(1–3), 45–61.

Marlowe, F. W. (2003). The mating system of foragers in the Standard Cross-Cultural Sample. *Cross-Cultural Research, 37*(3), 282–306.

Maslow, A. H. (1970). *Motivation and personality*. Harper (Original work published 1954).

Maslow, A. H. (1971). *The farther reaches of human nature*. McGraw-Hill.

Mass, M. K., Vasilnkno, S. A., & Willoughby, B. J. (2018). A dyadic approach to pornography use and relationship satisfaction among heterosexual couples: The role of pornography acceptance and anxious attachment. *The Journal of Sex Research, 55*(6), 772–782.

Masters, R. A. (2006). *The anatomy and evolution of anger: An integral exploration.* Tehmenos Press.

Masters, R. A. (2007). *Transformation through intimacy: The journey toward mature monogamy.* Tehmenos Press.

Matsick, J. L., Conley, T. D., Ziegler, A. C., Moors, A. C., & Rubin, J. D. (2014). Love and sex: Polyamorous relationships are perceived more favourably than swinging and open relationships. *Psychology and Sexuality, 5*(4), 339–348,

May, S. (2011). *Love: A history.* Yale University Press.

Mazur, R. (1973). *The new intimacy: Open-ended marriage and alternative lifestyles.* Boston, MA: Beacon Press.

McCall, L. (2005). The complexity of intersectionality. *Signs, 30*(3), 1771–1800.

McClelland, N. C. (2010). *Encyclopedia of reincarnation and karma.* McFarland & Company.

McGrane, B. (1989). *Beyond anthropology: Society and the other.* Columbia University Press.

McGraw, L. A., & Young, L. J. (2010). The prairie vole: An emerging model organism for understanding the social brain. *Trends in Neuroscience, 33*(2), 103–109.

McKeever, N. (2017). Is the requirement of sexual exclusivity consistent with romantic love? *Journal of Applied Philosophy, 34*(3), 353–369.

McKenzie, S. K., Collings, S., Jenkin, G., & River, J. (2018). Masculinity, social connectedness, and mental health: Men's diverse patterns of practice. *American Journal of Men's Health, 12*(5), 1247–1261.

McNulty, J. K., Wenner, C. A., & Fisher, T. D. (2016). Longitudinal associations among relationship satisfaction, sexual satisfaction, and frequency of sex in early marriage. *Archives of Sexual Behavior, 45*(1), 85–97.

McNulty, J. K., & Widman, L. (2014). Sexual narcissism and infidelity in early marriage. *Archives of Sexual Behavior, 43*(7), 1315–1325.

Mehling, W. E., Gopisetty, V., Daubenmier, J., Price, C. J., Hecht, F. M., & Stewart, A. (2009). Body awareness: Construct and self-report measures. *PLoS One, 4*(5), e5614. https://doi.org/10.1371/journal.pone.0005614

Melotti, U. (1981). Towards a new theory of the origin of the family. *Current Anthropology, 22*(6), 625–638.

Mellor, M. (2020, April 4). Coronavirus has created a sex boom—but maybe not a baby boom. *Wired UK.* https://www.wired.com/story/coronavirus-has-created-a-sex-boom-but-maybe-not-a-baby-boom/

Mercer, C. H., Aicken, C. R. H., Tanton, C., Estcourt, C. S., Gary Brook, M., Keane, F., & Cassell, J. A. (2013). Serial monogamy and biological concurrency: Measurement of the gaps between sexual partners to inform targeted strategies. *American Journal of Epidemiology, 178*(2), 249–259.

Michaels, M. A., & Johnson, P. (2015). *Designer relationships: A guide to happy monogamy, positive polyamory, and optimistic open relationships.* Cleis Press.

Michalski, R. L., Shackelford, T. K., & Salmon, C. A. (2007). Upset in response to a sibling's partner's infidelities. *Human Nature, 18*(1), 74–84.

Milanovic, B. (2020). The clash of capitalisms: The real fight for the global economy's future. *Foreign Affairs, 99*(1), 10–21.

Miller, L. C., & Fishkin, S. A. (1997). On the dynamics of human bonding and reproductive success: Seeking windows on the adapted-for human-environment interface. In J. A. Simpson & D. T. Kenrich (Eds.), *Evolutionary social psychology* (pp. 197–235). Lawrence Erlbaum Associates.

Miller, W. B. (2018). *Intimate relationships* (8th ed.). McGraw-Hill Education.

Miller, W. B., Sable, M. R., & Beckmeyer, J. J. (2009). Preconception motivation and pregnancy wantedness: Pathways to toddler attachment security. *Journal of Marriage and Family, 71*(5), 1174–1192.

Mint, P. (2004). The power dynamics of cheating: Effects on polyamory and bisexuality. In S. Anderlini D'Onofrio (Ed.), *Plural loves: Designs for bi and poly living* (pp. 55–76). Harrington Park Press.

Mint, P. (2010). The power mechanisms of jealousy. In M. Barker & D. Langdridge (Eds.), *Understanding non-monogamies* (pp. 201–206). Routledge.

Mitchell, M. E., Bartholomew, K., & Cobb, R. J. (2014). Need fulfillment in polyamorous relationships. *Journal of Sex Research, 51*(4), 329–339.

Mitchell, S. A. (2002). *Can love last? The fate of romance over time.* Norton.

Mogilski, J. K., Memering, S. L., Welling, L. L. M., & Shackelford, T. (2017). Monogamy versus consensual non-monogamy: Alternative approaches to pursuing strategically pluralistic mating strategy. *Archives of Sexual Behavior, 46*(2), 407–417.

Mogilski, J. K., Reeve, S. D., Nicolas, S. C. A., Donaldson, S. H., Mitchell, V. E., & Welling, L. L. M. (2019). Jealousy, consent, and compersion within monogamous and consensually non-monogamous romantic relationships. *Archives of Sexual Behavior, 48*(6), 1811–1828.

Mogilski, J. K., Mitchell, V. E., Reeve, S. D., Donaldson, S. H., Nicolas, S. C. A., & Welling, L. L. M. (2020). Life history and multi-partner mating: A novel explanation for moral stigma against consensual non-monogamy. *Frontiers in Psychology, 10*(3033). https://doi.org/10.3389/fpsyg.2019.03033

Moore, D. S. (2015). *The developing genome: An introduction to behavioral epigenetics.* Oxford University Press.

Moore, K. A., Lipsitch, M., Barry, J. M., & Osterholm, M. T. (2020). *Covid-19: The CIDRAP viewpoint.* Center for Infectious Disease Research and Policy (CIDRAP), University of Michigan.

Moore, P. (2016, October 3). *Young Americans are less wedded to monogamy than their elders.* YouGov, Lifestyle. https://today.yougov.com/topics/lifestyle/articles-reports/2016/10/03/young-americans-less-wedded-monogamy

Moore, T. (1998). *The soul of sex: Cultivating life as an act of love.* HarperCollins.

Moore, T. (2002). The temple of the body: Sex in an anti-erotic age. *Hidden Mysteries.* http://www.hiddenmysteries.org/spirit/ecstacy/bodytemple.shtml

Moors, A. C., Conley, T. D., Edelstein, R. S., & Chopin, W. J. (2015). Attached to monogamy? Avoidance predicts willingness to engage (but not actual engagement) in consensual non-monogamy. *Journal of Social and Personal Relationships, 32*(2), 222–240.

Moors, A. C., Gesselman, A. N., & Garcia, J. (2021). Desire, familiarity, and engagement in polyamory: Results from a national sample of single adults in the United States. *Frontiers in Psychology, 12*(619640). https://doi.org/10.3389/fpsyg.2021.619640

Moors, A. C., Matsick, J. L., & Schechinger, H. A. (2017). Unique and shared relationship benefits of consensually non-monogamous and monogamous relationships: A review and insights for moving forward. *European Psychologist, 22*(1), 55–71.

Moors, A. C., Matsick, J. L., Ziegler, A., Rubin, J., & Conley, T. D. (2013). Stigma toward individuals engaged in consensual non-monogamy: Robust and worthy of additional research. *Analyses of Social Issues and Public Policy, 13*(1), 52–69.

Moors, A. C., Rubin, J., Matsick, J. L., Ziegler, A., & Conley, T. D. (2014). It's not just a gay male thing: Sexual minority women and men are equally attracted to consensual non-monogamy. *Journal für Psychologie, 22*, 1–13.

Moors, A. C., Ryan, W., & Chopik, W. J. (2019). Multiple loves: The effects of attachment with multiple concurrent romantic partners on relational functioning. *Personality and Individual Differences, 147*, 102–110.

Moors, A. C., Selterman, D. F., & Conley, T. D. (2017). Personality correlates of desire to engage in consensual non-monogamy among lesbian, gay, and bisexual Individuals, *Journal of Bisexuality, 17*(4), 418–434.

Moradi, B., Wiseman, M. C., DeBlaere, C., Goodman, M. B., Sarkees, A., Brewster, M. E., & Huang, Y. (2010). LGB of color and White individuals' perceptions of heterosexist stigma, internalized homophobia, and outness: Comparisons of levels and links. *Counseling Psychologist, 38*(3), 397–424.

Morris, A. (2014, March 31). Tales from the Millennials' sexual revolution. *Rolling Stone.* https://www.rollingstone.com/interactive/feature-millennial-sexual-revolution-relationships-marriage/

Morrison, T. G., Beaulieu, D., Brockman, M., & Beaglaoich, C. Ó. (2013). A comparison of polyamorous and monoamorous persons: Are there differences in indices of relationship well-being and sociosexuality? *Psychology & Sexuality, 4*(1), 75–91.

Muise, A., Laughton, A. K., Moors, A., & Impett, E. A. (2019). Sexual need fulfillment and satisfaction in consensually nonmonogamous relationships. *Journal of Social and Personal Relationships, 36*(7), 1917–1938.

Muise, A., Schimmack, U., & Impett, E. A. (2016). Sexual frequency predicts greater well-being, but more is not always better. *Social Psychology and Personality Science, 7*(4), 295–302.

Mullen, P. E. (1993). The crime of passion and the changing cultural construction of jealousy. *Criminal Behaviour and Mental Health, 3*(1), 1–11.

Munson, M., & Stelboum, J. (Eds.). (1999). *The lesbian polyamory reader: Open relationships, non-monogamy, and casual sex.* Harrington Park Press.

Nack, A. (2000). Damaged goods: Women managing the stigma of STDs. *Deviant Behavior, 21*(2), 95–121.

Nash, J. (2008). Rethinking intersectionality. *Feminist Review, 89,* 1–15.

N'diaye, P. (2020, August 27). How to safely practice non-monogamy during the pandemic. *VICE.* https://www.vice.com/en/article/935vkd/safely-practice-non-monogamy-polyamory-during-covid-19-pandemic

Nelson, J. B. (1983). *Between two gardens: Reflections on sexuality and religious experience.* The Pilgrim Press.

Nelson, T. (2012). *The new monogamy: Redefining your relationship after infidelity.* New Harbinger Publications.

Nelson, T. (2016, January 7). A new monogamy? A fresh look at open marriage for 2016. *Huffington Post.* https://www.huffpost.com/entry/a-new-monogamy-a-fresh-look-at-open-marriage-for-2016_n_8916498

Neufeldt, R. W. (Ed.). (1986). *Karma and rebirth: Post classical developments.* State University of New York Press.

Neu, J. (2000). *A tear is an intellectual thing.* Oxford University Press.

Neuman, M. G. (2001). *Emotional infidelity: How to affair-proof your marriage and 10 other secrets for a great relationship.* Three Rivers Press.

Newitz, A. (2006, July 5). Love unlimited: The polyamorists. *New Scientist.* https://www.newscientist.com/article/mg19125591-800-love-unlimited-the-polyamorists/

Newmahr, S. (2010). Rethinking kink: Sadomasochism as serious leisure. *Qualitative Sociology, 33,* 313–331.

Newmann, S., Sarin, P., Kumarasamy, N., Amalraj, E., Rogers, M., Madhivanan, P., Flanigan, T., Cu-Uvin, S., McGarvey, S., Mayer, K., & Solomon, S. (2000). Marriage, monogamy and HIV: A profile of HIV-infected women in south India. *International Journal of STD & AIDS, 11*(4), 250–253.

Nhat Hanh, T. (2007). *For a future to be possible: Buddhist ethics for everyday life.* Parallax Press.

Nicolas, S. C. A., & Welling, L. L. M. (2015). The Darwinian mystique? Synthesizing evolutionary psychology and feminism. In V. Zeigler-Hill, L. L. M. Welling, & T. K. Shackelford (Eds.), *Evolutionary perspectives on social psychology* (pp. 203–214). Springer.

Nisbett, R. E., & Cohen, D. (1996). *Culture of honor: The psychology of violence in the South.* Westview Press.

Noël, M. J. (2006). Progressive polyamory: Considering issues of diversity. *Sexualities, 9*(5), 602–620.

Nozick, R. (1989). *The examined life: Philosophical meditations.* Simon & Schuster.

Numan, M. (2015). *Neurobiology of social behavior: Toward an understanding of the prosocial and antisocial brain.* Academic Press.

Numan, M., & Young, L. J. (2016). Neural mechanisms of mother-infant bonding and pair bonding: Similarities, differences, and broader implications. *Hormones and Behavior, 77,* 98–112.

Nunes-Costa, R. A., Lamela, D. J. P. V., & Figueiredo, B. F. C. (2009). Psychosocial adjustment and physical health in children of divorce. *Jornal of Pediatria, 85*(5), 385–396.

Nusinovici, S., Olliac, O., Flamant, C., Müller, J.-B., Olivier, M., Rouger, V., Gascoin, G., Basset, H., Bouvard, C., Rose, J-C., & Hanf, M. (2018). Impact of parental separation or divorce on school performance in preterm children: A population-based study. *PLOS ONE, 13*(9). https://doi.org/10.1371/journal.pone.0202080

Nygren, A. (1982). *Agape and eros: The Christian idea of love* (P. S. Watson, Trans.). University of Chicago Press (Originally published 1930 and 1936).

O'Connell Walshe, M. (1975). *Buddhism and sex.* Buddhist Publication Society.

Ogden, G. (2006). *The heart and soul of sex: Exploring the sexual mysteries.* Trumpeter Books.

Ogilvy, J. (1977). *Multidimensional man.* Oxford University Press.

Ogilvy, J. (2013). The new polytheism: Updating the dialogue between East and West. *East-West Affairs, 1*(2), 29–48.

O'Leary, A. (2000). Women at risk for HIV from a primary partner: Balancing risk and intimacy. *Annual Review of Sex Research, 11,* 191–243.

O'Neill, N., & O'Neill, G. (1972). *Open marriage: A new lifestyle for couples.* Owen.

Opie, C. F. (2013). *The evolution of social systems in human and non-human primates* [Doctoral dissertation, University of Oxford]. https://ethos.bl.uk/OrderDetails.do?did=1&uin=uk.bl.ethos.581239

Orion, R. (2018). *A therapist's guide to consensual nonmonogamy: Polyamory, swinging, and open marriage.* Routledge.

Otter, R. C. D. (2014). Three may not be a crowd: The case for a constitutional right to plural marriage. *Emory Law Journal, 64*(6), 1977–2046.

Over, R., & Koukonas, E. (1995). Habituation of sexual arousal: Product and process. *Annual Review of Sex Research, 6*(1), 187–223.

Overall, C. (1998). Monogamy, nonmonogamy, and identity. *Hypatia, 13*(4), 1–17.

Oxford English Dictionary (1989, 2nd ed.). Envy. 5.316.

Ozturk, Y. N. (1988). *The eye of the heart: An introduction to Sufism and the major tariqats of Anatolia and the Balkans* (R. Blakney, Trans.). Redhouse Press.

Pain, E. (2019). Race, class, gender and relationship power in queer polyamory. In B. L. Simula, J. E. Sumerau, & A. Miller (Eds.), *Expanding the rainbow: Exploring the relationships of bi+, polyamorous, kinky, ace, intersex, and trans people* (pp. 107–120). Brill Sense.

Pallotta-Chiarolli, M. (1995). Choosing not to choose: Beyond monogamy, beyond duality. In K. Lano & C. Perry (Eds.), *Breaking the barriers of desire: New approaches to multiple relationships* (pp. 41–67). Five Leaves Publications.

Pallotta-Chiarolli, M. (2006). Polyparents having children, raising children, schooling children. *Lesbian and Gay Psychology Review, 7*(1), 48–53.

Pallotta-Chiarolli, M. (2010). *Border sexualities, border families in schools*. Rowman & Littlefield.

Paloutzian, R. F., Bufford, R. K., & Wildman, A. J. (2012). Spiritual well-being scale: Mental and physical health relationships. In M. Cobb, C. Puchalski, & B. Rumbold (Eds.), *Oxford textbook of spirituality in healthcare* (pp. 353–358). Oxford University Press.

Pandita, S. U. (2017). *The state of mind called beautiful* (K. Wheeler, Ed.; Venerable Vivekananda, Trans.). Wisdom Publications.

Paper, J. (2005). *The deities are many: A polytheistic theology*. State University of New York Press.

Pappas, S., & LiveScience (2013, February 14). New sexual revolution: Polyamory may be good for you. *Scientific American*. http://www.scientificamerican.com/article.cfm?id=new-sexual-revolution-polyamory

Parker-Pope, T. (2009, June 3). When sex leaves marriage. *The New York Times*. https://well.blogs.nytimes.com/2009/06/03/when-sex-leaves-the-marriage/

Parsons, J. T., Starks, T. J., DuBois, S., Grov, C., & Golub, S. A. (2013). Alternatives to monogamy among gay male couples in a community survey: Implications for mental health and sexual risk. *Archives of Sexual Behavior, 42*(2), 303–312.

Parsons, J. T., Starks, T. J., Gamarel, K. E., & Grov, C. (2012). Non-monogamy and sexual relationship quality among same-sex male couples. *Journal of Family Psychology, 26*(5), 669–677.

Parsons, W. B. (Ed.). (2018). *Being Spiritual but Not Religious: Past, present, futures*. Routledge.

Pascoal, P. M., Narciso Ide, S., & Pereira, N. M. (2014). What is sexual satisfaction? Thematic analysis of lay people's definitions. *Journal of Sex Research, 51*(1), 22–30.

Patterson, K. (2018). *Love is not color blind: Race and representation in polyamorous and other alternative communities*. Thorntree Press.

Paul, K. (2020, April 1). Polyamory in a pandemic: Who do you quarantine with when you're not monogamous? *The Guardian*. https://www.theguardian.com/us-news/2020/apr/01/polyamory-quarantine-coronavirus-pandemic

Peabody, S. A. (1982). Alternative lifestyles to monogamous marriage: Variants of normal behavior in psychotherapy clients. *Family Relations, 31*(3), 425–434.

Perel, E. (2006). *Mating in captivity: Unlocking erotic intelligence.* HarperCollins.

Perel, E. (2017). *The state of affairs: Rethinking infidelity.* HarperCollins.

Perry, S. L. (2018). Pornography use and marital separation: Evidence from two–wave panel data. *Archives of Sexual Behavior, 47*(6), 1869–1880.

Perverts of Color Zine: Celebrating the Diversity of Perversity. Jaki Griot Productions.

Petrella, S. (2005). Only with you—maybe—if you make me happy: A genealogy of serial monogamy as governance and self-governance. In M. Sönser Breed & F. Peters (Eds.), *Genealogies of identity: Interdisciplinary readings on sex and sexuality* (pp. 169–182). Rodopi.

Petrella, S. (2007). Ethical sluts and closet polyamorists: Dissident eroticism, abject subjects and the normative cycle in self-help books on free love. In N. Rumens & A. Cervantes-Carson (Eds.), *Sexual politics of desire and belonging* (pp. 151–171). Rodopi.

Pew Research Center (2015). *The American family today.* https://www.pewsocialtrends.org/2015/12/17/1-the-american-family-today/

Pew Research Center (2019). *Generation Z looks a lot like millennials on key social and political issues.* https://www.pewsocialtrends.org/2019/01/17/generation-z-looks-a-lot-like-millennials-on-key-social-and-political-issues/

Pfeiffer, S. M., & Wong, P. T. (1989). Multidimensional jealousy. *Journal of Social and Personal Relationships, 6*(2), 181–196.

Phillips, L., & Stewart, M. R. (2008). "I am just so glad you are alive": New perspectives on non-traditional, non-conforming, and transgressive expressions of gender, sexuality, and race among African Americans. *Journal of African American Studies, 12*(4), 378–400.

Phillips, R. (1988). *Putting asunder: A history of divorce in Western society.* Cambridge University Press.

Pieper, M., & Bauer, R. (2005). *Polyamory and mono-normativity: Results of an empirical study of non-monogamous patterns of intimacy* [Unpublished manuscript]. Research Center for Feminist, Gender, and Queer Studies, University of Hamburg

Pines, A. (1998). *Romantic Jealousy: Causes, symptoms, cures.* Routledge.

Pitagora, D. (2016). The kink-poly confluence: Relationship intersectionality in marginalized communities. *Sexual and Relationship Therapy, 31*(3), 391–405.

Portwood-Stacer, L. (2010). Constructing anarchist sexuality: Queer identity, culture, and politics in the anarchist movement. *Sexualities, 13*(4), 479–493.

Posey, S. M., & Fowler, M. (2016). More different than the same: Customary characterization of alternative relationships groups and types. *New Directions in Folklore, 14*(2), 60–88.

Potter-Efron, R. T., & Potter-Efron, P. S. (2008). *The emotional affair: How to recognize emotional infidelity and what to do about it.* New Harbinger Publications.

Przybylo, E. (2019). *Asexual erotics: Intimate readings of compulsory sexuality.* The Ohio State University Press.

Puar, J. K. (2007). *Terrorist assemblages: Homonationalism in queer times.* Duke University Press.

Raab, M. (2014). Care in consensually non-monogamous relationship networks: Aspirations and practices in a contradictory field. *Graduate Journal of Social Science, 14*(1), 10–27.

Raley, B. G. (2018). *The more perfect union: Monogamy and the right to marriage* [Working paper]. Hanyang University School of Law. https://www.researchgate.net/public ation/317648478_The_More_Perfect_Union_Monogamy_and_the_Right_to_Marriage

Rambukkana, N. (2015). *Fraught intimacies: Non/monogamy in the public sphere.* The University of British Columbia.

Ransom, C. (2015). A critique of Ian Stevenson's rebirth research. In K. Augustine & M. Martin (Eds.), *The myth of an afterlife: The case against life after death* (pp. 571–574). Rowman & Littlefield.

Raskin, R., & Terry, H. (1988). A principal-components analysis of the narcissistic personality inventory and further evidence of its construct validity. *Journal of Personality and Social Psychology, 54*(5), 890–902.

Rauer, A. J., & Volling, B. L. (2007). Differential parenting and sibling jealousy: Developmental correlates of young adults' romantic relationships. *Personal Relationships, 14*(4), 495–511.

Razack, S. (2005). How is white supremacy embodied? Sexualized racial violence at Abu Ghraib. *Canadian Journal of Women and the Law, 17*(2), 341–363.

Regh, W., & Bohman, J. (Eds.). (2001). *Pluralism and the pragmatic turn: The transformation of critical theory—Essays in honor of Thomas McCarthy.* The MIT Press.

Regnerus, M. (2017). *Cheap sex: The transformation of men, marriage, and monogamy.* Oxford University Press.

Rifkin, J. (2009). *The empathic civilization: The race to global consciousness in a world in crisis.* Jeremy P. Tarcher/Penguin.

Rigoglioso, M. (2009). *The cult of divine birth in ancient Greece.* Palgrave Macmillan.

Rilke, R. M. (1934). *Letters to a young poet* (M. D. Herter Norton, Trans.). W. W. Norton & Co.

Ritchie, A. (2010). Discursive constructions of polyamory in mono-normative media culture. In M. Barker & D. Langdridge (Eds.), *Understanding non-monogamies* (pp. 47–51). Routledge.

Ritchie, A., & Barker, M. (2006). 'There aren't words for what we do or how we feel so we have to make them up': Constructing polyamorous languages in a culture of compulsory monogamy. *Sexualities, 9*(5), 584–601.

Roberson, P. N. E., Shorter, R. L., Woods, S., & Priest, J. (2018). How health behaviors link romantic relationship dysfunction and physical health across 20 years for middle-aged and older adults. *Social Science and Medicine, 201*, 18–26.

Roberts, R. (2000, October 4). White House welcome. *The Washington Post.* https://www.washingtonpost.com/archive/lifestyle/2000/10/04/white-house-welcome/2be3b fdd-e26b-420b-a7f0-f9df48cc373b/?utm_term=.22f17e8dc2a9

Robin, C. (2017). *Intimacy in marriage: 200 ways to seduce your husband: How to boost your marriage libido and actually enjoy sex: A couple's intimacy guide* [E-book].

Robinson, M. (2009). *Cupid's poisoned arrow: From habit to harmony in sexual relationships.* North Atlantic Books.

Robinson, M. (2013). Monogamy and polyamory as strategies identities. *Journal of Bisexuality, 13*, 21–38.

Robinson, S., White, A., & Anderson, E. (2017). Privileging the bromance: Appraisal of romantic and bromantic relationships. *Men and Masculinities, 22*(5), 850–871.

Robinson, V. (1997). My baby just cares for me: Feminism, heterosexuality, and non-monogamy. *Journal of Gender Studies, 6*(2), 143–157.

Rodrigues, D., Fasoli, F., Huic, A., & Lopes, D. (2017). Which partners are more human? Monogamy matters more than sexual orientation for dehumanization in three European countries. *Sexuality Research and Social Policy, 15*(48), 504–515.

Rodrigues, D., Lopes, D., & Smith, C. V. (2017). Caught in a "bad romance"? Reconsidering the negative association between sociosexuality and relationship functioning. *Journal of Sex Research, 54*(9), 1118–1127.

Rodriguez, L. M., DiBello, A. M., Øverup, C. S., & Neighbors, C. (2015). The prize of distrust: Trust, anxious attachment, and partner abuse. *Partner Abuse, 6*(3), 298–319.

Roisman, G. I., Masten, A. S., Coatsworth, J. D., & Tellegen, A. (2004). Salient and emerging developmental tasks in the transition to adulthood. *Child Development, 75*(1), 123-133.

Rosa, B. (1994). Anti-monogamy: A radical challenge to compulsory heterosexuality. In G. Griffin, M. Hester, S. Rai, & S. Roseneil (Eds.), *Stirring it: Challenges for feminism* (pp. 107–120). Taylor & Francis.

Rose, H., & Rose, S. (Eds.). (2000). *Alas, poor Darwin: Arguments against evolutionary psychology.* Harmony Books.

Rosenau, P. M. (1992). *Post-modernism and the social sciences.* Princeton University Press.

Rossman, K., Sinnard, M., & Budge, S. (2019). A qualitative examination of consideration and practice of consensual nonmonogamy among sexual and gender minority couples. *Psychology of Sexual Orientation and Gender Diversity, 6*(1), 11–21.

Rotello, G. (1997). *Sexual ecology: AIDS and the destiny of gay men.* Dutton Penguin.

Rowan, A. (1995). How to be not monogamous. In K. Lano & C. Perry (Eds.), *Breaking the barriers of desire: New approaches to multiple relationships* (pp. 13–19). Five Leaves Publications.

Rubel, A. N., & Bogaert, A. F. (2015). Consensual non-monogamy: Psychological well-being and relationship quality correlates. *Journal of Sex Research, 52*(9), 961–982.

Rubin, A. M. (1982). Sexually open versus sexually exclusive marriage: A comparison of dyadic adjustment. *Alternative Lifestyles, 5*(2), 101–106.

Rubin, A. M., & Adams, J. R. (1986). Outcomes of sexually open marriages. *The Journal of Sex Research, 22*(3), 311–319.

Rubin, H., & Campbell, L. (2012). Day-to-day changes in intimacy predict heightened relationship passion, sexual occurrence, and sexual satisfaction: A dyadic diary analysis. *Social Psychological and Personality Science, 3*(2), 224–231.

Rubin, R. (2001). Alternative family styles revisited, or whatever happened to swingers, group marriages and communes? *Journal of Family Issues, 7*(6), 711–726.

Rüdebusch, E. (1903/04). *Die eigenen: Ein tendenzroman für freie gesiter.* Johannes Räde.

Rust, P. C. (1996). Monogamy and polyamory: Relationship issues for bisexuals. In B. A. Firestein (Ed.), *Bisexuality: The psychology and politics of an invisible minority* (pp. 127–148). SAGE.

Ryan, C., & Jethá, C. (2010). *Sex at dawn: How we mate, how we stray, and what it means for modern sexuality.* HarperCollins.

Rycenga, J. (1995). Clearly God intended polemics to the threadbare: Some Christian theological justifications for monogamy and polygyny. In K. Lano & C. Perry (Eds.),

Breaking the barriers of desire: New approaches to multiple relationships (pp. 87–98). Five Leaves Publications.

Salmon, C., Townsend, J. M., & Hehman, J. (2016). Causal sex and college students: Sex differences and the impact of father absence. *Evolutionary Psychological Science, 2*, 254–261.

Salovey, P. (Ed.). (1991). *The psychology of jealousy and envy.* Guilford.

Salzberg, S. (1995). *Lovingkindness: The revolutionary art of happiness.* Shambhala.

Samuels, A. (2010). Promiscuities: Politics, imagination, spirituality and hypocrisy. In M. Barker & D. Langdridge (Eds.), *Understanding non-monogamies* (pp. 212–221). Routledge.

Sangharakshita (1999). *The Bodhisattva ideal: Wisdom and compassion in Buddhism.* Windhorse Publications.

Saraswati, L. A. (2013). Wikisexuality: Rethinking sexuality in cyberspace. *Sexualities, 16*(5/6), 587–603.

Sartorius, A. (2004). Three and more in love: Group marriage or integrating commitment and sexual freedom. In S. Anderlini-D'Onofrio (Ed.), *Plural loves: Designs for bi and poly living* (pp. 79–98). Harrington Park Press.

Sauer, S., Walach, H., Schmidt, S., Hinterberger, T., Lynch, S., Büssing, A., & Kohls, N. (2013). Assessment of mindfulness: Review on state of the art. *Mindfulness, 4*(1), 3–17.

Savage, D. (2012, January). *Meet the monogamish.* The Stranger. http://www.thestranger.com/seattle/ SavageLove?oid=11412386

Savage, D. (2020, March). *Savage love: Open and shut (on non-monogamy and pandemics).* digboston. https://digboston.com/savage-love-open-and-shut-on-non-monogamy-and-pandemics/

Saxon, L. (2011). *Sex at dusk: Lifting the shiny wrapping from Sex at dawn.* CreateSpace.

Schaupp, (2009). Free love for free persons: An anarchist utopia based on sexual self-ownership. In A. Moore & C. Zuccarini (Ed.), *Persons and sexuality: Interdisciplinary reflections* (pp. 67–76). Inter-Disciplinary Press.

Schechinger, H., Sakaluk, J., & Moors, A. (2018). Harmful and helpful therapy practices with consensually non-monogamous clients: Toward an inclusive framework. *Journal of Consulting and Clinical Psychology, 86*(11), 879–891.

Scheidel, W. (2009). A peculiar institution? Greco-Roman monogamy in global context. *The History of the Family: An International Quarterly, 14*(3), 280–291.

Scherrer, K. S. (2010). Asexual relationships: What does asexuality have to do with polyamory. In M. Barker & D. Langdridge (Eds.), *Understanding non-monogamies* (pp. 154–159). Taylor & Francis.

Schiavi, M.C., Spina, V., Zullo, M.A., Colagiovanni, V., Luffarelli, P., Rago, R., & Palazzctti, P. (2020). Love in the time of COVID-19: Sexual function and quality of life analysis during the social distancing measures in a group of Italian reproductive-age women. *The Journal of Sexual Medicine, 17*(8), 1407–1413.

Schippers, M. (2016). *Beyond monogamy: Polyamory and the future of polyqueer sexualities.* New York University Press.

Schippers, M. (2019). Polyamory and a queer orientation to the world. In B. L. Simula, J. E. Sumerau, & A. Miller (Eds.), *Expanding the rainbow: Exploring the relationships of bi+, polyamorous, kinky, ace, intersex, and trans people* (pp. 71–80). Brill Sense.

Schippers, M. (2020). *Polyamory, monogamy, and American dreams: The stories we tell about poly lives and the cultural production of inequality*. Routledge.

Schiralli, M. (1999). *Constructive postmodernism: Toward a renewal in cultural and literary studies*. Praeger.

Schmitt, D. E. (2005a). Sociosexuality from Argentina to Zimbanwe: A 48-nation study of sex, culture, and strategies of human mating. *Behavioral and Brain Sciences, 28*(2), 247–275.

Schmitt, D. E. (2005b). Fundamentals of human mating strategies. In D. Buss (Ed.), *Handbook of evolutionary psychology* (pp. 258–291). Wiley.

Schnarch, D. (2002). *Resurrecting sex: Solving sexual problems and revolutionizing your relationship*. HarperCollins.

Schnarch, D. (2009). *Passionate marriage: Keeping love and intimacy alive in committed relationships*. W. W. Norton & Company.

Schwartz, R. C. (1995). *Internal family systems therapy*. Guilford Press.

Scott, S. B., Rhoades, G. K., Stanley, S. M., Allen, E. S., & Markman, H. J. (2013). Reasons for divorce and recollections of premarital intervention: Implications for improving relationship education. *Couple and Family Psychology, 2*(2):131–45.

Seal, K. L., Doherty, W. J., & Harris, S. M. (2015). Confiding about problems in marriage and long-term committed relationships: A national study. *Journal of Marital and Family Therapy, 42*(3), 438–450.

Séguin, L. (2019). The good, the bad, and the ugly: Lay attitudes and perceptions of polyamory. *Sexualities, 22*(4), 669–690.

Séguin, L. J., Blais, M., Goyer, M. F., Adam, B. D., Lavoie, F., Rodrigue, C., & Magontier, C. (2017). Examining relationship quality across three types of relationship agreements. *Sexualities, 20*(1–2), 86–104.

Seiffge-Krenke, I., & Gelhaar, T. (2008). Does successful attainment of developmental tasks lead to happiness and success in later developmental tasks? A test of Havighurt's (1948) theses. *Journal of Adolescence, 31*(1), 33–52.

Senn, T. E., Carey, M. P., & Vanable, P. A. (2018). Childhood and adolescent sexual abuse and subsequent sexual risk behavior: Evidence from controlled studies, methodological critique, and suggestions for research. *Clinical Psychology Review, 28*(5), 711–735.

Sesardic, N. (2002). Evolution of human jealousy: A just-so story or just-so criticism. *Philosophy of the Social Sciences, 33*(4), 427–443.

Shannon, D., & Willis, A. (2010). Theoretical polyamory: Some thoughts on loving, thinking, and queering anarchism. *Sexualities, 13*(4), 433–443.

Sheets, V. L., & Wolfe., M. D. (2001). Sexual jealousy in heterosexual, lesbians, and gays. *Sex Roles: A Journal of Research, 44*(5–6), 255–276.

Sheff, E. (2005). Polyamorous women, sexual subjectivity, and power. *Journal of Contemporary Ethnography, 34*(3), 251–283.

Sheff, E. (2006). Poly-hegemonic masculinities. *Sexualities, 9*(5), 621–642.

Sheff, E. (2010). Strategies in polyamorous parenting. In M. Barker & D. Langdridge (Eds.), *Understanding non-monogamies* (pp. 169–181). Routledge.

Sheff, E. (2014). *The polyamorists next door: Inside multi-partner relationships and families*. Rowman & Littlefield.

Sheff, E., & Hammers, C. (2011). The privilege of perversities: Race, class, and education among polyamorists and kinksters. *Psychology and Sexuality, 2*(3), 198–223.

Sheff, E., & Tenese, M. M. (2015). Consensual non-monogamies in industrialized nations. In J. DeLamater & R. F. Plante (Eds.), *Handbook of the sociology of sexualities* (pp. 223–241). Springer.

Sheff, E. A. (n.d.). *Three waves of non-monogamy: A select history of polyamory in the United States.* https://elisabethsheff.com/2012/09/09/three-waves-of-polyamory-a-select-history-of-non-monogamy/

Sheff, E. A. (2019, April 4). Do kids from polyamorous families become poly themselves? A preview of findings emerging from a 20+ year study. *Psychology Today.* https://www.psychologytoday.com/us/blog/the-polyamorists-next-door/201904/do-kids-polyamorous-families-become-poly-themselves

Shoener, S. (2014, June 22). Two-parent households can be lethal: Domestic violence and two-parent households. *The New York Times.* http://nytimes.com/2014/06/22/opinion/sunday/domestic-violence-andtwo-parent-households.html

Shrage, L. (2013). Reforming marriage: A comparative approach. *Journal of Applied Philosophy, 30*(2), 107–121.

Simon, R. W. (2002). Revisiting the relationships among gender, marital status, and mental health. *American Journal of Sociology, 107*(4), 1065–1096.

Slater, D. (2013). *Love in the time of algorithms: What technology does to meeting and mating.* Current.

Smith, A., Lyons, A., Ferris, J., Ritchers, J., Pitts, M., Shelley, J., & Simpson, J. M. (2011). Sexual and relationship satisfaction among heterosexual men and women: The importance of desired frequency of sex. *Journal of Sex and Marital Therapy, 37*(2), 104–15.

Smith, C. A., & Konik, J. A. (Eds.) (2011). Feminist reappraisals of evolutionary psychology. [Special issue]. *Sex Roles: A Journal of Research, 64*(9–10).

Smith, C. N. (2017). Open to love: Polyamory and the Black American. *Journal of Black Sexuality and Relationships, 3*(2), 99–129.

Smith, D. J. (2007). Modern marriage, men's extramarital sex, and HIV risk in southeastern Nigeria. *American Journal of Public Health, 97*(6), 997–1005.

Smith, G. (2020, August 2020). 9 ways non-monogamous people are dealing with the pandemic. *Self.* https://www.self.com/story/non-monogamous-pandemic-dating

Smith, T. H. (2011). Romantic love. *Essays in Philosophy, 12*(1), 68–92.

Smothers, H. (2020). Sex toy sales are skyrocketing during the coronavirus pandemic. *VICE.* https://www.vice.com/en_us/article/y3m9bw/sex-toy-sales-up-during-coronavirus-covid-19pandemic

Snyder, S. (2018). *Love worth making: How to have ridiculously great sex in a long-lasting relationship.* St. Martin Press.

Soble, A. (1987). The unity of romantic love. *Philosophy and Theology, 1*(4), 374–397.

Solomon, R. C. (2006). *About love: Reinventing romance for our times.* Hackett (Original work published 1994).

Somé, M. (1999). *The healing wisdom of Africa: Finding life purpose through nature, ritual, and community.* J. P. Tarcher/Putnam.

Spanjer, N. (2015, August). *The rise of multi-parenting: These five people are about to have a baby together.* Stuff. https://www.stuff.co.nz/life-style/life/70873407/null

Spears, B., & Lowen, L. (2016). *Choices: Perspectives of gay men on monogamy, non-monogamy, and marriage.* CreateSpace.

Sprecher, S., & Regan, P. C. (1998). Passionate and companionate love in courting and young married couples. *Sociological Inquiry, 68*(2), 163–185.

Squire, S. (2008). *I don't: A contrarian history of marriage.* Bloomsbury.

Stacey, J. (1996). *In the name of the family: Rethinking family values in the postmodern age.* Beacon Press.

Stacey, J. (2011). *Unhitched: Love, marriage, and family values from West Hollywood to Western China.* New York University Press.

Statistic Brain Research Institute (2016). *Infidelity statistics.* https://www.statisticbrain.com/infidelity-statistics/

Stearns, P. N. (2009). *Sexuality in world history.* Routledge.

Stelboum, J. P. (2010). Patriarchal monogamy. *Journal of Lesbian Studies, 3*(1–2), 39–46.

Sternlicht, A. (2020, May 20). With the new COVID-19 outbreak linked to gay man, homophobia on the rise in South Korea. *Forbes.* https://www.forbes.com/sites/alexandrasternlicht/2020/05/12/with-new-covid-19-outbreak-linked-to-gay-man-homophobia-on-rise-in-south-korea/#b4fe02349099

Stevenson, I. (1997). *Reincarnation and biology: A contribution to the etiology of birthmarks and birth defects* (2 Vols.). Praeger.

Stewart, H. (2018). Parents of "pets"? A defense of interspecies parenting and family building. *Analyze: Journal of Gender and Feminist Studies, 11,* 239–263.

Stirling Hastings, A. (1996). *America's sexual crisis: Discovering healthy sex by healing culturally caused shame, addiction, and sexual distortion.* SelfHelpBooks/Wellness Institute.

Strassberg, M. I. (2003). The challenge of post-modern polygamy: Considering polyamory. *Capital University Law Review, 31,* 439–560.

Strohschein, L. (2005). Parental divorce and child mental health trajectories. *Journal of Marriage and Family, 67*(5), 1286–1300.

Stryker, S. (2008). *Transgender history.* Seal Press.

Sumerau, J. E., & Nowakowski, A. "X." C. H. (2019). Relational fluidity: Somewhere between polyamory and monogamy (personal reflection). In B. L. Simula, J. E. Sumeray, & A. Miller (Eds.), *Expanding the rainbow: Exploring the relationships of bi+, polyamorous, kinky, ace, intersex, and trans people* (pp. 121–132). Brill Sense.

Summers, K. (2005). The evolutionary ecology of despotism. *Evolution and Human Behavior, 26*(1), 106–135.

Swan, D. J., & Thompson, S. C. (2016). Monogamy, the protective fallacy: Sexual versus emotional exclusivity and the implication for sexual health risk. *The Journal of Sex Research, 53*(1), 64–73.

Sweetman, R. (2019, October 27). How was it for you? The dark side of the 1960s sexual revolution. *The Irish Times.* https://www.irishtimes.com/culture/books/how-was-it-for-you-the-dark-side-of-the-1960s-sexual-revolution

Symons, D. (1979). *The evolution of human sexuality.* Oxford University Press.

Szabrowicz, Z. M. (2018). *The relationship between adult attachment theory, jealousy, and attitudes toward monogamy* [Unpublished master's thesis, Eastern Washington University].

Tafoya, M. A., & Spitzberg, B. H. (2007). The dark side of infidelity: Its nature, prevalence, and communicative functions. In B. H. Spitzberg & W. R. Cupach (Eds), *The dark side of interpersonal communication* (pp. 201–242). Lawrence Erlbaum Associates.

Talmey, B. S. (1938). Evolution of marriage from promiscuity to monogamy. In B. S. Talmey (Ed.), *Love: A treatise on the science of sex-attraction* (Rev. ed.) (pp. 427–434). Eugenics Publishing Company. (Original work published 1933)

Tanenbaum, L. (1999). *Slut*. Seven Stories Press.

Taormino, T. (2008). *Opening up: A guide to creating and sustaining open relationships*. Simon and Schuster.

Tatkin, S., & Hendrix, H. (2011). *Wired for love: How understanding your partner's brain and attachment style can help you defuse conflict and build a secure relationship*. New Harbinger Publications.

Tay, L., & Diener, E. (2011). Needs and subjective well-being around the world. *Journal of Personality and Social Psychology, 101*(2), 354–365.

Taylor, C. (1989). *Sources of the self: The making of the modern identity*. Cambridge University Press.

Taylor, C. (2007). *A secular age*. Belknap.

Tennov, D. (1979). *Love and limerance: The experience of being in love in New York*. Stein and Day.

Tenzin Gyatso (H. H. the XIVth Dalai Lama) (1998). *The art of happiness: A handbook for living*. Penguin Putnam.

Thanissaro Bhikkhu (1994). *The Buddha's Kalama Sutta: To the Kalamas*. https://www.accesstoinsight.org/tipitaka/an/an03/an03.065.than.html

Thompson, A. E., Moore, E. A., Haedtke, K., & Karst, A. T. (2020). Assessing implicit associations with consensual non-monogamy among U.S. early emerging adults: An application of the Single-Target Implicit Association Test. *Archives of Sexual Behavior*. https://doi.org/10.1007/s10508-020-01625-x

Thompson, M. J. (2017). What is critical theory? In M. J. Thompson (Ed.), *The Palgrave handbook of critical theory* (pp. 1–14). Palgrave Macmillan.

Thornhill, R., & Palmer, C. T. (2000). *A natural history of rape: Biological bases of social coercion*. The MIT Press.

Thrangu Rimponche, K. (2013). *The five Buddha families and the eight consciousnesses* (P. E. Roberts, Trans.). Namo Buddha Publications.

Thurer, S. L. (2005). *The end of gender: A psychological autopsy*. Routledge.

Tibbets, L. (2001). Commitment in monogamous and polyamorous relationships. *Social Work, 521*. Washburn University.

Todd, L., Laier, C., Brand, M., Hatch, L., & Hajela, R. (2015). Neuroscience of Internet pornography addiction: A review and update. *Behavioral Sciences, 5*(3), 388–433.

Toft, A. & Yip, A. K. T. (2018). Intimacy negotiated: The management of relationships and the construction of personal communities in the lives of bisexual women and men. *Sexualities, 12*(2), 233–250.

Toohey, P. (2014). *Jealousy*. Yale University Press.

Torres, J. B., Solberg, V. H., & Carlstrom, A. H. (2002). The myth of sameness among Latino men and their machismo. *American Journal of Orthopsychiatry, 72*(2), 163–181.

Treas, J., & Giesen, D. (2000). Sexual infidelity among married and cohabiting Americans. *Journal of Marriage and the Family, 62*(1), 48–60.

Tricycle (n.d.). *Tricycle teachings: Love and relationships* [eBook]. https://tricycle.org/ebooks/tricycle-teachings-love-relationships/

Trungpa, C. (1991). *Orderly chaos: The mandala principle* (S. Chözdin, Ed.). Shambhala.

Tsoulis, A. (1987). Heterosexuality—A feminist option. *Spare Rib, 179*, 22–26.

Tucker, W. (2014). *Marriage and civilization: How monogamy made us human.* Regnery.

Tuffley, T. (2012). *The four sublime states: The Brahmaviharas. Contemplations on love, compassion, sympathetic joy and equanimity.* Altiora Publications.

Turner, P. (2019, April 9). *You have heard about polyamory, but what about ambiamory?* Kinkly. https://www.kinkly.com/youve-heard-of-polyamory-but-what-about-ambiamory/2/17832?fbclid=IwAR0L7iaxRxR5TOze6HJP3SF77pwuc5HXcpm4ub48eOpag1-hRwDYwMVnSLo

Tweedy, A. (2011). Polyamory as a sexual orientation. *University of Cincinnati Law Review, 79*(4), 1461–1515.

Uhlendorff, U. (2004). The concept of developmental tasks and its significance for education and social work. *Social Work and Society, 2*(1), 54–63.

Urban, H. (2003). *Tantra: Sex, secrecy, politics, and power in the study of religion.* University of California Press.

Valenti, J. (2008). *He is a stud, she is a slut and 49 other double standards every women should know.* Seal Press.

van Anders, S. M. (2015). Beyond sexual orientation: Integrating gender/sex and diverse sexualities via sexual configurations theory. *Archives of Sexual Behavior, 44*(5), 1177–1213.

van Anders, S. M., Hamilton, L. D., & Watson, N. V. (2007). Multiple partners are associated with higher testosterone in North American men and women. *Hormones and Behavior, 51*(3), 454–459.

Van Fraassen, B. C. (2008). *Scientific representations: Paradoxes of perspective.* Clarendon Press.

Vandello, J. A., & Cohen, D. (2003). Male honor and female fidelity: Implicit cultural scripts that perpetuate domestic violence. *Journal of Personality and Social Psychology, 84*(5), 997–1010.

VandenBos, G. R. (Ed.). (2007). *APA dictionary of psychology.* American Psychological Association.

Vandermassen, G. (2005). *Who's afraid of Charles Darwin? Debating feminism and evolutionary theory.* Rowman & Littlefield.

VanderVoort, L., & Duck, S. (2004). Sex, lies…and transformation. In J. Duncombe, K. Harrison, G. Allen, & D. Marsden (Eds.), *The state of affairs: Explorations in infidelity and commitment* (pp. 1–13). Lawrence Erlbaum Associates.

Vangelisti, A. L., & Gerstenberger, M. (2004). Men, women, and infidelity: Sex differences in extradyadic sex and jealousy. In J. Duncombe, K. Harrison, G. Allen, & D. Marsden (Eds.), *The state of affairs: Explorations in infidelity and commitment* (pp. 59–78). Lawrence Erlbaum Associates.

Vaughan, P. (2003). *The monogamy myth: A personal handbook for recovering from affairs* (3rd ed.). New Market Press.

Veaux, F., & Rickert, F. (2014). *More than two: A practical guide to ethical polyamory.* Thorntree Press.

Vicedo, M. (2013). *The nature and nurture of love: From imprinting to attachment in cold war America.* University of Chicago Press

Voegelin, E. (2000). *Order and history, Vol. III: Plato and Aristotle.* In. D. Germino (Ed.), *The collected works of Eric Voegelin* (Vol. 16). University of Missouri Press.

Vossler, A., & Moller, N. P. (2020). Internet affairs: Partners' perceptions and experiences of internet infidelity. *Journal of Sex and Marital Therapy, 46*(1), 67–77.

Wade, J. (2004). *Transcendent sex: When lovemaking opens the veil.* Pocket Books.

Wade, L. (2017). *American hookup: The new culture of sex on campus.* W. W. Norton & Company.

Waite, L., & Gallagher, M. (2000). *The case for marriage: Why married people are happier, healthier, and better off financially.* Doubleday.

Wakeman, J. (2016, November 16). Virtual brothels: How teledildonics is revolutionizing sex work. *Rolling Stone.* https://www.rollingstone.com/culture/culture-features/virtual-brothels-how-teledildonics-is-revolutionizing-sex-work-108209/

Waldby, C. (1996). *AIDS and the body politic: Biomedicine and sexual difference.* Routledge.

Walker, A. M. (2017). *The secret life of the cheating wife: Power, pragmatism, and pleasure in women's infidelity.* Lexington Press.

Walker, R. S., Hill, K. R., Flinn, M. V., & Ellsworth, R. M. (2011). Evolutionary history of hunter-gatherer marriage practices. *PLoS One, 6*(4), 1–6.

Wallerstein, J. S., & Lewis, J. M. (2004). The unexpected legacy of divorce: Report of a 25-year study. *Psychoanalytic Psychology, 21*(3), 353–370.

Walum, H., Lichtenstein, P., Pedersen, N. L., Larsson, H., Anckarster, H., Westberg, L., Neiderhiser, J. M., Reiss, D., Ganiban, J. M., & Spotts, E. L. (2012). Variation in the oxytocin receptor gene (OXTR) is associated with pair-boding and social behavior. *Biological Psychiatry, 71*(5), 419–426.

Walum, H., Westberg, L., Henningsson, S., Neiderhiser, J. M., Reiss, D., Igl, W., Ganiban, J. M., Spotts, E. L., Pedersen, N. L., Eriksson, E., & Lichtenstein, P. (2008). Genetic variation in the vasopressin receptor 1a gene (AVPRIA) associates with pair-bonding behavior in humans. *Proceedings of the National Academy of Sciences, 105*(37), 14153–14156.

Wang, C. T. L., & Schofer, E. (2018). Coming out of the penumbras: World culture and cross-national variation in divorce rates. *Social Forces, 97*(2), 675–704.

Warren, J. T., Harvey, S. M., & Agnew, C. R. (2012). One love: Explicit monogamy agreements among heterosexual young adult couples at increased risk of sexually transmitted infections. *Journal of Sex Research, 49*(2–3), 282–289.

Waskul, D., Douglass, M., & Edgley, C. (2004) Outercourse: Body and self in text cybersex. In D. Waskul (Ed.), *net.seXXX: Readings of Sex, Pornography, and the Internet* (pp. 13–33). Peter Lang.

Wayland-Smith, E. (2016). *Oneida: From free love utopia to the well-set table.* Picador.

Weaver, B. R., & Woollard, F. (2008). Marriage and the norm of monogamy. *The Monist, 91*(3–4), 506–522.

Webb, H. S. (2012). *Yanantin and Masintin in the Andean world: Complementary dualism in modern Peru.* University of New Mexico Press.

Weeks, J. (2007). *The world we have won: The remaking of erotic and intimate life.* Routledge.

Weiser-Hanks, M. E. (2000). *Christianity and sexuality in the early modern world: Regulating desire, reforming practice.* Routledge.

Weitzman, G. (2006). Therapy with clients who are bisexual and polyamorous. *Journal of Bisexuality, 6*(1/2), 137–164.

Weitzman, G., Davidson, J., & Phillips, Jr., R. A. (2012). *What psychology professionals should know about polyamory.* (James R. Fleckenstein & C. Morotti-Meeker, Eds.). National Coalition for Sexual Freedom. http://instituteforsexuality.com/wp-content/uploads/2014/05/What-therapists-shouldknow-about-Polyamory-1.pdf

Welwood, J. (1996). *Love and awakening: Discovering the sacred path of intimate relationship.* HarperCollins.

West, C. (2007). *The love that satisfies: Reflections on eros and agape.* Ascension Press.

Whisman, M. A., Dixon, A. E., & Johnson, B. (1997). Therapists' perspectives of couple problems and treatment issues in couple therapy. *Journal of Family Psychology, 11*(3), 361–366.

Whitman, W. (2007). *Leaves of grass: The original 1855 edition* (Dover Thrifts ed.). Dover (Original work published 1855).

Whitty, M. T., & Carr, A. N. (2003). Cyberspace as potential space: Considering the web as a playground to cyber-flirt. *Human Relations, 56*(7), 861–891.

Wiederman, M. W. (1997). Extramarital sex: Prevalence and correlates in a national survey. *Journal of Sex Research, 34*, 167–174.

Wilkinson, E. (2010). What's queer about non-monogamy now? M. Barker & D. Langdridge (Eds.), *Understanding non-monogamies* (pp. 243–254). Routledge.

Wilkinson, E. (2012). The romantic imaginary: Compulsory coupledom and single existence. In S. Hines & Y. Taylor (Eds.), *Sexualities: Past reflections, future directions* (pp. 130–145). Palgrave Macmillan.

Wilkinson, E. (2014). Single people's geographies of home: Intimacy and friendship beyond "the family." *Environment and Planning, 46*(10), 2452–2468.

Willey, A. (2006). "Christian nations," "polygamic races" and women's rights: Toward a genealogy of non/monogamy and whiteness. *Sexualities, 9*(5), 530–546.

Willey, A. (2015). Constituting compulsory monogamy: Normative femininity and the limits of imagination. *Journal of Gender Studies, 24*(6), 621–633.

Willey, A. (2016). *Undoing monogamy: The politics of science and the possibilities of biology.* Duke University Press.

Willey, A. (2018). Monogamy's nature: Global sexual science and the secularization of Christian marriage. In V. Fuechtner (Ed.), *A global history of sexual science, 1880–1960* (pp. 97–117). University of California Press.

Williams, C. (1987). *Descent of the dove: A history of the Holy Spirit in the Church.* Regent College Publishing.

Willoughby, B. J., Carroll, J. S., Busby, D. M., & Brown, C. C. (2016). Differences in pornography use among couples: Associations with satisfaction, stability, and relationship processes. *Archives of Sexual Behavior, 45*(1), 145–158.

Wilson, M., & Daly, M. (1996). Male sexual proprietariness and violence against wives. *Current Directions in Psychological Science, 5*(1), 2–7.

Witt, E. (2016). *Future sex.* Ferrar, Straus, and Giroux.

Witte, J., Jr. (2015). *The Western case of monogamy over polygamy.* Cambridge University Press.

Wolf, N. (1997). *Promiscuities.* Chatto & Windus.

Wolfe, L. (2003). *Jealousy and transformation in polyamorous relationships* [Unpublished doctoral dissertation, Institute for Advanced Study of Human Sexuality].

Wolkomir, M. (2019). Monogamy vs. polyamory: Negotiating gender hierarchy. In B. L. Simula, J. E. Sumerau, & A. Miller (Eds.), *Expanding the rainbow: Exploring the relationships of bi+, polyamorous, kinky, ace, intersex, and trans people* (pp. 81–93). Brill Sense.

Wood, J., Desmarais, S., Burleigh, T., & Milhausen, R. (2018). Reasons for sex and relational outcomes in consensually nonmonogamous and monogamous relationships. *Journal of Social and Personal Relationships, 35*(4), 632–654.

Woodword Thomas, K. (2015, May 21). Why serial monogamy is the new marriage. *Glamour.* https://www.glamour.com/story/serial-monogamy-marriage-consci ous-uncoupling

Woolever, M. (2010). *When God had sex: The practice of spirit marriage in ecstatic spirituality* [Unpublished manuscript]. Department of East-West Psychology, California Institute of Integral Studies.

Wosick, K. R. (2012). *Sex, love, and fidelity: A study of contemporary romantic relationships.* Cambria Press.

Wosick-Correa, K. (2010). Agreements, rules, and agentic fidelity in polyamorous relationships. *Psychology & Sexuality, 1,* 44–61.

Wright, P. J., Tokunaga, R. S., Kraus, A., & Klann, E. (2017). Pornography consumption and satisfaction: A meta-analysis. *Human Communication Research, 43*(3), 315–343.

Yalom, M. (2001). *A history of the wife.* HarperCollins.

Yamaguchi, M. (2019, April 24). Japan apologizes to victims of forced sterilization and promises compensation. *Time.* http://time.com/5577075/japan-apologizes-forced-st erilization-eugenics-program/

Yeo, C., Kaushal, S., & Yeo, D. (2020). Enteric involvement of coronaviruses: Is faecal-oral transmission of SarS-coV-2 possible? *The Lancet Gastroenterology & Hepatology, 5*(4), 335–337.

Young, A. (2004). Review of *The ethical slut: A guide to infinite sexual possibilities* (by D. Easton & C. L. Liszt). *Off Our Backs* (May/June), 38–39.

Young, A. H. (1998). Reconceiving the family: Challenging the paradigm of the exclusive family. *Journal of Gender & the Law, 6* (Summer), 505–555.

Young, K. A., Gobrogge, K. L., Liu, Y., & Wang, Z. (2011). The neurobiology of pair bonding: Insights from a socially monogamous rodent. *Frontiers in Neuroendocrinology, 32,* 53–69.

Young, L. J., Nilsen, R., Waymire, K. G., MacGregor, G. R., & Insel, T. R. (1999). Increased affiliative response to vasopressin in mice expressing the V1a receptor from a monogamous vole. *Nature, 400*(6746), 766–768.

Zandbergen, D. L., & Brown, S. G. (2015). Culture and gender differences in romantic jealousy. *Personality and Individual Differences, 72,* 122–127.

Zanin, A. (2013, January 24). *The problem with polynormativity.* Sex geek. https://sexgeek.wordpress.com/2013/01/24/theproblemwithpolynormativity

Zhu, J. (2018). "We are not cheaters": Polyamory, mixed-orientation marriage and the construction of radical honesty. *Graduate Journal of Social Science, 14*(1), 57–78.

Ziegler, A., Matsick, J. L., Moors, A. C., Rubin, J. D., & Conley, T. D. (2014). Does monogamy harm women? Deconstructing monogamy with a feminist lens. *Journal für Psychologie, 22*(1), 1–18.

Ziff, B. H., & Rao, P. V. (Eds.). (1997). *Borrowed power: Essays on cultural appropriation.* Rutgers University Press.

Zimmer, C., Corum, J., & Wee, S.-L. (2021, January 9). Coronavirus vaccine tracker. *The New York Times.* https://www.nytimes.com/interactive/2020/science/coronavirus-vaccine-tracker.html

Zimmerman, K. J. (2012). Clients in sexually open relationships: Considerations for therapists. *Journal of Feminist Family Therapy, 24*(3), 272–289.

Zussman, M., & Pierce, A. (1998). Shifts of consciousness in consensual S/M, bondage, and fetish play. *Anthropology of Consciousness, 9*(4), 15–38.

Index

About the Author

Jorge N. Ferrer, PhD, is a clinical psychologist, public speaker, and educator. He was a professor of psychology for more than twenty years at California Institute of Integral Studies, San Francisco, where he also served as chair of the Department of East–West Psychology. He has published several books and dozens of articles on psychology, education, and religious studies, and his work on alternative intimate relationships has been featured in journals such as *Sexuality and Culture* and *Psychology and Sexuality*. In his international private practice, Jorge offers professional counseling to individuals and couples focused on the management of jealousy, infidelities, sexual incompatibilities, open relationships, and the design of more satisfying intimate relationships. He was selected to become an advisor to the organization Religions for Peace at the United Nations. Learn more at www.jorgenferrer.com.

Printed in Great Britain
by Amazon

81556137R00123